DISCARD

# Edmund Husserl's Origin of Geometry: An Introduction

## Jacques Derrida

**TRANSLATED, WITH A PREFACE, BY
JOHN P. LEAVEY, JR.**

David B. Allison, Editor

## NICOLAS HAYS, LTD.
*Distributed by Great Eastern Book Co.*

**Library of Congress Cataloging in Publication Data**

Derrida, Jacques.
    Edmund Husserl's The origin of geometry: an introduction.

    Appendix (p. 155): The origin of geometry, by
E. Husserl, first published in 1939 under title: Die
Frage nach dem Ursprung der Geometrie als intentional-
historisches Problem.
    "French and English bibliography of Jacques
Derrida": p. 181
    Includes indexes.
    1. Husserl, Edmund, 1859–1938.  Die Frage nach dem
Ursprung der Geometrie als intentional-historisches
Problem.  2. Phenomenology.  I. Husserl, Edmund,
1859–1938.  Die Frage nach dem Ursprung der Geometrie
als intentional-historisches Problem. English. 1977.
II. Title.
QA447.D4713 1977        142'.7        77-13723
ISBN 0-89254-006-0

QA
447
.D4713
1978

© **1978** by Nicolas Hays, Ltd.

**Nicolas Hays, Ltd.**
**Box 596**
**Stony Brook, N.Y. 11790**

*Distributed by:*
*Great Eastern Book Co.*
*1123 Spruce St.*
*Boulder, Colorado 80302*

Library of Congress Catalog Card Number 77–13723

International Standard Book Number 0-89254-006-0

Printed in the United States of America

# Contents

---

\* These headings, added for the convenience of the reader, do not appear in the French edition.

# Acknowledgments

The 1974 second, revised French edition of EDMUND HUSSERL'S *L'ORIGINE DE LA GÉOMÉTRIE,* traduction et introduction par JAC-QUES DERRIDA, in Epiméthée, Essais Philosophiques, Collection fondée par Jean Hyppolite, copyright © 1962 by Presses Universitaires de France, 108, Boulevard Saint-Germain, Paris, is the source of this English translation.

We are grateful to the PRESSES UNIVERSITAIRES DE FRANCE for their authorization to present this text in English.

HUSSERL'S *ORIGIN OF GEOMETRY* is here reprinted from *THE CRISIS OF EUROPEAN SCIENCES AND TRANSCENDENTAL PHENOMENOLOGY* by EDMUND HUSSERL, translated by David Carr. Copyright © 1970 by Northwestern University Press, Evanston. Pp. 353–78.

We are also grateful to NORTHWESTERN UNIVERSITY PRESS for their authorization to reprint Husserl's text in full.

# Preface
# Undecidables and Old Names

## UNDECIDABLES AND DECONSTRUCTION

*Tympaniser–la philosophie.*

Marges

On the present French intellectual scene, the advent and demise of structuralism has accompanied what has been called the book's supersedure by the text.[1] The French philosopher and critic Jacques Derrida is situated at the juncture of the two, the book and the text; he writes about the origins, delays, and different paths at their crossroads. His "method" is the "deconstruction" of the very idea of *writing*.

Texts occur for Derrida only in writing, a writing understood not in the ordinary sense, but as the place of *rature*—the always incomplete erasure or scratching out of Western metaphysics.[2] The book as an

---

[1] See, for example, Eugenio Donato, "Structuralism: The Aftermath," *Sub-Stance*, No. 7 (Fall 1973), 9–26; Phillippe Sollers, "Programme," in his *Logiques* (Paris: Seuil, 1968), pp. 9–14; or Julia Kristeva, *Semeiotike: Recherches pour une sémanalyse* (Paris: Seuil, 1969); as well as any number of works by Roland Barthes or Derrida himself.

[2] "Like all the notions I am using, it belongs to the history of metaphysics and we can only use it under erasure [*sous rature* (added by tr.)]," Jacques Derrida, *Of Grammatology*, tr. Gayatri Spivak (Baltimore: The Johns Hopkins University Press, 1977), p. 60. Since this translation, with an excellent preface by the translator, appeared after the present work was completed, I was unable to compare translations for consistency of terminology (as I did with Allison's translation of *Speech and Phenomena*), nor was I able to comment on Mrs. Spivak's Preface. However, I have added references in the notes to relevant sections of her preface. Her discussion of *rature* occurs on pp. xiii–xx. It forms the backdrop for her lengthy discussion of Derrida's "acknowledged 'precursors'—Nietzsche, Freud, Heidegger, Husserl," pp. xxi–liv. In his translation of "La 'différance,'" contained in Derrida's *Speech and Phenomena: And Other Essays on Husserl's Theory of Signs* (Evanston: Northwestern University Press, 1973), p. 143, David Allison notes: "Derrida often brackets or 'crosses out' certain key terms taken from metaphysics and logic, and in doing this, he follows Heidegger's usage in *Zur Seinsfrage*. The terms in question no longer have their full meaning, they no longer have the status of a purely signified content of expression—no longer, that is, after the deconstruction of metaphysics. Generated out of the play of difference, they still retain a vestigial trace of sense, however, a trace that cannot simply be gotten around (*incontourable*)."

archives of metaphysical inscriptions, as the encyclopedia of knowledge or the complete presence of the signified (transcendental or not), is foreign to Derrida's new "concept" of writing, *l'écriture*. Derrida explains: "If I distinguish the text from the book, I shall be saying that the destruction of the book, as it is now under way in all domains, denudes the surface of the text. That necessary violence responds to a violence that was no less necessary." The book's own violence, its "protection of theology and of logocentricism against the disruption of writing, against its aphoristic energy, and . . . against difference in general,"[3] forces the present-day violent distinction of the book and the text, in order for "writing" to be understood.

*Rature* and the text of Derrida wherein it occurs are themselves crossed out or somehow suspended in his thought,[4] a thought seemingly too abstract. His method of criticism, deconstruction, could be seen, as Ricoeur says, as "consisting in laying waste to metaphysical discourse by aporia"[5]—i.e., as a kind of mental gymnastics. This common, but important, criticism of Derrida actually strikes at the heart of his enterprise. His continual insistence on the failure of metaphysics as onto-theo-logy seems to support Ricoeur's criticism. Derrida still writes "books" in the ordinary sense, and all the words of his text are, by necessity, not erased. In fact, deconstruction seems to be the violent *mis*interpretation of Western thought. However, the above criticism also misses the point, or preferably, the non-point, of Derrida's work, all of which could be considered as outside of books, *hors-livre*, as

---

[3] *Of Grammatology*, p. 18.

[4] "If there were only perception, pure permeability to fraying [facilitation, *Bahnung*], there would be no fraying. We would be written but nothing would be recorded; no writing would be produced, retained, repeated as readability. *But pure perception does not exist* [*my emphasis*]: we are written only by writing . . . by the instance within us which always already governs perception, be it internal or external. The 'subject' of writing does not exist if we mean by that some sovereign solitude of the author. The subject of writing is a *system* of relations between strata: of the Mystic Pad, of the psyche, of society, of the world. Within that scene the punctual simplicity of the classical subject is not to be found. In order to describe that structure, it is not enough to recall that one always writes for someone; and the oppositions sender-receiver, code-message, etc., remain extremely coarse instruments. We would search the 'public' in vain for the first reader: i.e., the first author of a work. And the 'sociology of literature' is blind to the war and ruses—whose stakes are the origin of the work—between the author who reads and the first reader who dictates. The *sociality* of writing as *drama* requires an entirely different discipline" (Jacques Derrida, "Freud et la scène de l'écriture," in his *L'Ecriture et la différence* [Paris: Seuil, 1967], p. 335; ET: "Freud and the Scene of Writing," tr. Jeffrey Mehlman, in *Yale French Studies,* No. 48: *French Freud* [1972], 113–14).

[5] *La Métaphore vive* (Paris: Seuil, 1975), p. 365.

*prefaces,* as marginal comments written in the margins of other books or texts.[6]

The preface, Derrida says, is "a fourth text. Simulating the postface, the recapitulation.and the recurrent anticipation, the auto-movement of the concept, it is an entirely other, different text, but at the same time, as 'discourse of assistance, it is the 'double' of what it exceeds."[7] The fourth text, as text, is "the beyond everything [which] insofar as it withstands all *ontology* . . . is not a *primum movens.* However, it imparts [*imprime*] to everything . . . a movement of fiction."[8] Derrida *fictionalizes* Western tradition, an action, in part, of tearing down or apart, deconstructing or demolishing.[9]

How does Derrida fictionalize? In other words, what is the fictional motion that his prefaces impress on everything? As the fourth text, it is *dissemination,*[10] deconstruction,[11] *differance*:[12]

---

[6] "All these texts . . . no doubt are the interminable preface to another text that I would one day like to have the strength to write, or again the epigraph to another [text] of which I would never have had the audacity to write . . . " (*Positions* [Paris: Minuit, 1972], p. 14). On marginality, see David Allison, "Derrida's Critique of Husserl: The Philosophy of Presence," Diss. The Pennsylvania State University, 1974, p. 177.

[7] Jacques Derrida, *La Dissémination* (Paris: Seuil, 1972), pp. 33–35.

[8] *Ibid.,* p. 65; my emphasis on *fiction.*

[9] This unbuilding at times seems close to the negative moment often assigned to the creative imagination. See Ray Hart, *Unfinished Man and the Imagination* (New York: Herder, 1968), pp. 247–49.

[10] "*Dissémination* ultimately has no meaning and cannot be channeled into a definition. . . . If it is not possible to summarize dissemination, the seminal differance, in its conceptual tenor, it is because the force and form of its disruption *break through* the semantic horizon. . . . Dissemination . . . by producing a non-finite number of semantic effects, does not allow itself to be reduced either to a present of simple origin (*La Dissémination, La Double Séance, La Mythologie Blanche* are practical re-stagings of all the false starts, beginnings, incipits, titles, exergues, fictitious pretexts, etc.: decapitations) or to an eschatological presence. It marks an irreducible and *generative* multiplicity. The *supplément* and the turbulence of a certain lack break down the limit of the text, exempt it from exhaustive and enclosing formalization or at least prohibit a saturating taxonomy of its themes, of its signified, of its intended meaning *(vouloir-dire).*

"Here we are *playing,* of course, upon the fortuitious resemblance, upon the purely simulative kinship between *seme* and *semen.* They are in no way interconnected by meaning. And yet, in this skidding and this purely external collusion, the accident does produce a sort of semantic mirage: the deviance of the intended meaning, its reflective-effect *(effet-reflet)* in writing sets a process in motion." Taken from *Positions,* pp. 61–62; ET: "Positions," *Diacritics,* 2, No. 4 (Winter 1972), 37. See Spivak's Preface in *Of Grammatology,* pp. lxv–lxvi.

[11] Allison in his Translator's Introduction to *Speech and Phenomena* notes: "The term 'deconstruction' *(déconstruction),* while perhaps unusual, should present no difficulties

> *Dissemination* **displaces** *the three of onto-theo-logy according to an angle of a certain bending-back. A crisis of* **versus:** *these marks no longer allow themselves to be resumed or 'decided' in the two of the binary opposition nor sublated [*relever*] in the three of speculative dialectics . . . they* **destroy** *the trinitarian horizon. They textually destroy it: they are the marks of dissemination (and not of polysemy) because they do not allow themselves at any point to be pinned down by the concept or content of a signified. They 'add' there the more or less of a fourth term.*[13]

here. It signifies a project of critical thought whose task is to locate and 'take apart' those concepts which serve as the axioms or rules for a period of thought, those concepts which command the unfolding of an entire epoch of metaphysics. 'Deconstruction' is somewhat less negative than the Heideggerian or Nietzschean terms 'destruction' or 'reversal'; it suggests that certain foundational concepts of metaphysics will never be entirely eliminated, even if their importance may seem to be effectively diminished. There is no simple 'overcoming' of metaphysics or the language of metaphysics. Derrida recognizes, nonetheless, that the system of Western thought is finite; it has a finite number of axioms and a finite number of permutations that will continue to work themselves out in a given period of time as particular moments within this tradition, e.g., as particular schools or movements of philosophy. In this sense, Derrida also speaks of the 'completion' of metaphysics, the terminal point of 'closure' *(clôture)* for the system. But the work of deconstruction does not consist in simply pointing out the structural limits of metaphysics. Rather, in breaking down and disassembling the ground of this tradition, its task is both to exhibit the source of paradox and contradiction within the system, within the very axioms themselves, and to set forth the possibilities for a new kind of meditation, one no longer founded on the metaphysics of presence" (pp. xxxii–xxxiii).

[12] The *a* of differance inscribes the at onceness of differing and deferring in differance (the French verb *différer* has both significations: to differ, to defer or delay; etymologically the English words "differ" and "defer" stem from the same root). Derrida explains in "La différance," translated in *Speech and Phenomena*, p. 137: "the word 'difference' (with an *e*) could never refer to differing as temporalizing or to difference as *polemos* [to difference as division or spacing]. It is this loss of sense that the word differance (with an *a*) will have to schematically compensate for. Differance . . . refers to [its] whole complex of meanings not only when it is supported by a language or interpretive context (like any signification), but it already does so somehow of itself. Or at least it does so more easily by itself than does any other word: here the *a* comes more immediately from the present participle [*différant* (added by tr.)] and brings us closer to the action of 'differing' that is in progress. . . . But while bringing us closer to the infinitive and active core of differing, 'differance' with an *a* neutralizes what the infinitive denotes as simply active, in the same way that 'parlance' does not signify the simple fact of speaking, of speaking to or being spoken to. . . . Here in the usage of our language we must consider that the ending *-ance* is undecided between active and passive. And we shall see why what is designated by 'differance' is neither simply active nor simply passive, that it announces or rather recalls something like the middle voice, that it speaks of an operation which is not an operation, which cannot be thought of either as a passion or as an action of a subject upon an object, as starting from an agent or from a patient, or on the basis of, or in view of, any of these terms."

[13] *La Dissémination*, p. 32.

This textual *crisis* (a crisis of the line, of the line of writing), this addition of the fourth term—that of *fiction*—"must be conceived of in terms other than as a calculus or mechanics of choice."[14] In other words, a new calculus, that of differance or dissemination, is needed, since the crisis of the text is not brought about by polysemy or the overabundance of meaning, but rather by the very inability to decide meaning.

Non-choice runs throughout Derrida's texts. In "Structure, Sign, and Play in the Discourse of the Human Sciences," concerning the "two interpretations of interpretation," that which "dreams of deciphering" the truth or origin and that which "affirms freeplay and tries to pass beyond man and humanism," Derrida says he does not believe "that today there is any question of *choosing*."[15] Or again, in "The Ends of Man," there is no "simple and unique" choice between two forms of deconstruction, either Heidegger's deconstruction of onto-theo-logy by means of its own language or the structuralist way—by "affirming absolute rupture and difference." "A new writing must weave and intertwine the two motifs."[16] This logic of non-choice is the very foundation, if there is one, of Derrida's enterprise. It is the notion of the undecidable—that which, *by analogy,* Derrida says—cannot be decided. By analogy because, as Sarah Kofman notes, undecidability has a reference to decidability, a reference that must be "crossed out."[17]

The undecidable[18] takes into itself this non-choice, as well as the figure of the ellipsis. Derrida says in "Form and Meaning":

*There is, then, probably no choice to be made between two lines of thought; our task is rather to reflect on the circularity which makes the*

[14] "Freud et la scène de l'écriture," p. 302; ET p. 81.

[15] In *L'Ecriture et la différence,* pp. 427–28; ET: in *The Structuralist Controversy: The Languages of Criticism and the Sciences of Man* (Baltimore: The Johns Hopkins Press, 1970), pp. 265–66.

[16] "The Ends of Man," *Philosophy and Phenomenological Research,* 30, No. 1 (1969), 56. A French version of this article was published in Derrida's *Marges de la philosophie* (Paris: Minuit, 1972). The above citations occur on pp. 162–63.

[17] Sarah Kofman, "Un philosophe 'unheimlich,' " in *Ecarts: Quatre Essais à propos de Jacques Derrida* (Paris: Fayard, 1973), p. 148, n. 1. The whole essay of Kofman is invaluable for "understanding" Derrida.

[18] "It was necessary to analyze, to put to work, *in* the text of the history of philosophy as well as *in* the so-called 'literary' text . . . certain marks . . . which I called *by analogy* (I emphasize this) undecidables, i.e., simulative units, 'false' verbal, nominal or semantic properties, which escape from inclusion in the philosophical (binary) opposition and which nonetheless inhabit it, resist and disorganize it, but *without ever* constituting a third term, without ever occasioning a solution in the form of speculative dialectics" (*Positions,* p. 58; ET p. 36).

*one pass into the other indefinitely. And, by strictly repeating this*
**circle** *in its own historical possibility, we allow the production of some*
**elliptical** *change of site, within the difference involved in repetition; this*
*displacement is no doubt deficient, but with a deficiency that is not yet,*
*or is already no longer, absence, negativity, nonbeing, lack, silence.*
*Neither matter nor form, it is nothing that any philosopheme, that is,*
*any dialectic, however determinate, can capture. It is an ellipsis of*
*both meaning and form; it is neither plenary speech nor perfectly*
*circular. More and less, neither more nor less—it is perhaps an*
*entirely different question.*[19]

The undecidable's logic is that of the ellipsis of the circle, a deformed,
decentered circle. Along with the circle, this logic of the undecidable,
of differance, unhinges the point, line, and space and time themselves:

*differance already suggests a mode of writing (**écriture**) without*
*presence and absence—without history, cause, **arche,** or **telos**—which*
*would overturn all dialectic, theology, teleology, and ontology. This*
*mode of writing would exceed everything that the history of*
*metaphysics has conceived in the form of the Aristotelian **gramme**: the*
*point, the line, the circle, as well as time and space themselves.*[20]

This logic of "differance" is what animates, finally, the early text of
Derrida translated here, his *Introduction* to Husserl's *The Origin of
Geometry.* In *Of Grammatology,* Derrida says what can also be said of
this *Introduction:* "Here as elsewhere, to pose the problem in terms of
choice, to oblige or to believe oneself obliged to answer it by a *yes* or
*no,* to conceive of appurtenance as an allegiance or nonappurtenance as
plain speaking, is to confuse very different levels, paths, and styles. In
the deconstruction of the arche [the proto-], one does not make a
choice." Even more important for our purposes is the line just before
this. Derrida says: "*That is why a thought of the trace [differance] can no
more break with a transcendental phenomenology than be reduced to
it.*"[21]

In other words, Derrida is as much a phenomenologist as not, is as

[19] "La Forme et le vouloir-dire: note sur la phénoménologie du langage," in *Marges,* p.
207; ET in *Speech and Phenomena,* p. 128.

[20] "Ousia et grammè: note sur une note de *Sein und Zeit,*" in *Marges,* p. 78; ET:
" '*Ousia* and *Gramme*': A Note to a Footnote in *Being and Time,*" tr. Edward S. Casey,
in *Phenomenology in Perspective,* ed. F. J. Smith (The Hague: Nijhoff, 1970), p. 93.

[21] P. 62.

much a structuralist as not, an atheist as well as thinker of the sacred,[22] as neither. Choices need not be made here, in fact, cannot be made!

## DERRIDA'S *INTRODUCTION* TO *THE ORIGIN OF GEOMETRY*

> *"To deconstruct" philosophy would . . . be to think the*
> *structured genealogy of its concepts in the most faithful or*
> *interior manner, but at the same time it would be to determine*
> *from a certain outside unqualifiable or unnameable by*
> *philosophy itself what this history could dissemble or prohibit,*
> *becoming history through this somewhere interested*
> *suppression.*
>      Positions

*Speech and Phenomena,* Derrida says, is the "essay I value the most."[23] In this work he questions "the privilege of the voice [speech] and phonetic writing in relation to all of Western history, such as this question lets itself be depicted in the history of metaphysics and in its most modern, critical, and vigilant form: Husserl's transcendental phenomenology."[24] It can be considered, Derrida feels, as a long note to *Of Grammatology,* but a note that has the first place "in a classic philosophic architecture." Or, he says, *Speech and Phenomena* can be considered as "the other side (front or back as you wish) of another essay, published in 1962, as an Introduction to Husserl's *Origin of Geometry.* There the problems concerning writing were already in place as such and connected to the irreducible structure of '*différer*' in its relations to consciousness, presence, science, history and the history of science, the disappearance or delaying of the origin, and so on."[25]

---

[22] E. Donato in "Structuralism: The Aftermath," p. 25, sees *Of Grammatology,* along with Foucault's *The Order of Things,* as "the only quest for time past and time regained that a fundamentally *atheist* [my emphasis] epistemological configuration might offer." Also see on this Mikel Dufrenne, "Pour une philosophie non théologique," in his *Le Poétique,* 2nd revised and enlarged ed. (Paris: Presses Universitaires de France, 1973), pp. 7–57. On Derrida and the sacred, see Henri Meschonnic, *Le Signe et le poème* (Paris: Gallimard, 1975), pp. 401–92.

[23] *Positions,* p. 13.

[24] *Ibid.*

[25] *Ibid.* Derrida has an even earlier essay on Husserl, given at a conference in 1959, entitled " 'Genèse et structure' et la phénoménologie." It was reprinted in *L'Ecriture et la différence* in 1967, but first appeared in 1965 in *Entretiens sur les notions de genèse et de structure,* ed. Maurice de Gandillac et al. (Paris: Mouton, 1965), pp. 243–60. This, then, is both before and after the work on the *Origin,* having obviously undergone changes by the time of its reprinting in *L'Ecriture* (the use of the concept *différance* on p. 239 is the clearest and simplest example of this change). The article is very helpful for understanding Derrida's *Introduction.*

In these comments Derrida presents us with an option. As he suggests, we could take *Speech and Phenomena* as the reverse of his *Introduction,* which becomes the obverse, the right or proper *(recto)* side. In light of the comments above, the *Introduction* would then be the essay Derrida valued the most. Or, if this is to go too far, as the reverse (or improper) side, Derrida's *Introduction* is still to be highly prized (and is so by Derrida[26]), since it is the whole which has value. More perversely, the improper side, attacking by its very impropriety the proper side, "supplements" the value of the second essay, *Speech and Phenomena.* In this option, the *Introduction* is both proper (since it was written first, in 1961, six years before the publication of *Speech and Phenomena*) and improper (since it is the reverse of the second essay).

The above comments, taken from Henri Ronse's interview with Derrida in 1967, and the options they present provide further justification for a close reading of Derrida's first major published essay, his *Introduction* to *The Origin of Geometry.* It is also an introduction to the work of Derrida in general and furnishes a basic part of the framework for his later, present work. *That basic framework*—and here framework should possibly be changed immediately to set of problems, optic, method, if all these terms were not already inadequate to what we are going to consider—*is phenomenology.* However, as will become clear, the phenomenology in question is not that rejected by Michel Foucault in his Foreword to the English edition of *The Order of Things,* a phenomenology "which gives absolute priority to the observing subject, which attributes a constitutent role to an act, which places its own point of view at the origin of all historicity—which, in short, leads to a transcendental consciousness."[27] What I wish to claim by saying that Derrida's framework is phenomenological is not that he is Husserlian or Heideggerian, or even idealist or existential, or that his method is phenomenological. Rather, I want to suggest that Derrida has found in and *at the limits* precisely where phenomenology fails (i.e., where it becomes the modern, exemplary recapitulation of Western metaphysics) a fertile ground for cultivating questions about the non-

---

[26] Derrida often refers to and summarizes the results obtained in this study in his later work. See, for example, *Speech and Phenomena,* pp. 80–81; or *L'Ecriture et la différence,* pp. 22 and 248.

[27] *The Order of Things: An Archaeology of the Human Sciences* (New York: Vintage Books, 1973), p. xiv. I cannot resist citing Foucault's statement to the "English-speaking reader" concerning his relation to the other half of the phenomenological-structural debate: "In France, certain half-witted 'commentators' persist in labelling me a 'structuralist'. I have been unable to get it into their tiny minds that I have used none of the methods, concepts, or key terms that characterize structural analysis" (xiv).

philosophical *per se* (the limits or "margins" of philosophy), about writing, origins and history, and differance.

Moreover, the phenomenology Derrida examines and argues with is the "phenomenology of signification."[28] Subtitled "Introduction to the Problem of Signs in Husserl's Phenomenology," *Speech and Phenomena* leads to the conclusion: "There never was any 'perception.' "[29] Further: "And contrary to what phenomenology—which is always phenomenology of perception—has tried to make us believe, contrary to what our desire cannot fail to be tempted into believing, *the thing itself always escapes*."[30] Based on the *"absolute will-to-hear-oneself-speak,"*[31] phenomenology must always fail, must always delay-defer-differentiate *the thing itself,* even the absolute foundation for so much of today's thought, i.e., self-consciousness. What remains is "for us to *speak,* to make our voices resonate throughout the corridors in order to make up for the breakup of presence, in order to supplement the impact of one's presence."[32]

Derrida's work to date remains *inside* this *failure* and *need to speak* of phenomenology. As he shows, phenomenology breaks upon the rock of presence; it is "a subjection of *sense* to seeing, of sense to the sense of sight, since sense in general is in fact the concept of every phenomenological field."[33] Yet "before" this breaking up, in the midst of it, is where Derrida works. Prior to the metaphysical claims that phenomenology exercises and within the possibility of a deconstructive reversal of the hierarchy of sight and sense, since they are undecidable—that is where fruitful Husserlian work can be done. The problem of method within these limits is what we will see developed in Derrida's *Introduction.*

The *Introduction* to *The Origin of Geometry* is a long, extensive essay concerned with a short independent fragment included, according to Husserl's probable intent, as an Appendix to *The Crisis of European*

[28] See Paul Ricoeur, "Negativity and Primary Affirmation," in his *History and Truth,* tr. Charles A. Kelbley (Evanston: Northwestern University Press, 1965), p. 312.

[29] p. 103. Also see the comments of Newton Garver in his Preface to this work, xxiii–xxiv, as well as Note 4 above.

[30] *Ibid.,* p. 104.

[31] *Ibid.,* p. 102.

[32] *Ibid.,* p. 104 and xxviii–xxix.

[33] "Form and Meaning," in *Marges,* p. 188; ET in *Speech and Phenomena,* pp. 108–09.

*Sciences and Transcendental Phenomenology*. The major thread guiding Husserl's reflections in the *Origin* is the question of beginnings or origins within *history* and their sense. Derrida's *Introduction* respects Husserl's manner of proceeding therein. His commentary–interpretation follows the order of questioning and the problems raised by Husserl, and within this structure Derrida elaborates and elucidates—and finally "supplements"—what Husserl writes. In what follows, however, I will not proceed so rigorously. Instead, I will elucidate the architectural "concept" of historicity (sense-history) and the related areas of questioning it entails: language, writing, ideality, the Living Present, and the transcendental. These comments will be pursued within Derrida's attempt to understand the interplay of phenomenology's "principle of all principles" and its final institution: the interplay within consciousness of the definite thing present in person and the infinite Idea as an always deferred Telos. Derrida wants to understand phenomenology as it is "*stretched* between the *finitizing* consciousness of its *principle* and the *infinitizing* consciousness of its final *institution, the Endstiftung* indefinitely deferred in its content but always evident in its regulative value."[34] The dialectic of these two, phenomenon and Idea, are what Derrida seems to feel implicitly guided Husserl in his reflections on historicity, and a study of Derrida's commentary reveals what happens when these implications are made explicit.

## Historicity

For Husserl, historicity *(Geschichtlichkeit)*[35] concerns the origins and traditions of ideal objects, and tradition itself is understood to be both the process of handing down and the endurance of this process, a

[34] Jacques Derrida, *Introduction* et Traduction de *L'Origine de la géométrie* de Husserl, 2nd ed. (Paris: Presses Universitaires de France, 1974). Translations will be taken from the text as presented below and the page references will be cited in the text within parenthesis. For this quote: (138).

[35] It should be noted that *Geschichtlichkeit* is the term used many years earlier by Martin Heidegger in *Being and Time,* §§72–77: "Temporality and *Geschichtlichkeit.*" Although the English translators of Heidegger's work, John Macquarrie and Edward Robinson, have rendered the term as *historicality,* most translators, including Derrida, prefer the term *historicity* for *Geschichtlichkeit.* I have followed the latter, using historicity throughout. However, although both Heidegger and Husserl use the same term, their senses are different, as Derrida's *Introduction* should make clear.

In addition, David Carr, who translated Husserl's *Crisis,* explains in his *Phenomenology and the Problem of History* (Evanston: Northwestern University Press, 1974), pp. 66–67, that Husserl's concern with the problem of history did not arise from his

heritage. Ideal objects are what alone guarantee "the possibility of historicity, i.e., the always intersubjective consciousness of history" (29). In other words, historicity is always a *sense-history*. It operates on the level of sense and is related to the problems of language, ideality, truth, and humankind in its Living Present—the source of all sense and history.

According to Derrida there are two consequences to this view for Husserl. First, Husserl's inquiry back to the origin (in this case) of geometry is an inquiry into the sense-history of *geometrical* truths, into the origin and transmission of *geometrical* ideal objectivities or objects, an inquiry that can only be a "sense-investigation" (as Husserl used the term) *of geometry*.[36] Derrida says about this: "To meditate on or investigate the sense *(besinnen)* of origins is at the same time to: make oneself responsible *(verantworten)* for the sense *(Sinn)* of science and philosophy, bring this sense to the clarity of its 'fulfil[ment],' and put oneself in a position of *responsibility* for this sense starting from the total sense of our existence" (31). Sense-investigation reveals the conditions for and the sense of historicity, but only through personal responsibility and response.

Secondly, the origin of ideal objects, as *origin,* raises for Husserl the problem of their enduring heritage, their tradition. In other words, if ideal objects are truly original and primordial, how can they be recognized or known. What places them in history is their *"essence-of-the-first-time,"* their *Erstmaligkeit;* they do not occur, Husserl says, in a

---

acquaintance with Heidegger's *Being and Time:* "It is hardly to be expected, however, that a problem with which Husserl is so preoccupied could have occurred to him overnight, as it were, or even have entered his thinking from an outside source—such as Heidegger's *Being and Time* (with its chapter on *Geschichtlichkeit*), which Husserl seems to have studied carefully, for the first time, in 1932. We intend to show, in fact, that the concept of historicity has its roots in reflections on various subjects going back as far as 1913, and that its emergence in the *Crisis* is the effect of an accumulation and confluence of trains of thought which ultimately force Husserl's new introduction to phenomenology to take on its peculiar form." Carr refers, then, to Gadamer's support of this position in his *Truth and Method,* tr. ed. Garrett Barden and John Cumming (New York: Seabury Press, 1975), p. 215: "These statements of the later Husserl [concerning historicity] might be motivated by the debate with *Being and Time,* but they are preceded by so many other attempts to formulate his position that it is clear that Husserl had always had in mind the application of his ideas to the problems of the historical sciences."

[36] Sense-investigation, *Besinnung, prise de conscience*—George Steiner explains this notion well in *After Babel: Aspects of Language and Translation* (New York: Oxford University Press, 1975): "The complete penetrative grasp of a text, the complete discovery and recreative apprehension of its life-forms *(prise de conscience),* is an act whose realization can be precisely felt but is nearly impossible to paraphrase or systematize" (p. 25).

*"topos ouranios,"* in some heavenly locale, and then descend to the earth. Rather, ideal objects are "traditional objects," and they possess historicity as one of their "eidetic components" (48). Thus any attempt to get at the "origin" of these ideal objects, any historical "reduction," would be *"reactivating* and noetic," and it would have to work through free phantasy (imaginary) variation. However, as *tradition,* ideal objects have accreted (and continue to do so) sedimentations in their transmission, their delivery to the present and future. They have picked up lateral and latent strata which the historical reduction must finally reduce in order to reach back and grasp the origins of the idealities under discussion.

Since the origin in question here is a phenomenological one, its reactivation entails a return inquiry *(Rückfrage).* This inquiry always starts with an origin's *tradition,* which must in turn be reduced to the very origin the inquiry is seeking to reactivate. In other words, tradition is essential to both the inquiry back to and the reactivation of an origin. *Rückfrage* is the questioning back *through tradition* to the origin of ideality. Yet, as Husserl's term suggests, this questioning responds to an already received message that the tradition hands over. *Reactivation* is the human capacity or ability to reawaken the primordial sense that sedimented (traditional) sense covers over. A finite and mediate capacity, reactivation must work through equivocal language to regain a primordial sense. It is, according to Derrida, *Verantwortung* and *Besinnung,* the reawakening and being responsible for the primordial sense that the equivocal tradition conceals. As finite and mediate (i.e., traditional), the ability to reactivate sense can be lost, a plight that Husserl felt gave rise to the crisis in philosophy which characterized modern times. And yet, Husserl continued, reactivation as a capacity of humankind in general can be infinitized through the idealizing power of geometry.

The role of tradition in Husserl's thought becomes clearer, Derrida points out, when we notice that tradition operates analogously to the "dialectic" of internal time-consciousness, the dialectic of protention and retention within the Living Present. The historical sedimentation of sense interplays with the creation of new sense within the horizon of present sense. All of which is possible for Husserl, we shall see, because of language, particularly written language (87). Thus, historicity becomes possible through return inquiry and reactivation, and yet both are possible only because there is an origin and tradition of ideal objects, because there is historicity. This circle, Derrida explains, is what concerns Husserl: "what seems to be of utmost importance to Husserl is as much an operation (reactivation itself as the ability to open a hidden historical field) as the nature of the field itself (as the possibility of something like reactivation)'' (51).

So far we have seen that historicity is concerned with the origin and tradition of ideal objects. For Husserl the latter notion, that of ideal objects, requires examination of both objectivity and ideality. First the problem of the former, then the latter.

Origins are beginnings of something new; as such, they raise the problem of recognizability. Husserl answers by saying that there must be some objectivity in the origin of an ideality for the ideality to be recognizable.[37] This means, Derrida says, that the ''sense of the constituting act can only be deciphered in the web of the constituted object. And this necessity is not an external fate, but an essential necessity of intentionality. The *primordial* sense of every intentional act is *only* its *final* sense, i.e., the constitution of an object'' (64). In other words, objectivity, a correlate of intentionality, forces intentionality—the problem of recognizability—to be grasped first through its final product: the constituted object. So the question is narrowed: what allows for the objectivity of a primordial sense, an origin-al sense, since the conditions of objectivity are those of historicity?

This brings us to the problem of language, that by which sense itself—or rather, expressive meaning, linguistic meaning—obtains its ideal objectivity. In his comments, Derrida elaborates three degrees of ideal objectivity implicit in Husserl's analysis. First, there is the level of the word's ideal objectivity. The word ''lion,'' for instance, is recognizable within several languages, but is bound to those languages in which the word itself makes sense. Secondly, there is the level of the word's sense. The intended content or signification of the word ''lion'' is available to many languages, for example, *Leo, Löwe,* lion, such that the ideality signified thereby is free ''from all factual linguistic subjectivity'' (71). Thirdly, there is the level of absolute ideal objectivity, such

[37] Dorion Cairns, in his review-abstract of Husserl's ''Die Frage nach dem Ursprung der Geometrie als intentional-historisches Problem'' (''Inquiry Concerning the Origin of Geometry: a Problem of Intentional History''), *Philosophy and Phenomenological Research,* 1, No. 1 (1940), p. 100, accurately presents Husserl's answer to this problem (he is abstracting from the German transcription Fink published in the same journal in 1939): ''Our mathematics, however, exists as an age-long advance from acquisition to acquisition. Therefore it must have been a more primitive sense that first was projected and appeared in the evidence of a successful execution. But the phrase is redundant. Evidence means the grasping of a being in the consciousness of its original 'itself-thereness.' And grasping covers other acts besides simply perceptive seeing. The sense of the meant object indicates the way to grasp it *originaliter.* Sense-formations whose nature it is to exist as subjectively produced results are 'grasped' *originaliter* in being produced. Successfully realizing a project *is* evidence; in the realizing, the effect is there as 'itself.' ''

as the free idealities of geometry. The ideality in question here is that of "the object itself." On this level of objectivity, there is no adherence to any de facto language, only adherence to the possibility of language in general.[38] This means that translation is infinitely open. Derrida has elucidated these three degrees in order to show that when Husserl, in the *Origin,* does not distinguish between the object itself and its sense, this can only occur within the third region of ideal objectivity, the absolutely free ideal objectivity of language. Thus language is the tool for revealing ideal objectivity, which in turn reveals, since it does not live in a *"topos ouranios,"* that objectivity itself is intrinsically historical and must be connected with transcendental subjectivity. The ground for transcendental historicity is uncovered.

Husserl's question then becomes the "how" of ideality (and not yet that of its origin): how does ideality, particularly geometrical ideality, arrive at absolute ideal objectivity from its *intra*personal origin in the inventor's mind? Paradoxically, he goes back once again to language. He says that ideality arrives at its absolute objectivity by means of language, the very thing from which it was trying to escape just a moment ago. "The paradox," Derrida says, "is that, without the apparent fall back into language and thereby into history, a fall which would alienate the ideal purity of sense, sense would remain an empirical formation imprisoned as fact in a psychological subjectivity—*in the inventor's head.* Historical incarnation [in language] sets free the transcendental, instead of binding it. The last notion, the transcendental, must then be rethought" (77). I will return to this rethinking in a moment.

This "how" is achieved because humankind is "in one and the same world," and consciousness of this fact "establishes the possibility of a universal language. Mankind is first conscious of itself [Husserl says] 'as an immediate and mediate linguistic community'" (79). In addition, our Earth, as the place of all objects, is not an object itself and cannot become one for an objective science. In fact, Derrida comments, "the possibility of a geometry strictly complements the impossibility of what could be called a 'geo-logy,' the objective science of the Earth itself" (83). Geology is as radically impossible, then, as is an objective science of transcendental subjectivity. And geometry is possible only insofar as the above is true, since phenomenology's basic principle of finitude always interplays with an infinite (and nonobjec-

---

[38] However, as Derrida points out in a note, p. 72 below, this ideality occurs and is discovered in a factual language, and this occurrence is "the crucial difficulty of all [Husserl's] philosophy of history: what is the sense of this last [type of] factuality?"

tive) ideal pole—here, our Earth—the zero-point of all perception, the "infinite horizon" of every object.

The problem of language and ideality, however, is first encountered *intra*personally. The first inventor of geometry, for example, must have been able to recognize and communicate a geometrical ideality within his own individual consciousness. Sense must be recognized and communicated as the same sense from one moment of the ego to another absolutely different moment of the same ego. Here again Husserl returns to the unique form of temporalization, the Living Present, whose dialectical character and primordiality permit intrapersonal communication. In a sense, then, Derrida concludes, *inter*subjectivity is first *intra*subjectivity, a fact that explains Husserl's reversion once more to the Living Present in his discussion about the crucial role of writing.

As *inter*personal communication par excellence, writing guarantees for Husserl the possibility of absolute ideal objectivity. And Derrida argues that, since the *possibility* of writing gives sense the ability to become *nonspatiotemporal,* writing "sanctions and completes the existence of pure transcendental historicity" (87), thus pushing humankind, Husserl feels, across a new threshold—that of transcendental community. Derrida's comment on this result, that the "authentic act of writing is a transcendental reduction performed by and toward the *we*" (92), indicates that writing is a counterpart to the Living Present in interpersonal communication. In order not to have truth disappear from the world, from *inter*subjectivity, both men revert to the Living Present, to the intentional act of the ego, to *intra*subjectivity. Since writing is *intentional*—i.e., it makes sense—Husserl argues back to writing's intentionality, to the ego's intentional act in the act of writing, to the Living Present which grounds every intentional act in both its alterity and sameness. Adapting Derrida's succinct remarks about the Living Present, we could say, then, that writing "constitutes the other as other in itself and the same as same in the other" (86).

## Historicity and the Transcendental

Historicity, Husserl says, is humankind's essential horizon: the Living Present founds the historic Present, and the historic Present as traditionalization (the incessant totalization of the Past in the Present) reveals the universal Apriori of history. The Living Present *is,* to adapt Husserl's words twice quoted by Derrida, "the vital movement of the coexistence and the interweaving . . . of primordial formations and sedimentations of sense" (109). Humankind is a community of speaking beings in their Living Presents, the Living Present being the "final retrenchment" and "security," Derrida says, "of every phenomenological reduction" (110–11). He wonders if Husserl's merit was not in having described, in a truly *transcendental* move, "the conditions of possibility for history which were at the same time *concrete* . . . because they are experienced under the form of *horizon*" (117)? Horizon is the Living Present's dialectical form, the how of its temporalization, the "already there" of its dialectics of sense.

So far the problem of ideality's origin has been left in abeyance. Derrida points out that Husserl will leave the question open. Geometrical ideality is always *based on* the morphological idealities of imagination and sense, yet it is always already a rupture with that sensible-morphological idealization. We could say, perhaps, that Husserl leaves each strand undecided: geometry is what has taken place in the Greek creative infinitization, and yet this *scientific, theoretical* leap is always based on the morphological, sensible idealization of the prescientific world, the *Lebenswelt*. Thus he saves, Derrida concludes, both the absolutely original sense of each traditional line (its historicity) and its "relativity" within history in general (131).

However, the idealizing activity of *understanding,* of "pure thinking," i.e., of the nonimaginative and nonsensible, is never studied in itself; nor are its conditions. It is a radical operation, a *passage to the limit* whose structure is that of mathematical idealization, the "again and again" which Derrida feels must have its *protentional* correlate in intentionality. Once again we are led back to the Living Present, "the phenomenological absolute," the now needing a past which in turn needs a future toward which the present always already tends, so that the present is the horizon for past and future. However, Derrida says, the unity of this movement is never given, it must be experienced or *thought* (thereby making the phenomenalization of time possible). This unity, the work of the Idea in the Kantian sense,[39] is never phenomenalized in itself. Here again we see the "conflict" between the finitizing consciousness of phenomenology's principle and the infinitizing consciousness of its final institution, the infinite Idea that authorizes finitude.

What then is the historicity of the mathematical (philosophical) origin, if the Idea is what allows for ideality's origin? Both the Idea and Reason are historicities, both must expose "themselves" in order to be, although neither are exhausted in this exposition. They are eternal yet

---

[39] See *L'Ecriture,* pp. 242 and 250 on the concept of the Idea in the Kantian sense.

historical, since eternity is a mode of historicity. Derrida states, in a decisive sentence, that the absoluteness of the Idea "is the Absolute *of* intentional historicity" (142), adding that the "of" designates neither a subjective nor objective genetive, i.e., neither the "Absolute" nor "intentional historicity" has first place. In other words, the Idea as authorization of ideality, as the limit toward which ideality passes, *reveals* the limit of historicity (and thereby its own limit): the progressive— *creative*—movement of intentionality. This progressive movement is tradition, or as Derrida says, "intentionality is traditionality." Moreover, since it is the dialectical root of the Living Present, "intentionality is the root of historicity." Consequently, Derrida concludes, there is no need to inquire about the sense of historicity, "historicity is *sense*" (150). In other words, sense is *traditionality* and "the *Absolute is Passage*" (149). The absolute is the act of all tradition (and of historicity and intentionality): transmission in the act of creation.

Now Derrida also says that sense is "the appearing of being" (148), which means that being is historical. So the question for him becomes: what is "the origin of Being as History" (151)? Ontology may ask the question, but only phenomenology can provide the apparatus for an answer. Being, Derrida says, "is *silently* shown under the negativity of the *apeiron*" *(ibid)*. The *delay* or *lateness* of speech in this manifestation of Being is finally the philosophical, not just the phenomenological, absolute. Derrida says:

> Here delay is the philosophical absolute, because the beginning of
> methodic reflection can only consist in the consciousness of the
> implication of **another** previous, possible, and absolute origin in
> general. Since this alterity of the absolute origin structurally appears in
> my **Living Present** and since it can appear and be recognized only
> in the primordiality of something like my **Living Present**, this very fact
> signifies the authenticity of phenomenological delay and limitation. In
> the lackluster guise of a technique, the Reduction is only pure thought
> as that delay, pure thought investigating the sense of itself as delay
> within philosophy. (152–53)

Pure thought is always delay. Consciousness of this delay, Derrida says, is consciousness of Difference: consciousness of the impossibility of remaining in the simple now of the Living Present as well as the "inability to live enclosed in" a simple undivided Absolute. The Living Present, the never present origin of Being and Sense, interplays with the always deferred Absolute within this consciousness, a consciousness without which, Derrida concludes, "nothing would appear."

Without "its own proper dehiscence," there would be no historicity, no sense, nothing.

More abstractly, then, an Origin, an absolute Origin, must be a dif-fer*a*nt Origin—the never–yet–always–already–there as the "beyond" or "before" that makes all sense possible. That Difference, Derrida con-jectures, "is perhaps what always has been said under the concept of *'transcendental'* through the enigmatic history of its displacements." So Primordial Difference would be transcendental—as must be, finally, historicity and reflections thereon.

## DECONSTRUCTION AND THE SCIENCE OF OLD NAMES

*The "rationality"—but perhaps that word should be abandoned*
*for reasons that will appear at the end of this sentence—which*
*governs a writing thus enlarged and radicalized, no longer*
*issues from a logos. Further, it inaugurates the destruction, not*
*the demolition but the de-sedimentation, the de-construction, of*
*all the significations that have their source in that of the logos.*
*Particularly the signification of truth.*
Of Grammatology

Prior to elaborating the "structure" of historicity, I described the deconstructive logic of the undecidable, of non-choice, of *differance*. However, differance is also an *old name*, a name *sous rature*, obliterated by old senses, parenthesized. The deconstruction of differance includes then a de-sedimentation and supplementation (or substitution) of an old name for a new "concept." This paleonymic supplementarity is a sec-ond moment or level of Derrida's deconstruction, second moment or level being understood neither hierarchically nor chronologically. This supplementary grafting is noteworthy in Derrida's *Introduction*. He has *added* something new, something different, to the old name of phenomenology in that text.

The movement of supplementarity, as one of "a certain number of nonsynonymic substitutions" for differance,[40] involves, according to Derrida, two major senses (taken from the French verb *suppléer*): to fill a deficiency (to complete) and to take the place of (to replace).[41] This is

---

[40] "Differance," in *Speech and Phenomena*, p. 147.

[41] On the "concept" of supplementarity, see: *Speech and Phenomena*, ch. 7; *Of Grammatology*, Part II, ch. 2; *La Dissémination*, pp. 180–96; and Alan Bass, " 'Literature'/Literature," *Velocities of Change: Critical Essays from MLN*, ed. Richard Macksey (Baltimore: The Johns Hopkins Press, 1974), pp. 348–49.

deconstruction as the science of old names: it fills a deficiency in the old concept and replaces it while using its old name. Derrida asks:

> What is, then, the "strategic" necessity which sometimes requires that an **old name** be preserved in order to initiate a new concept? With all the reservations imposed by the traditional distinction between the name and the concept, one ought to be able to begin to describe this operation: aware of the fact that a name does not name the punctual simplicity of a concept but the system of predicates defining the concept, the conceptual structure **centered** on such and such a predicate, one proceeds: (1) to the setting-aside (**prélèvement**) of a reduced predicative trait, which is held in reserve and limited within a given conceptual structure (limited for some motivations and relations of force which are to be analyzed) **named** x; (2) to the de-limitation, the grafting, and the controlled extension of this predicate which was set aside, the name x being maintained as a **tool of intervention (levier d'intervention)** in order to maintain a hold on the former organization which it is effectively a question of transforming. Setting-aside, grafting, extension: you know that this is what I called, according to the process that I have just described, **writing**.[42]

The science of old names is writing, an old name itself.

Let me now rehearse some of the supplementations that Derrida advances in the *Introduction*. He says Difference is transcendental—transcendental being the primordial Difference of a different Origin. Thus transcendental is equivalent to differ*a*nt (with an *a*).

Consciousness of Difference, that without which nothing would appear, is transcendental consciousness, i.e., differant consciousness. So we could say that consciousness is differance (with an *a*).[43]

Similarly, the Reduction, pure thought of its own delay, is transcendental. Derrida says: "The pure and interminable disquietude of thought striving to 'reduce' Difference by going beyond factual infinity toward the infinity of its sense and value, i.e., while maintaining Difference—that disquietude would be transcendental" (153). The Reduction, thought's own disquietude at Difference, can only be a differant Reduction.

Primordial Difference is transcendental. And transcendental Difference, i.e., the always deferred-differing difference of the origin, is differance (with an *a*).

---

[42] *Positions*, p. 96; ET: *Diacritics*, 3, No. 1 (Spring 1973), p. 37.

[43] See *Speech and Phenomena*, ch. 5: "Signs and the Blink of an Eye," pp. 60–69, as well as Note 4 above.

And, finally, because it is a method for reflecting on historicity, *Rückfrage* is thereby transcendental: it is a *differant* process. Derrida says: "And Thought's pure certainty would be transcendental, since it can look forward to the already announced Telos only by advancing on (or being in advance of) the Origin that indefinitely reserves itself. Such a certainty never had to learn that Thought would always be to come" *(ibid.).*

Thus the Reduction, *Rückfrage,* consciousness, and intentionality—all basic concepts of phenomenology—have been supplemented by *differance;* they all partake of its logic. Yet they are still *named* Reduction, *Rückfrage,* and so on. Phenomenology has been supplemented, its metaphysical text deconstructed, and the old names retained. Phenomenology is no longer, but still is, phenomenology. Its "is" is that of all metaphysics, *sous rature:* i̶s̶.

Is there a *need* to choose here between undecidables and old names? Is one choice more faithful to Derrida's intent than the other, is one in fact different from the other? The exemplary case here seems to be *differance* itself, in which undecidables and old names are both *present* and *deferred* in the silent tomb of the *a,* in a fragile letter that is easily erased, crossed out, or misprinted, an *a* that is hardly readable and definitely undecidable.

## TRANSLATOR'S NOTE

The translation offered here is that of the second edition of Derrida's *Introduction,* published by Presses Universitaires de France in 1974. The first edition was published in 1962. In the text itself, I have indicated references to present English translations of works to which Derrida refers, but have modified them where necessary to underscore Derrida's argumentation. These modifications have been indicated by the word "modified" inserted within brackets in the text. Texts unavailable in English translation I have translated from the French. The Husserl texts have been modified in accordance with many of the suggestions of Dorion Cairns' *Guide for Translating Husserl,* particularly when they bear on a point that Derrida is arguing.

All German terms in parentheses are Derrida's additions. Similarly, all explanatory brackets that occur within quotations are Derrida's additions. I have included certain French and German terms within brackets where necessary in the text.

Such terms as *de facto* and *de jure* have been underscored only where Derrida has stressed them himself, since they are often translations of the French "en fait" and "en droit." The same is true of *apriori* (adjec-tival form) and *a priori* (adverbial or substantive form). Likewise, I have followed Cairns' suggestion in differentiating between *Objektivität* and *Gegenständlichkeit* by the capital or lower case "o" respectively. (Der-rida, following the French tradition, indicates *Gegenständlichkeit* by the neologism *objectité* and *Objektivität* by *objectivité*.) However, since the French *objet* comprises both the meaning of *Gegenstand* and that of *Objekt,* no differentiation is possible for the word "object," although in quotations from Husserl it has been retained. For further details on this problem, see the Translator's Preface of Lester E. Embree to Suzanne Bachelard's *A Study of Husserl's* Formal and Transcendental Logic. Finally, the translation has been done in light of and in accordance with David Allison's earlier translation of Derrida's *Speech and Phenomena*.

I would like to thank various people for their invaluable aid in the process of this translation. To Professors Robert Detweiler, William Beardslee, and Arthur Evans, I extend my sincerest thanks for their long-term encouragement. I would also like to thank Professor Evans for his patient checking of the complete first draft with the French text. The same appreciation is extended to Professor James Dagenais for his invaluable suggestions in relation to the first half of the translation. And I am particularly grateful to Professor David Allison for his personal friendship and editorial aid, as well as his invaluable translation of Derrida's other major work on Husserl. Professor J. Hillis Miller was also very helpful with his many bibliographical aids and goodwill. And, finally, I am most deeply indebted to Professor Derrida himself for his personal help and patient advice during this time. His cordiality and support were greatly appreciated.

I would also like to thank friends who kindly helped in the prepara-tion of the final draft: Bernard Matt, Ron Rembert, and most particu-larly Barbara DeConcini and Carla Schissel. Also, to Walter Russell I want to extend gratitude for persistent good humor and friendship dur-ing this period. Finally, I would like to thank the Belgian American Educational Foundation for providing me with time to complete this work.

I wish to dedicate this work to the memory of my father, who only saw half its completion, and to my mother.

*John P. Leavey*

*Louvain-Leuven*
*December 1976*

# Introduction
## to
## "The Origin of Geometry"

By its date and themes, this meditation of Husserl [*The Origin of Geometry*] belongs to the last group of writings that surround *The Crisis of European Sciences and Transcendental Phenomenology*.[1] It is deeply rooted there and to that extent its originality runs the risk of not being immediately apparent. If *The Origin of Geometry* is distinguishable from the *Crisis,* it is not because of its descriptive novelty. Nearly all its motifs are already present in other investigations, whether they be largely prior to or almost contemporary with it. In fact, *The Origin of Geometry* still concerns the status of the ideal objects of science (of which geometry is one example), their production, by identifying acts, as "the same," and the constitution of exactitude through idealization and passage to the limit—a process which starts with the life-world's sensible, finite, and prescientific materials. Also in question are the

[1] *Die Krisis der europäischen Wissenschaften und die tranzendentale Phänomenologie: Eine Einleitung in die phänomenologische Philosophie,* ed. Walter Biemel, in *Husserliana,* Vol. 6 (The Hague: Nijhoff, 1954); English translation [hereafter abbreviated as ET]: *The Crisis of European Sciences and Transcendental Phenomenology: An Introduction to Phenomenological Philosophy,* tr. David Carr (Evanston: Northwestern University Press, 1970). [Since the ET does not contain all the appendices that the German edition does, it will be necessary at times to refer to the German pagination.] Hereafter the ET will be cited as *C,* the German as *K. The Origin of Geometry (C,* pp. 353–78) is a text appended to §9*a* on "Pure Geometry" (*C,* pp. 24–28). In a forewording note Derrida says, after stating that he will translate the version presented in *K:* "The original manuscript dates from 1936. Its typed transcription bears no title. The author of this transcription, Eugen Fink, has also published an elaboration of it in *Revue Internationale de Philosophie,* 1, No. 2 (January 15, 1939), pp. 203–25, under the title 'Die Frage nach dem Ursprung der Geometrie als intentional-historisches Problem.' Since then, this text has been read and frequently cited under this form. Its history, at least, then, already conferred on it a certain right to independence."

interrelated and concrete conditions for the possibility of these ideal objects: language, intersubjectivity, and the world as the unity of ground and horizon. Finally, the techniques of phenomenological description, notably those of the various reductions, are always utilized. Less than ever do their validity and fruitfulness appear impaired in Husserl's eyes.

To begin with, *The Origin of Geometry* is no longer distinguishable by its twofold critique: a critique directed, on the one hand, against a certain technicist and objectivist irresponsibility in the practice of science and philosophy, and on the other hand, against a historicism blinded by the empiricist cult of *fact* and causalist presumption. The first criticism was the starting point for *Formal and Transcendental Logic,* the *Cartesian Meditations,* and the *Crisis.* The second had appeared much earlier, in the *Logical Investigations,* in "Philosophy as Rigorous Science" (in which it was the fundamental preoccupation), and in *Ideas I.* The reduction, if not condemnation, of historicist geneticism was always interrelated with that of psycho-geneticism; even when a certain historicity has become phenomenology's theme, despite the high cost of its difficulties, this action cannot possibly be retracted.

But never had the two denunciations of historicism and objectivism been so organically united as in *The Origin of Geometry,* where they proceed from the same impulse and are mutually involved throughout an itinerary whose bearing is sometimes disconcerting.[2] Now the singularity of our text rests on the fact that the conjunction of these two standing and tested refusals creates a new scheme: on the one hand, it brings to light a new type or profundity of historicity; on the other hand, and correlatively, it determines the new tools and original direction of historic reflection. The historicity of ideal objectivities, i.e., their *origin* and *tradition* (in the ambiguous sense of this word which includes both the movement of transmission and the perdurance of heritage), obeys different rules, which are neither the factual interconnections of empirical history, nor an ideal and ahistoric adding on. The birth and development of science must then be accessible to an unheard-of style of historical intuition in which the intentional reactivation of sense should—*de jure*—precede and condition the empirical determination of fact.

[2] In effect these pages of Husserl, first written for himself, have the rhythm of a thought feeling its way rather than setting itself forth. But here the apparent discontinuity also depends on an always regressive method, a method which chooses its interruptions and multiplies the returns toward its beginning in order to reach back and grasp it again each time in a recurrent light.

In their irreducible originality, the historicity of science and the re-flection that it invites, *Geschichtlichkeit* and *Historie*,[3] have certain common apriori conditions. For Husserl, their disclosure is possible in principle and this should lead us to reconsider the problems of universal historicity in their broadest extension. In other words, the possibility of something like a history of science imposes a rereading and a re-awakening of the "sense" of history in general: ultimately, its phenomenological *sense* will merge with its teleological *sense*.

Husserl tries to accomplish a singular proof of these essential pos-sibilities in connection with geometry and to decipher therein the pre-scription of a general task. Thus, like most of Husserl's texts, *The Origin of Geometry* has both a programmatic and an exemplary value. Consequently, our reading of it must be marked by the exemplary consciousness proper to all eidetic attention and be guided by the pole of this infinite task, from which phenomenology alone can make its way. In the introduction we now attempt, our sole ambition will be to recognize and situate one stage of Husserl's thought, with its specific presuppositions and its particular unfinished state. Though this moment of Husserl's radicalness is ultimate according to the facts, it is perhaps not so de jure. Husserl repeatedly seems to agree with this. Therefore, we will always try to be guided by his own intentions, even when we get caught up in certain difficulties.

## I

The mathematical object seems to be the privileged example and most permanent thread guiding Husserl's reflection. This is because the mathematical object is *ideal*. Its being is thoroughly transparent and exhausted by its phenomenality. Absolutely objective, i.e., totally rid of empirical subjectivity, it nevertheless is only what it appears to be. Therefore, it is always already *reduced* to its phenomenal sense, and its being is, from the outset, to be an object [*être-objet*] for a pure consciousness.[4]

[3] In our translation [of *The Origin of Geometry*], we will indicate the distinction be-tween *Historie* and *Geschichte* in parentheses only when this distinction corresponds to Husserl's explicit intention, which is not—indeed, far from it—always the case.

[4] On the question of knowing whether, for Husserl, the mathematical object is the mode of every object's constitution, and on the consequences of such a hypothesis, cf. the discussion in which Walter Biemel, Eugen Fink, and Roman Ingarden participated follow-ing Biemel's lecture on "Les phases décisives dans le développement de la philosophie de Husserl," in *Husserl* (Cahiers de Royaumont, Philosophie No. 3) (Paris: Minuit, 1959), pp. 63–71.

The *Philosophy of Arithmetic,* Husserl's first important work, could have been entitled *The Origin of Arithmetic.* Despite a psychologistic inflection whose originality has often and justly been emphasized,[5] it already concerns, as does *The Origin of Geometry,* the reactivation of the primordial sense of arithmetic's ideal unities by returning to the structure of perception and the acts of a concrete subjectivity. Husserl himself already proposed to account *at once* for the normative ideality of number (which is never an empirical fact accessible to a history in precisely this same style) and for its grounding in and through the lived act of its production.[6]

In such a case, however, the genesis of arithmetic is not thought of as a history of arithmetic, i.e., as a cultural form and adventure of humanity. In 1887–91, the origin of arithmetic was described in terms of *psychological genesis.* In *The Origin of Geometry,* after fifty years of meditation, Husserl repeats the same project under the species of a *phenomenological history.* This fidelity is all the more remarkable since the path traversed is immense. It passes first through the reduction of all historical or psychological genesis. After that, when the genetic dimension of phenomenology is discovered, genesis is still not history. In passing from static to genetic constitution, as announced in *Ideas I* and then accomplished between the years 1915 and 1920, Husserl still had not engaged phenomenological description in the problems of historicity. The thematization of transcendental genesis maintained the reduction of history; all that could be placed under the category of objective

[5] Cf. in particular Biemel, *ibid.,* pp. 35ff. [A German version of Biemel's lecture, "Die entscheidenden Phasen in Husserls Philosophie," appeared in *Zeitschrift für philosophische Forschung,* 13 (1959), pp. 187–213. An ET of this German version, entitled "The Decisive Phases in the Development of Husserl's Philosophy," is in *The Phenomenology of Husserl: Selected Critical Readings,* ed. and tr. R. O. Elveton (Chicago: Quadrangle, 1970), pp. 148–73. Reference above begins on p. 148ff. The German and English versions differ from the French version published in *Husserl;* they also do not include the discussion mentioned in note 4 above.] Despite his severity as regards this psychologistic tendency, Husserl continually refers to his first book, especially in *Formal and Transcendental Logic.*

[6] "Numbers are mental creations insofar as they form the results of activities exercised upon concrete contents; what these activities create, however, are not new and absolute contents which we could find again in space or in the 'external world'; rather are they unique relation-concepts which can only be produced again and again and which are in no way capable of being found somewhere ready-made." This remarkable passage, which already designates the production, therefore the primordial historicity, of idealities which no longer will ever belong to the time and space of empirical history, is from *Concerning the Concept of Number* (1887), which is taken up again as the first chapter of *Philosophy of Arithmetic* (1891). The passage is translated in Biemel's article, in *Husserl,* p. 37 [ET: p. 150].

spirit and the cultural world was repressed within the sphere of intra-worldliness. The return to prepredicative experience, in *Experience and Judgment* and in *Formal and Transcendental Logic,* extended down to a precultural and prehistoric stratum of lived experience.

And in the *Cartesian Meditations,* when Husserl speaks about the unity of a history, it is a question of the unity of traces, of "references," of synthetic "residues" *within* the pure egological sphere.[7] Husserl underscores this: the ideal objects, "the higher forms of *products* of reason," which alone assure the possibility of historicity, i.e., the always intersubjective consciousness of history, do not belong to the *eidos* of the concrete *ego* (*CM,* §38, p. 78). At the end of the Third Cartesian Meditation, the investigations that particularly concern the "*theory* . . . of man, of human community, of culture, and so forth," are defined as ulterior, regional, and dependent tasks (*ibid.,* §29, p. 63). All these reductions hold *a fortiori* for the descriptions of primordial temporality and immanent duration.[8]

Thus the neutralization of psychological genesis and that of history are still on equal footing in the texts which place the transcendental development in focus. But when, in the period of the *Crisis,* history itself breaks through into phenomenology, a new space of questioning is opened, one that will be difficult to maintain in the regional limits which were so long prescribed for it.

While constantly *practiced* in the *Crisis* itself, this new access to history is never *made a problem.* At least not directly and as such. On the one hand, the consciousness of a crisis and the affirmation of a teleology of reason are *only* new paths or means for legitimizing transcendental idealism once again. On the other hand, to put the whole development of Western philosophy into perspective, to define the European *eidos* and the man of infinite tasks, and to recount the adventures and misadventures of the transcendental motif, concealed each time by the very gesture that uncovers it: all this would give credit to a kind of synoptic retrospection that no criticism of historic reason had explicitly justified from the start. Neither the structures of historicity in

[7] Edmund Husserl, *Cartesian Meditations: An Introduction to Phenomenology,* tr. Dorion Cairns (The Hague: Nijhoff, 1970), Meditation IV, §§37 and 38, pp. 75–80 —hereafter cited as *CM.*

[8] On the problem of history in Husserl's philosophy, we refer particularly to Paul Ricoeur's very fine article, "Husserl and the Sense of History," in Paul Ricoeur, *Husserl: An Analysis of His Phenomenology,* tr. Edward G. Ballard and Lester E. Embree (Evanston: Northwestern University Press, 1967), pp. 143–74. On what obstructs the direct thematization of history in a transcendental phenomenology which at the same time calls for this thematization, cf. more particularly pp. 145–51.

general (and we do not yet know whether the historicity of science and philosophy are examples or exceptions, whether they are the highest and most revelatory possibilities, or if they are simply beyond history itself), nor the methods of the phenomenology of history were made the objects of specific, original questions. This confidence was supported by the system of apodictic certainties of phenomenology itself, which could be considered as a criticism of reason in general. If this teleological reading of history could not be characterized in Husserl's eyes by the dogmatic imprudence with which so many philosophers (from Aristotle to Hegel to Brunschvicg) perceive in the past only the labored presentiment of their own thought, it is because this reading referred to the very Idea of transcendental phenomenology—which is not itself a philosophical system.

But this reading referred to that Idea only *mediately*. It was still necessary to show in a specific, concrete, and direct manner:

1. that history, as empirical science, was, like all empirical sciences, dependent on phenomenology—which alone could reveal to it its fund of eidetic presuppositions (this dependence, frequently affirmed, had always been treated by preterition, signaled rather than explored);[9]

2. that history—whose own content (contrary to that of the other material and dependent sciences) was, by virtue of its sense of being, always marked by oneness and irreversibility, i.e., by non-exemplariness—still lent itself to imaginary variations and to eidetic intuitions;

3. that, in addition to the empirical and non-exemplary content of history, certain eidetic content (for example, that of geometry as the eidetic analysis of spatial nature) had itself been produced or revealed in a history which irreducibly inhabits its being-sense. If, as Husserl affirms, the history of the geometrical eidetic is exemplary, then history in general no longer risks being a distinct and dependent sector of a more radical phenomenology. By remaining completely within a determined relativity, history in general no less completely engages phenomenology with all its possibilities and responsibilities, its original techniques and attitudes.

[9] That, for example, was not the case with psychology, whose relations with phenomenology have been most abundantly defined, notably in *Ideen II* [*Ideen zu einer reinen Phänomenologie und phänomenologischen Philosophie*, Vol. II, ed. M. Biemel, in *Husserliana*, Vol. 4 (The Hague: Nijhoff, 1952)], in the *Cartesian Meditations*, and in the third part of the *Crisis*. The recent publication by Walter Biemel of the Lectures of 1925 and of appended texts devoted to *Phänomenologische Psychologie* (in *Husserliana*, Vol. 9 [The Hague: Nijhoff, 1962]) is a very rich testimony to this.

No doubt these three ambitions, which are also difficult ones, animate the *Crisis,* and to all intents and purposes, the earlier works. But it is in *The Origin of Geometry* and in the short fragments of the same period that these ambitions, it seems, are most immediately assumed.

We must be careful here: these ambitions are only *served* by already familiar themes which they orient in a new direction. Instead of seeing it as a prolongation of the *Crisis,* we might be strongly tempted to see *The Origin of Geometry* (after taking into account the brevity of this sketch) only as the preface to a re-issue of *Formal and Transcendental Logic,* whose purpose simply would be adapted to a material ontology. In his Introduction to that work, Husserl perceives the motif of "radical investigations of sense" within the "present condition of European sciences."[10] But we know that for Husserl the critical significance of this situation results less from some epistemological conflict inherent in the internal development of these sciences than from a divorce between a) the theoretical and practical activity of the science in the very renown of its progress and success, and b) its sense for life and the possibility of being related to *our* whole world. This freeing of science with respect to its bases in the *Lebenswelt* and its founding subjective acts undoubtedly remains a necessary condition for its conquests. But this freeing also involves the threat of an objectivist alienation, which conceals the instituting origins and renders them strange and inaccessible to us. This occultation, which is also a technicization and supposes the *"naïveté of a higher level"* of an investigator become irresponsible, has simultaneously ruined the "great belief" of the sciences and philosophy in themselves; it has made our world "unintelligible." To meditate on or investigate the sense *(besinnen)* of origins is at the same time to: make oneself responsible *(verantworten)* for the sense *(Sinn)* of science and philosophy, bring this sense to the clarity of its "fulfil[ment]," and put oneself in a position of *responsibility* for this sense starting from the total sense of our existence.[11]

The same disquietude and the same will are underscored and expressed in rigorously identical terms from the first pages of *The Origin*

---

[10] *Formal and Transcendental Logic,* tr. Dorion Cairns (The Hague: Nijhoff, 1969), p. 5—hereafter cited as *FTL.* Also cf. the commentary of Suzanne Bachelard, *A Study of Husserl's* Formal and Transcendental Logic, tr. Lester E. Embree (Evanston: Northwestern University Press, 1968), notably pp. xxxiii–liii.

[11] "We must place ourselves above this whole life and all this cultural tradition and, by radical sense-investigations, seek for ourselves singly and in common the ultimate possibilities and necessities, on the basis of which we can take our position toward actualities in judging, valuing, and acting" *(FTL,* pp. 5–6). The citations are from *FTL,* pp. 2, 5, and 9.

*of Geometry*. And the question asked there appears at first sight to be only a specification of the general question begun and defined in *Formal and Transcendental Logic*. Is it not a question here of applying a general project whose program had already been organized to a singular and dependent science? Did not Husserl write: "These investigations, concerning the possible sense and possible method of genuine science as such, are naturally directed first of all to what is essentially common to all possible sciences. They should be followed secondarily by corresponding sense-investigations for particular groups of sciences and single sciences" (*ibid.*, p. 6)?[12]

The anteriority of *Formal and Transcendental Logic* in relation to the problems of origin for the other sciences has a systematic and juridical significance. This necessary anteriority first derives from the nature of traditional logic, which is always presented as the general theory of science, as the science of science. This statement also refers to the hierarchy of ontologies already elaborated in *Ideas I*. Materially determined ontologies are subordinated to formal ontology, which treats the pure rules of Objectivity in general.[13] Now geometry is a material ontology whose object is determined as the spatiality of the thing belonging to Nature.[14]

The fact that every dimension of *The Origin of Geometry* accentuates this dependence and this relative superficiality of description will thus be explained. On several occasions Husserl notes that he presupposes the constitution of the ideal objectivities[15] of logic and language in

---

[12] On the "directive" character of logic, also cf. *FTL*, §71, pp. 181–82.

[13] Cf. *Ideas: General Introduction to Pure Phenomenology*, tr. W. R. Boyce Gibson (1931; rpt. New York: Collier Books, 1962), §§8–10, 17, pp. 56–62 and 70–71—hereafter cited as *Ideas I*. [At times Derrida refers to the notes of Paul Ricoeur in his invaluable French translation, *Idées directrices pour une phénoménologie et une philosophie phénoménologique pures*. Tome I: *Introduction générale à la phénoménologie pure* (Paris: Gallimard, 1950). We will refer to this translation as *Idées*.] Here formal ontology designates formal logic "in the narrower sense" and "all the other disciplines which constitute the formal '*mathesis universalis*' (thus arithmetic also, pure analysis, theory of multiplicities)," *Ideas I*, p. 57 [modified].

[14] "It is clearly realized that it is the *essence* of a material thing to be a *res extensa*, and that consequently *geometry is an ontological discipline relating to an essential phase of such thinghood* (Dinglichkeit), *the spatial form*" (Husserl's emphasis), *Ideas I*, §9, pp. 58–59.

Also cf. *Ideas I*, §25, p. 84: there geometry and kinematics (which Husserl always associates with geometry in the *Crisis* and in the *Origin*) are also defined as "pure mathematical . . . material" disciplines.

[15] On the translation of *Gegenständlichkeit* by objectivity [FT: *objectité* (and *Objektivität* or *objectivité* by Objectivity], cf. the French translation of *FTL*, p. 18, n. 3, and the

general, the correlative constitution of intersubjectivity, and all related investigations. In a certain sense, it is truly necessary to see that this order of dependence is not reversed. The phenomenon of "crisis," as forgetfulness of origins, has precisely the sense of this type of "reversal" *(Umkehrung)*. [16]

But while completely justifying the priority of his reflections on logic, Husserl also specifies in *Formal and Transcendental Logic* that this is only one path among others: "*Other paths* are possible for sense-investigations with a radical aim; and the present work attempts to open up, at least in main sections, one suggested by the historically given relation of the idea of genuine science to logic as its antecendent norm" (*FTL*, p. 7; Husserl's emphasis).

Also, by a *spiraling movement* which is the major find of our text, a

---

ET, p. 3, tr. note 2. Of course the notion of objectivity here is not in any sense tied to Schopenhauer's concept of *Objektität*. [On matters of translation related to Husserl we have followed in the main the suggestions of Dorion Cairns in *Guide for Translating Husserl* (The Hague: Nijhoff, 1973).] As for translations which we have had to do, we will be led to justify them in the course of this Introduction.

[16] Cf. *FTL*, p. 2: "the original relationship between logic and science has undergone a remarkable *reversal* in modern times. The sciences made themselves independent. Without being able to satisfy completely the spirit of critical self-justification, they fashioned extremely differentiated methods, whose fruitfulness, it is true, was practically certain, but whose productivity *(Leistung)* was not clarified by ultimate insight." Our emphasis. Moreover, concerning geometrical science and mathematics in general, Husserl has principally and most often defined this *Umkehrung* as the falsification of sense, the displacement of ground, and the forgetting of origins. He has done this under at least three forms:

1. Geometry, the model of exact science, is responsible for the naturalization of the psychic sphere—a fact that was pointed out in the first part of "Philosophy as Rigorous Science," in *Phenomenology and the Crisis of Philosophy*, tr. Quentin Lauer (New York: Harper and Row, 1965), pp. 71–147—hereafter cited as "PRS" (cf. in particular pp. 82, 84, and 93). We should also remember that in *Ideas I* (§§72–75, pp. 185–93), Husserl denounces the absurdity of geometrizing lived experience, on account of both geometrical *exactitude* and *deductivity*.

2. The geometrical ideal (or that of mathematical physics), dogmatically received, is what impelled Descartes to cover over again the transcendental motif that he had ingeniously brought to light. The certitude of the *cogito* becomes the *axiomatic* ground, and philosophy is transformed into a *deductive* system, *ordine geometrico:* "only this axiomatic foundation lies even deeper than that of geometry and is called on to participate in the ultimate grounding even of geometrical knowledge" (*CM*, §3, p. 8); cf. also *C*, Part II, in particular § 21.

3. Finally, the whole *Crisis* tends to show how geometry, the ground for the mathematization of nature, hides *true* Nature. Perhaps this is one of the reasons why later on Husserl will hardly use—yet without explicitly questioning again—the definition of geometry as an eidetic science or as the material ontology of spatially extended, natural things, a definition often proposed as an example up to *Ideas I*.

bold clearing is brought about within the regional limits of the investigation and transgresses them toward a new form of radicality. Concerning the intentional history of a particular eidetic science, a sense-investigation of its conditions of possibility will reveal to us exemplarily the conditions and sense of the historicity of science in general, then of universal historicity—the last horizon for all sense and Objectivity in general. Consequently, the architectonic relations evoked a moment ago are complicated, if not inverted. This would demonstrate, if it were still necessary, at what point the juridical order of implications is not so linear and how difficult it is to recognize the starting point.

It is in the midst of these difficulties and with extreme prudence that Husserl tries to make his purpose understood in *The Origin of Geometry*.

## II

Husserl takes numerous, diverse, and rather intricate methodological precautions in the first pages.

**1.** Provided the notion of history is conceived in a new sense, the question posed must be understood in its most historic resonance. It is a question of repeating an origin. In other words, reflection does not work upon or within geometry itself as "ready-made, handed-down" (157).[17] The attitude taken, then, is not that of a geometer: the latter has at his disposal an already given system of truths that he supposes or utilizes in his geometrizing activity; or, further, at his disposal are possibilities of new axiomatizations which (even with their problems and difficulties) *already* are announced as *geometrical* possibilities. The required attitude is no longer that of the classic epistemologist who, within a kind of horizontal and ahistoric cut, would study the systematic structure of geometrical science or of various geometries. Both these attitudes would depend on what Husserl had defined in *Formal and Transcendental Logic* and recalled in the *Crisis* as a "naiveté of a priori self-evidence that keeps every normal geometrical project in motion" (*C*, §9*b*, p. 29). Not only are the intelligence and the practice of geometry always possible and ocasionally profound and creative, but so is a certain second reflection on constituted geometry, all without disturbing or shaking [*sollicitée*] geometry in its buried sense of origin. The *Crisis* always echoed this. "There is no need for [the question of the origin] in the attitude of the geometer: one has, after all, studied geometry, one 'understands' geometrical concepts and propositions, is

---

[17] *The Origin of Geometry*, p. 157 in Appendix. Hereafter all references to the *Origin* will be placed in parentheses, as done here. [When placed in brackets, they indicate the addition of the translator.]

familiar with methods of operation as ways of dealing with precisely defined structures . . ." *(ibid.).*[18]

No geometrizing activity as such, however critical, can return to a point short of that "familiarity."

**2.** But if we leave the actual or virtual givens of the received geometry, and if we then come to history's vertical dimension, three confusions again lie in wait for us:

**A)** In the first place, we are not interested here in "the manner of being which the sense [of geometry] had in [Galileo's] thinking," or "in that of all the late inheritors of the older geometric knowledge" (157 [modified]). Despite the value which would be attached to such an approach, the latter depends, in the best hypothesis, only on a psychology or history of cognition. And even if, by virtue of their descriptive style, this history and psychology escaped what Husserl always suspected, even if they did not reduce the normativity of ideal objects and geometrical *truth* to the empirical facts of lived experience, they would only inform us about the factual rootedness of truth in a historical or psychological milieu of fact. No doubt this rootedness may be accessible to a descriptive phenomenology which would respect all its originality, but it would teach us nothing about the truth of geometry and its sense of origin.

For Galileo—whose name here is the exemplary index of an attitude and a moment, rather than a proper name[19]—was already an inheritor of geometry.[20] If, in the *Crisis,* a very important place is reserved for

---

[18] Naturally, here "geometry" serves in an exemplary way to designate mathematics and even logic in general.

[19] Cf. *C*, §9*l*, p. 57: ". . . I have linked all our considerations to his name [Galileo's], in a certain sense simplifying and idealizing the matter; a more exact historical analysis would have to take account of how much of his thought he owed to his 'predecessors.' (I shall continue, incidentally, and for good reasons, in a similar fashion.)"

[20] What Galileo inaugurated, opening the way for objectivism by making mathematized Nature an "in itself," marks the birth of a crisis in the sciences and in philosophy. All the more, then, does it command the attention of the author of the *Crisis.* Besides, Husserl already insists a great deal on the secondary character of Galileo's revolution and on the scientific heritage that it supposed, notably that of " 'pure geometry,' the pure mathematics of spatiotemporal shapes in general, pregiven to Galileo as an old tradition" (*C*, §9*a*, p. 24), "the relatively advanced geometry known to Galileo, already broadly applied not only to the earth but also in astronomy" (*ibid.*, §9*b*, p. 28). For Galileo, the sense of the geometrical tradition's origin was already lost: "Galileo was himself an heir in respect to pure geometry. The *inherited geometry,* the inherited manner of 'intuitive' conceptualizing, proving, constructing, was *no longer original geometry:* in this sort of 'intuitiveness' it was already *empty of its sense*" (*ibid.*, §9*h*, p. 49 [modified]; Husserl's emphasis).

Galileo and his revolution (which Husserl situates at the origin of the modern spirit's perils), here the radicalist demand wants to undo the sedimentations upon which the enterprise of an infinite mathematization was based. We must *reduce* the very remarkableness of the Galilean naiveté to free the question as to the origin of geometry.

In the *Crisis,* while invoking Galileo's blindness to the traditional space of his own adventure and designating his "fateful omission,"[21] Husserl announces very precisely the task that he will undertake a little later on in the *Origin:* "For Galileo, then, [pure geometry as tradition] was given—and of course he, quite understandably, did not feel the need to go into the manner in which the accomplishment of idealization originally arose (i.e., how it grew on the underlying basis of the pre-geometrical, sensible world and its practical arts) or to occupy himself

---

[21] "It was a fateful omission that Galileo did not inquire in return as to the original sense-bestowing production which, as idealization practiced on the original ground of all theoretical and practical life—the immediately intuited world (and here especially the empirically intuited world of bodies)—resulted in the geometrical ideal formations)" (*C,* §9*h*, p. 49 [modified]).

Like all forgetfulness in general, the "fatefulness" of this "omission" or negligence *(Versäumnis),* which is never questioned for or in itself, assumes one of the three following significations, each varying according to text and context:

**a)** that of an empirical necessity (on the order of individual or social psychology as well as that of factual history), and thus, of an extrinsic necessity, one which is thereby contingent in comparison with the sense and teleology of reason. This necessity, then, has the inconsistent negativity of the "non-essence" *(das Unwesen),* of the *"apparent"* defeat of reason. Illuminated by the teleology of Reason, it ceases to be "an obscure fate, an impenetrable destiny" (cf. "Philosophy and the Crisis of European Humanity," Appendix I in *C,* p. 299). [The ET of *das Unwesen* offered by Carr is "disarray." Paul Ricoeur in his French translation of this text points out the literal translation as "non-essence": "La Crise de l'humanité européenne et la philosophie," *Revue de Métaphysique et de Morale,* 55, No. 3 (July–October, 1950), p. 258. For the relation of Ricoeur's translation and the English one, see note 149 below.]

**b)** that of a radical ethico-philosophical fault: the bankruptcy of philosophical freedom and responsibility.

**c)** that of an eidetic necessity: the necessity of sedimentation prescribed for all constitution and all traditionalization of sense, therefore for all history. This prescription in turn is sometimes valued as the condition of historicity and the progressive advent of reason, sometimes devalued as what makes origins and accumulated sense become dormant. It truly is a threatening value.

It is a matter of course that these three significations, apparently irreducible to one another, are conceived by Husserl on the basis of one and the same latent intuition. History itself is what this intuition announces. Even if we managed simultaneously and without contradiction to think the unitary ground on the basis of which these three propositions can be received, it is history itself that would be thought. But then the possibility of a crisis of reason would disappear, the negativity of which ought to be unthinkable in itself.

with questions about the origins of apodictic, mathematical self-evidence" (*C*, §9*b*, p. 29).

And if in the *Origin* Husserl speaks of engaging himself "in reflections which surely never occurred to Galileo" (157), it is because, as he had said in the *Crisis:* "It did not enter the mind of a Galileo that it would ever become relevant, indeed of fundamental importance, to geometry, as a branch of a universal knowledge of what is (philosophy), to make geometrical self-evidence—the 'how' of its origin—into a problem. For us, proceeding beyond Galileo in our historical reflections, it will be of considerable interest to see how a shift of focus became urgent and how the 'origin' of knowledge had to become a major problem" (§9*b*, p. 29).[22]

If the Galilean discovery resides especially in a formalizing infinitization of ancient mathematics, does not the return to them as an origin tie primordiality to a certain finitude? No simple response is possible to such a question. We will see that the infinite had already broken through, was already at work, when the first geometry began—that it, too, was already an infinitization.

**B)** But if we return to a point this side of Galileo, is the question now one of studying for itself the heritage which was given to him? Not any more. The question of origin will not be a "philological-historical . . . search" in the investigation of "particular propositions" (158) that the first geometers discovered or formulated. There, it would only be a matter for the history of science in the classical sense to take stock of the already constituted contents of geometrical cognitions, in particular of the first postulates, axioms, theorems, and so forth, contents that must be explored and determined as precisely and as completely as possible from archeological documents. Despite its incontestable interest, such an investigation can teach us nothing about the geometrical sense of the first geometrical acts. It cannot even recognize and isolate those acts as such except by supposing that the primordial sense of geometry is already known.

**C)** Finally, if one must return to the instituting sense of first acts, it is not at all a question of determining what *in fact* were the first[23] acts, the first experiences, the first geometers who were *in fact* responsible

---

[22] These sentences announce what follows in the *Crisis*, devoted to the transcendental motif in post-Galilean philosophy, as well as investigations like that of the *Origin*.

[23] "First" *(erste)* nearly always designates in Husserl either an undetermined primacy, or, most often, a de facto chronological priority in constituted cosmic time, i.e., an original factuality. *Proto-, Arch-,* and *Ur-* refer to phenomenological primordiality, i.e., to that of sense, of ground, of the de jure, after the reduction of all factuality.

for the advent of geometry. Such a determination, even if possible, would flatter our historical curiosity (and everything that Husserl attributes to a certain "romanticism"); it would enrich our knowledge of empirical circumstances, of names, dates, and so forth. But even if, at its limit, this determination would embrace all the historical facts that have constituted the empirical milieu for truth's founding, it would still leave us blind about the very sense of such a founding: a sense that is necessary and compared to which these facts have at best only an exemplary signification. Such empirical knowledge can justifiably present itself as historical knowledge *of* things related to geometry only by supposing a fully developed clarity about the very sense of what is called *the* geometrical science. And here, this means clarity about its sense of origin. The juridical priority of the question of phenomenological origin is therefore absolute.

But this question can be asked only *secondarily* and *at the end* of an itinerary which, in its turn, enjoys a methodological and rightful priority. In fact, all these various kinds of inquiries we just dismissed have been caught up in the element of a constituted geometry. Their object supposed or was confused with the results of a *ready-made* geometry that would have to be *reduced* in order to attain a consciousness of its origin, a consciousness which was at the same time an intuition of its essence. In other words, although it only has for its content ideal essences, *ready-made* geometry holds here in bulk the status of a fact which must be reduced in its factuality so that its sense can be read. Indeed, in this case, the *fact* has the forgotten sense of the *ready-made*. But this reduction needs as its starting point the constituted result it neutralizes. There must always already have been the fact of a history of geometry, so that the reduction can be performed. I must already have a naïve knowledge of geometry and must not *begin* at its origin. Here the method's juridical necessity overlaps history's factual necessity. Despite certain appearances, philosophers of method are perhaps more profoundly sensitive to historicity, even though they seem to remove digressions from history's path.

Both the necessity to proceed from the fact of constituted science and the regression towards the nonempirical origins are at the same time conditions of possibility: such are, as we know, the imperatives of every transcendental philosophy faced with something like the history of mathematics.[24] A fundamental difference remains, however, between

---

[24] On the necessity of starting from existing sciences that are utilized as the thread guiding the transcendental regression, cf. *FTL,* pp. 8–9: "Thus we are presupposing the sciences, as well as logic itself, on the basis of the 'experience' that gives them to us

Kant's intention and that of Husserl, one that is perhaps less easily distinguishable than would first be imagined.

In a historical retrospection towards origins, Kant also evokes this mutation or transformation *(Umänderung)*, this *"revolution"* which gave birth to mathematics out of some empirical "gropings" in the Egyptian tradition *(Kritik der reinen Vernunft,* Preface to 2nd ed., p. x).

"The history of this revolution," attributed to the "happy thought of a single man" in "an experiment from which the path that *had* to be taken *must* no longer be missed and from which the sure way of science was *opened* and *prescribed (eingeschlagen und vorgezeichnet war) for all times and in endless expansion (für alle Zeiten und in unendlich Weiten),"* was more "decisive" than the empirical discovery "of the path around the famous Cape [of Good Hope]" *(ibid.,* p. xi).[25]

Thus, like Husserl, Kant is attentive to the historical dimension of apriori possibilities and to the original genesis of a truth, whose birth (or birth certificate) inscribes and prescribes omnitemporality and universality—not only for the opening of its possibility, but also for each of its developments and for the totality of its becoming. Like Husserl, he neutralizes the factual contents of this "revolution in the mode of thinking" with the same indifference. In effect, it is of little consequence for him that its "history" has "not reached" us. The sense of the first demonstration can be rigorously grasped, even though we know nothing of the first factual experience or the first geometer; "whether," as Kant specifies, "he be called Thales or whatever one desires" *(ibid.).*

Nevertheless, Kant's indifference to the factual origin (as well as to the content of the example—the isosceles triangle—concerning which he develops the implications of its discovery) is more immediately legitimate than Husserl's. For the inaugural mutation which interests Kant *hands over* geometry rather than creates it; it sets free a possibility, which is nothing less than historical, in order to hand it to us. At first this "revolution" is only a "revelation for" the first geometer. It is

---

beforehand. Because of this, our procedure seems not to be at all radical, since the genuine sense of all sciences . . . is the very thing in question. . . . Nevertheless, whether sciences and logic be genuine or spurious, we do have experience of them as cultural formations given to us beforehand and bearing within themselves their meaning, their 'sense.'" Cf. also on this *FTL,* Introd., pp. 13–14, and §102, pp. 268–69; and *CM,* §3, pp. 8–9.

[25] We emphasize those Kantian expressions which are also among the most frequent in *The Origin of Geometry.* [The bracketed expression "of Good Hope" is added in conformity to the English translation of Norman Kemp Smith.]

not produced by him. It is understood under a dative category, and the activity of the geometer to which the "happy thought" occurred is only the empirical unfolding of a profound reception. What is most often translated by "revelation" is the allusion to "a light that is given," to "a light dawns on": *"Dem ersten . . . dem ging ein Licht auf"* (*ibid.*, p. x).[26]

Undoubtedly, Husserl's production *(Leistung)*[27] also involves a stratum of receptive intuition. But what matters here is that this Husserlian intuition, as it concerns the ideal objects of mathematics, is absolutely constitutive and creative: the objects or objectivities that it intends did *not* exist *before* it; and this *"before"* of the ideal objectivity marks more than the chronological eve of a fact: it marks a transcendental prehistory. In the Kantian revelation, on the contrary, the first geometer merely becomes conscious that it suffices for his mathematical activity to remain within a concept that it *already possesses*. The "construction" to which he gives himself, then, is only the explication of an already constituted concept that he encounters, as it were, in himself—a description which no doubt for Husserl as well would be true of every noncreative geometrical act, and which teaches us about the sense of ready-made geometry as such, but not about geometry in the act of being instituted. "For," as Kant says, "he discovered that he must not follow the trace of what he saw in the figure

---

[26] Cf. for example the French translation of A. Tremesaygues and B. Pacaud, *Critique de la raison pure* (Paris: Presses Universitaries de France, 1950), p. 17. Of course, we are authorized to pay such attention to these Kantian expressions only by the confirmation that all of Kant's philosophy seems to give them.

[27] Among all the translations already proposed for the notion of *Leistung*, so frequently utilized in the *Origin*, the word "production" seemed to overlay most properly all the significations that Husserl recognizes in this act that he also designates by some complementary notions: *pro-duction*, which leads to the light, constitutes the "over against us" of Objectivity; but this bringing to light is also, like all production *(Erzeugung)* in general, a creation *(Schöpfung)* and an act of formation *(Bildung, Gestaltung)*, from which comes ideal objectivity as *Gebilde, Gestalt, Erzeugnis,* and so on. To be clear on this, we have translated by "formation" the notion of *Gebilde*, which appears so often in the *Origin*, and which up to now has been very diversely translated. The very vague character of the word "formation" seemed to us to suit the indetermination of Husserl's notion. It also agrees with the geological metaphor which runs throughout the text, where allusions to sedimentation, to deposits, to stages, to strata, and to substrata of sense are everywhere. But we were also unable to designate the act which engenders *das Gebilde*, namely, *die Bildung,* except by "formation." Each time *Bildung* has this active sense, we will insert the German word between parentheses. Do not forget, finally (and this is especially important here), that in German *Bildung* also carries the general sense of *culture*. There again, the notion of *formation* seemed the least foreign to this virtual signification.

or in the bare concept of that same figure. Rather he must beget *(hervor-bringen)* (its object) with the help of what he himself put into it and what *a priori* was represented in it through the concept (through construction). And to know something *a priori* with complete security, he must attribute to things *(Sache)* nothing but what necessarily followed from what he had put there himself in accordance with his concept" *(ibid.)*.[28]

No doubt, once the geometrical concept has revealed its freedom with respect to empirical sensibility, the synthesis of the "construction" is irreducible. And indeed it is an ideal history. But it is the history of an operation, and not of a founding. It unfolds explicative gestures in the space of a possibility already open to the geometer. The moment geometry is established as such, the moment, that is, something can be said of it, then geometry already will be on the point of being revealed to the consciousness of the *first* geometer, who is not, as in the *Origin,* protogeometer, the primally instituting *(urstiftende)* geometer. At least it will be ready to be revealed in its initial concept, that concept whose apriori Objectivity will presently strike any subject whatever with geometrical insight [*lumière*]. And since Kant is interested in the possibility of geometry for a subject in general, it is not only less constricting, but also de jure necessary, that the de facto subject of such a "revelation" be "anyone at all," and that the geometrical example serving as guide—the demonstration of the isosceles triangle—be indifferent. The apriori nature of that concept within which we operate precludes all historical investigation whatever about its subject matter. Contrary to its synthetic explication, the concept itself, as a structure of apriori prescription, could not be historical, because it is not, as such, produced and grounded by the act of a concrete subject.[29] Here all history can only be empirical. And if there is a birth of geometry for Kant, it seems to be only the extrinsic *circumstance* for the emergence of a truth (which is itself always already constituted for any factual consciousness). Thus the spontaneous eidetic reduction which frees the geometrical essence from all empirical reality—that of sensible figuration as well as from the geometer's psychological lived experience—is for Kant always already done.[30] Strictly speaking, the

---

[28] The Erdmann edition notes that *hervorbringen* has no "object" in Kant's text.

[29] The absence of the decisive notion of "material" or "contingent" a priori, such as Husserl defined it, thus seems to uproot Kant's formalist apriorism from all concrete history and to inhibit the theme of a transcendental history.

On the notion of the contingent a priori, cf. in particular *FTL,* §6, pp. 29–30. The level of geometry as a material ontology is precisely that of such a "material a priori."

[30] This seems true, furthermore, of the whole of Kant's transcendental analysis.

reduction is not for or by a subject who makes himself responsible for it in a transcendental adventure, a protogeometer or philosopher reflecting on protogeometry; it is always already made possible and necessary by the nature of geometrical space and the geometrical object. Barring a "scarcely altered" conventional Platonism, Kant's indifference to empirical history is only legitimated from the moment that a more profound history has already created nonempirical objects. This history remains hidden for Kant. Can we not say here that the theory of ideal space and time both requires and suppresses the bringing to light of an intrinsic and nonempirical historicity of the sciences of space and motion? If space and time were transcendental realities, a way would be opened both for an ahistoric metaphysics and for a historicist empirical science, two interrelated possibilities that Kant always denounced in one and the same move. But to avoid empiricism from the start and at any price, Kant had to confine his transcendental discourse to a world of ideal constituted objects, whose correlate was therefore itself a constituted subject.[31] This notion of a protohistory, which the whole of Kantian philosophy seems to make contradictory even while invoking it, becomes Husserl's theme.

Husserl's task is thus all the more hazardous,[32] and his freedom with respect to empirical knowledge is more difficult to justify at first sight. In fact, we now wonder about the sense of the production of geometrical concepts before and this side of the Kantian "revelation," before and this side of the constitution of an ideally pure and exact space and time. Since every ideal objectivity is produced by the act of a concrete consciousness (the only starting point for a transcendental phenomenology), every ideal objectivity has a history which is always already announced in that consciousness, even if we know nothing of its determined content.[33]

Up to *Ideas I* the methodological or constitutive analyses remained structural and static, and all history was *"reduced"* as factuality or

---

[31] Here we find, locally and through a different approach, the interpretation proposed by Fink and approved by Husserl concerning the intraworldliness of the Kantian critique compared with Husserl's investigation of the *"origin of the world."* Cf. Eugen Fink, "The Phenomenological Philosophy of Edmund Husserl and Contemporary Criticism," in R. O. Elveton, ed., *The Phenomenology of Husserl,* pp. 73-147. [The above quote is found on p. 95.]

[32] Perhaps the depth of vigilance in this Kantian "limitation" can only be measured by its difficulty, its failure.

[33] Husserl often stresses that the reference to a historical birth be inscribed within the sense itself of every cultural ideality, especially in Beilage XXVII in the *Krisis,* pp. 503–07.

science of constituted and intraworldly factuality. Thus, this history of geometry had remained in the dark and was judged of doubtful possibility or mediocre interest for the phenomenologist or mathematician as such.[34] Geometry's truth, its normative value, is radically independent of its history which, at this moment of Husserl's itinerary, is considered only as a factual history falling under the stroke of the suspension *(Ausschaltung)*.[35] Husserl says this (in the period of "Philosophy as Rigorous Science" and *Ideas I*) in some frank phrases which, if the levels of explication and the senses of the word "history" had not been clearly distinguished, would be in flagrant contradiction with those of the *Origin*. Thus: "Certainly the mathematician too will not turn to historical science to be taught about the truth of mathematical theories. It will not occur to him to relate the historical development of mathematical representations [the German and French editions add: and judgments] with the question of truth" ("PRS," p. 126). Or again, at the end of criticizing an empiricist theory of the origin of geometry: "Instead of philosophizing and psychologizing about geometrical thought and intuition from an outside standpoint, we should enter vitally into these activities, and through direct analyses determine their immanent sense. It may well be that we have inherited dispositions for cognition from the cognitions of past generations; *but for the question concerning the sense and value of what we cognize, the history of this heritage is as indifferent as is that of our gold currency to its real value*" (*Ideas I*,§25, pp. 85–86 [modified]; our emphasis).

[34] Cf. in particular *Ideas I*, §1, n. 1, p. 45, and p. 46, where both historical origin and history as a human science are excluded. Concerning the human sciences, the question is "provisionally" left open whether they are "natural sciences or . . . sciences of an essentially new type."

Of course, it is as *facts* and not as *norms* that the historical "givens" are parenthesized. In asking himself, "*'which sciences'*" can phenomenology "*'draw from'*" insofar as phenomenology is itself "a science of 'origins,'" and what sciences must it " 'not depend on,' " Husserl writes: "In the first place it goes without saying that with the suspending of the natural world, physical and psychological, all individual objectivities which are constituted through the functional activities of consciousness in valuation and in practice are suspended—all varieties of cultural expression, works of the technical and of the fine arts, of the sciences also *(so far as we accept them as cultural facts and not as validity-systems)* [our emphasis], aesthetic and practical values of every shape and form. Natural in the same sense are also realities of such kinds of state, moral custom, law, religion. Therewith *all the natural and human sciences*, with the entire knowledge they have accumulated, *undergo suspension* as sciences which require for their development the natural standpoint" (*Ideas I*, §56, p. 155 [modified]).

[35] Cf. the definitions of history as an empirical human science in "PRS," in particular pp. 124–26.

The continuity and coherence of these observations are truly remarkable: first, factual history must be reduced in order to respect and show the normative independence of the ideal object in its own right; then and only then, by thus avoiding all historicist or logicist confusion, in order to respect and show the unique historicity of the ideal object itself. That is why these first reductions of factual history will never be removed in the *Origin*—even less so than elsewhere.

This is because "Philosophy as Rigorous Science" was concerned with responding to the kind of historicism which reduced norm to fact, and *Ideas I*, with situating geometry in an exemplary fashion among the pure essential sciences. Since no *existential thesis (Daseinsthesis)* was necessary or permitted, these sciences were immediately freed from all factuality. No sensible figuration in the real world,[36] no psychological experience, no factual [*événementiel*] content have any instituting sense as such. The geometrical *eidos* is recognized in that it withstood the test of hallucination:

> There are pure **sciences of essences,** such as pure logic, pure
> mathematics, pure time-theory, space-theory, theory of movement, etc.
> These, in all their thought-constructions, are free throughout from any
> positings of actual fact; or, what comes to the same thing, **in them no
> experience qua experience,** i.e., **qua** consciousness that apprehends or
> sets up reality or factual existence, **can take over the function of
> supplying a logical grounding.** Where experience functions in them, it
> is not **as** experience. The **geometer** who draws his figures on the
> blackboard produces in so doing strokes that are actually there on a
> board that is actually there. But his experience of what he thus
> produces, **qua** experience, affords just as little **ground** for his seeing
> and thinking of the geometrical essence as does the physical act of
> production itself. Whether or not he thereby hallucinates, and whether
> instead of actually drawing lines he draws his lines and figures in a
> world of phantasy, does not really matter. The **scientific investigator of
> Nature** behaves quite differently. (**Ideas I**, §7, p. 55 [modified]; Hus-
> serl's emphasis)[37]

---

[36] The essential uselessness or the "inadequacy" of sensible "illustration" is already underscored in the *Logical Investigations,* tr. J. N. Findlay, 2 vols. (New York: Humanities Press, 1970)—hereafter cited as *LI.* [All future references will list the volume number, the investigation number or Prologomena, the section number, and the page: e.g., *LI,* I, 1, §18, pp. 301–02 means the first volume, First Investigation, etc.] Husserl does this in a passage (*LI,* I, 1, §18, pp. 301–02) where he recalls the Cartesian distinction between *imaginatio* and *intellectio* concerning the *chiliagon* and very precisely announces the theory of geometrical "idealization" that he will maintain in the *Origin.*

[37] This autonomy of mathematical truth compared to perception and natural reality (on which mathematical truth could not be based) is described here only in a negative way. Non-dependence is what is stressed. The positive ground of truth is not investigated for

Here the hypothesis of hallucination takes up the role assigned, in eidetic determination, to fiction in general, *"the vital element of phenomenology" (Ideas I, §70, p. 184 [modified])*. But if hallucination does not undermine the *eidos* of the constituted ideal object (because the *eidos* in general and the ideal object in particular are "irreal," though not phantasy realities—even if hallucination reveals them as such); if, on the other hand, the *eidos* and the ideal object do not preexist every subjective act, as in a [conventional] Platonism; so if they do have a history, they must be related to, i.e., they must be primordially grounded in, the protoidealizations based on the substrate of an actually perceived real world. But they must do this through the element of an original history.

---

itself. Starting from an analysis of the mathematical "phenomenon," or in order to better isolate its "sense," one simply reduces what is indicated in this sense as what cannot presently be retained by virtue of this ground. Husserl measures the eidetic intangibility of mathematical sense by *hallucination*. In the *Theaetetus* (190b), Plato had recourse to *dream*. Husserl's development is also situated on the same plane and dons the same style as the Cartesian analysis *before* the hypothesis of the Evil Demon in the First Meditation: "At this rate we might be justified in concluding that . . . arithmetic, geometry, and so on, which treat only of the simplest and most general subject-matter, and are indifferent whether it exists in nature or not, have an element of indubitable certainty. *Whether I am awake or asleep,* two and three add up to five, and a square has only four sides; and it seems impossible for such obvious truths to fall under a suspicion of being false" [par. 7; ET: in *Descartes: Philosophical Writings,* tr. Elizabeth Anscombe and Peter Thomas Geach (New York: Bobbs-Merrill, 1971, p. 63].

For Descartes, only *after* this phenomenology of mathematical evidence and with the hypothesis of the Evil Demon will the critical or juridical question be posed of the ground that guarantees the *truth* of náive evidence. The description itself and the "natural" validity of this truth, moreover, will never be put into question on their own specific level. The primordial ground of these constituted truths, whose mode of appearing is thus clearly recognized, will be delegated to a veracious God who is also the creator of eternal truths. Husserl, after an analogous descriptive stage, will investigate this in primally instituting acts *(Urstiftung),* themselves historical. In this respect, Descartes' God, like that of the great classic rationalists, would only be the name given to a hidden history and "would function" as the necessary reduction of empirical history and the natural world, a reduction which pertains to the sense of these sciences.

But we will see that, despite this extraordinary revolution which grounds the absolute and eternal truth without the aid of God or infinite Reason, and which seems thus to disclose (and redescend toward) a primordially instituted finitude while completely avoiding empiricism, Husserl is less distant from Descartes than it seems. This hidden history will take its sense from an infinite Telos that Husserl will not hesitate to call God in his last unpublished writings. It is true that this infinite, which is always already at work in the origins, is not a positive and actual infinite. It is given as an Idea in the Kantian sense, as a regulative "indefinite" whose negativity gives up its rights to history. Not only the morality but also the historicity of truth itself would here prevent this "falsification" of the actual *infinite* into an *indefinite* or an *ad infinitum,* a falsification of which Hegel accused Kant and Fichte.

Hallucination, then, is truth's accomplice only in a static world of constituted significations. To proceed to the ground and primordial constitution of truth, we must return, starting from the real world, to a creative experience. Even were it unique and buried, this experience remains, de jure as well as de facto, first. We recognize, then, that for the sphere of sense, the true contrary of hallucination (and imagination in general) is not directly perception, but history. Or, if you prefer, it is the consciousness of historicity and the reawakening of origins.

Thus only at the level and point marked by *Ideas I* does Husserl rejoin Kant's indifference to a kind of history that would simply be extrinsic and empirical. Also, as soon as Husserl's account becomes concerned with the genesis of geometry and getting beyond this preliminary stage, we might expect to see him remove the eidetic and transcendental reductions purely and simply, and return to a constitutive history, a history in which the consideration of facts themselves would become indispensable,[38] because here for the first time, as singular historical origin, the instituting fact would be irreplaceable, therefore *invariable*. This invariance of the fact (of what can never be *repeated* as such) would de jure carry over its eidetic invariance (what can be *repeated* voluntarily and indefinitely) into a history of origins. History as institutive would be the profound area where sense is indissociable from being, where the de facto is indissociable from the de jure. The notion of "origin" or genesis could no longer be recognized in

[38] The interpretation of Trân-Dúc-Tháo, *Phénoménologie et matérialisme dialectique* (1951; rpt. New York: Gordon and Breach, 1971), is strongly oriented toward this kind of a conclusion. At the end of Husserl's itinerary, the return to the "*technical* and *economic* forms of production" (namely, in Husserlian language, the return to real, factual, and extrinsic causality outside of every reduction) seems inevitable to that author, who thinks Husserl himself "obscurely" resigned to this at the time of *The Origin of Geometry:* "Moreover, this is what Husserl was obscurely presenting when he was searching in the famous fragment on *The Origin of Geometry* to ground geometrical truth on human *praxis*" (p. 220). "The phenomenological explication is thus oriented towards determining the actual conditions in which truth is engendered" (p. 221).

Husserl's reduction never had the sense (quite the contrary) of a negation—of an ignorance or a forgetfulness that would "leave" the real conditions of sense and factuality in general in order to "come back" or not, in order to "pass on" or not, to the real analysis of what is (for sense is *nothing other than* the *sense of* reality or *of* factuality). Otherwise, his reduction might seem vain and dissembling, and the "return" to an empiricist historicism, fatal. That does not appear to be the case, since, with dialectical materialism, "we find ourselves on a *plane subsequent [posterieur] to the reduction*, the latter having suppressed the abstract conception of nature but not the actually real nature which implies in its development the whole *movement of subjectivity*" (the author's emphasis; pp. 227–28).

the pure phenomenological sense that Husserl so doggedly distinguished.[39]

Because, for Husserl, it has the characteristic which defines fact—namely, singular and empirical existence, the irreducibility of a *here and now*—the total fact marking geometry's establishment would be invariable. Indeed, Husserl says that the upsurge of geometry interests him here insofar as it had taken place "once" *(dereinst),* "for the first time" *(erstmalig),* starting from a *"first* acquisition" *(aus einem ersten Erwerben)* (158–59). But what authorized the essential reading *of* and *within* constituted geometry was the possibility of imaginatively varying the natural *here and now* of the figure or the psychological experience of the geometer who, as we have seen, was not its institutor. Here, on the contrary, the *here and now* of the "first time" is institutive and creative. Is this experience, unique of its kind, not a singular fact—one for which we should not be able to substitute another fact as an example in order to decipher its essence?

Is this to say that this inseparability of fact and sense in the oneness of an instituting act precludes access for phenomenology to all history and to the pure *eidos* of a forever submerged origin?

Not at all. The indissociability itself has a rigorously determinable phenomenological sense. The imaginary variation of static phenomenology simply supposed a type of reduction whose style will have to be renewed in a historical phenomenology. The eidetic aspect of this reduction was the *iteration* of a noema: since the *eidos* is constituted and objective, the series of acts which intended it could not but indefinitely restore the ideal identity of a sense which was not obscured by any historical opacity, and it would only be a question of clarifying, isolating, and determining its evidence, invariance, and objective independence. The historical reduction, which also operates by variation, will be *reactivating* and noetic. Instead of repeating the constituted sense of an ideal object, one will have to reawaken the dependence of

[39] Opening *Ideas I* (Chapter 1, §1*a,* p. 45, passage already cited), this definition of phenomenological origin (in distinction to genesis in the worldly human and natural sciences) was already clearly specified in the *LI,* I, Prol., §67, pp. 237–38; in *The Phenomenology of Internal Time-Consciousness,* ed. Martin Heidegger, tr. James S. Churchill (Bloomington, Ind.: Indiana University Press, 1971), §2, pp. 27–28; and in "PRS," pp. 115–16. This distinction, which Husserl will always judge as decisive, will still be underscored quite frequently in *Experience and Judgment: Investigations in a Genealogy of Logic,* tr. from rev. ed. of Landgrebe by James S. Churchill and Karl Ameriks (Evanston: Northwestern University Press, 1973)—hereafter cited as *EJ*—particularly §1, p. 11; in *FTL,* in particular §102, p. 269; in the *CM,* §37, pp. 75–76; and of course in the *Origin.*

sense with respect to an inaugural and institutive act concealed under secondary passivities and infinite sedimentations—a primordial act which created the object whose *eidos* is determined by the iterative reduction. Here again we are going to see that there is no simple response to the question of the priority of one reduction over another.

The singularity of the invariable *first time* already has a necessity whose eidetic fund is indeed rather complex.

*First,* there is an *essence-of-the-first-time* in general, an *Erstmaligkeit,*[40] an inaugural signification that is always reproducible, whatever its de facto example may be. Whatever were the empirical content of the origin, it is apodictically and a priori necessary that geometry has had an origin and thus has appeared a first time. Ideal geometrical objects cannot have their original place in some *topos ouranios.* Husserl already emphasized this in the *Logical Investigations,* where he discussed all ideal significations and objects.[41] Their historicity, then, is one of their eidetic components, and there is no concrete historicity which does not necessarily implicate in itself the reference to an *Erstmaligkeit.* We said, a moment ago, that it would be impossible to substitute *another* fact for the unique fact of the *first time.* Undoubtedly. But only if *other* is meant to qualify essence and not empirical existence as such. For a unique fact already has its essence as unique fact which, by being nothing other than the fact itself (this is the thesis of the non-fictive irreality of the essence), is not the factuality of fact but the sense of fact—that without which the fact could not appear and give rise to any determination or discourse. Already, when Husserl wrote in "Philosophy as Rigorous Science" that, "for [the phenomenological subsumption], the singular is eternally the *apeiron.* Phenomenology can recognize with Objective validity only essences and essential relations" (p. 116 [modified]), he evidently understood by singularity only the oneness of fact in its pure factuality and not that of the eidetic singularities defined in *Ideas I* (§§11, 14, 15, pp. 62–63 and 66–69) as ultimate material essences which,

---

[40] In its substantive form, this notion does not seem to have been employed by Husserl himself. It is found in place of the adverbial expression *erstmalig* in the transcript of the *Origin* published by Fink in *Revue Internationale de Philosophie* (1939), pp. 203–225: Fink, who also italicizes *erstmalig* (p. 207), speaks of *Erstamaligkeitsmodus* [p. 208] and thus gives a thematic value to a signification aimed at by a profound intention of Husserl.

[41] Cf. in particular I, 1, §31, p. 330. There Husserl completely condemns in a Platonic manner those who, like the "sons of the earth," can "understand by 'being' *(Sein)* only real being," i.e., "being" in the world of natural reality, and he simultaneously rejects the hypothesis of the intelligible heaven. "They [the significations] are not for that reason objects which, though existing nowhere in the world, have being in a *topos ouranios* or in a divine mind, for such metaphysical hypostatization would be absurd."

as Ricoeur notes, exclude "only empirical individuality, only 'factuality' " (*Idées I*, p. 239, n. 1 of tr.), i.e., the *tode ti* of brute existence. The problem of dependence or independence, of the abstract or concrete character of these eidetic singularities, posed in *Ideas I* from the notions of the Third Logical Investigation, is really more difficult to solve when it concerns historical singularities, whose empirical *fact* is never immediately present. It could be said that the eidetic phenomenology of history, having to treat only singularities as such, is in one sense the most dependent and the most abstract of sciences. But inversely, since certain nonempirical singularities, as Husserl says, can be considered in certain respects as the most concrete and most independent, since the singularities of origins are those of instituting acts of every ideal signification and, in particular, of the possibilities of science and of philosophy, then their history is the most independent, the most concrete, and the first of sciences.

Indeed, the theme of eidetic singularities is already ticklish enough in *Ideas I*. However, since the clue there is the immanent lived experience or the sensible thing perceived *originaliter,* singular factuality is always present, although reduced, to guide and control the intuition of the ultimate material essence. But as soon as historical distance is interposed, the investigation of origins no longer proceeds in this way. A doctrine of *tradition* as the ether of historical perception then becomes necessary: it is at the center of *The Origin of Geometry.*

Only under these conditions can Husserl write: "our interest shall be the inquiry back into the most original sense in which geometry once arose, was present as the tradition of millennia . . . we inquire into that sense in which it appeared in history for the first time—*in which it must have appeared* [our emphasis], even though we know nothing of the first creators and are not even asking after them" (158 [modified]).

Here, the *"in which it must have appeared"* clearly reveals Husserl's intention and sums up the sense of every reduction. This *"must"* (have appeared) marks the necessity now recognized and timelessly assigned to a past fact of an eidetic pre-scription and of an apriori norm. I can state this value of necessity independently of all factual cognition. Moreover, this is a double necessity: it is that of a *Quod* and a *Quomodo,* a necessity of *having had a* historical *origin* and of having had *such* an origin, such a sense of origin. But an irreducible historicity is recognized in that this *"must"* is announced only *after* the fact of the event.[42] I could not define the necessary sense and the necessity of the

---

[42] This notion of "must," of apriori requisite, concerning a *past* is frequently utilized in the *Origin.* It marks the possibility of a recurrent structural determination in the absence

origin before geometry was *in fact* born and before it had in fact been given to me. Absolutely free with respect to what it governs, the lawfulness of sense is nothing in itself.

Also, and *second,* whatever *in fact* the first produced or discovered geometrical idealities were, it is *a priori* necessary that they followed from a sort of non-geometry, that they sprang from the soil of pre-geometrical experience. A phenomenology of the experience is possible thanks to a reduction and to an appropriate de-sedimentation.

*Third,* and finally, whoever *in fact* the first geometers were, and whatever *in fact* the empirical content of their acts was, it is *a priori* necessary that the establishing gestures had a sense, such that geometry issued from them *with the sense as we now know it.* For, of course, the reactivating reduction supposes the iterative reduction of the static and structural analysis, which teaches us once and for all what the geometrical "phenomenon" is and when its possibility is constituted. This means—by a necessity which is no less than an accidental and exterior fate—that I must start with ready-made geometry, such as it is now in circulation and which I can always phenomenologically read, in order to go back through it and question the sense of its origin. Thus, both thanks to and despite the sedimentations, I can restore history to its traditional diaphaneity. Husserl here speaks of *Rückfrage,* a notion no doubt current enough, but which now takes on a sharp and precise sense. We have translated it by *return inquiry (question en retour).* Like its German synonym, return inquiry (and *question en retour* as well) is marked by the postal and epistolary reference or resonance of a communication from a distance. Like *Rückfrage,* return inquiry is asked on the basis of a first posting. From a received and *already* readable *document,* the possibility is offered me of asking again, and *in return,* about the primordial and final intention of what has been given me by tradition. The latter, which is only mediacy itself and openness to a telecommunication in general, is then, as Husserl says, "open . . . to continued inquiry" (158).

These analogies, the metaphorical focus of our text, confirm at what point is required the *"zigzag"* way of proceeding—a procedure that the

---

of every material determination. And if this apriori normativity of history is recognized starting from the fact, *after* the fact, this *after* is not the indication of a dependence. The fact does not teach us through its factual content but as an *example*. It is due to this *after*'s own specific character, in the necessity of preserving transcendence or reduced factuality as clue, that the particular historicity of phenomenological discourse is announced.

*Crisis* proposes as a sort of necessary *"circle"*[43] and which is only the pure form of every historical experience.

Return inquiry, the reactionary and therefore revolutionary moment of this interplay *(Wechselspiel)*, would be impracticable if geometry were essentially something which continually circulated as common coin in the validity of ideality. Undoubtedly, no more than the history of its transmission grounds the value of gold,[44] can any wordly history give the sense of this circulation as common coin, since, on the contrary, history supposes it. Rather, the maintenance of this circulation permits the neutralization of worldly history. Neutralization then opens the space for an intentional and intrinsic history of this very circulation and permits the comprehension of how a tradition of truth is possible in general. In short, what seems to be of utmost importance to Husserl is as much an operation (reactivation itself as the ability to open a hidden historical field) as the nature of that field itself (as the possibility of something like reactivation).

Thus only under the cover of static phenomenology's reductions can we make other infinitely more subtle and hazardous reductions, which yield both the singular essences of institutive acts and, in their exemplary web, the whole sense of an open history in general. Without the *Wechselspiel* of this double reduction, the phenomenology of historicity would be an exercise in vanity, as would be all phenomenology. If we take for granted the philosophical nonsense of a purely empirical history and the impotence of an ahistorical rationalism, then we realize the seriousness of what is at stake.

### III

All these precautions have made us sensitive to the extreme difficulty of the task. Thus Husserl underscores the preliminary and general character of this meditation in a sentence which appears borrowed word

---

[43] "Thus we find ourselves in a sort of *circle*. The understanding of the beginnings is to be gained fully only by starting with science as given in its present-day form, looking back at its development. But in the absence of an understanding of the *beginnings* the development is mute as a *development of sense*. Thus we have no other choice than to proceed forward and backward in a 'zigzag' pattern . . ." (§9*l*, p. 58 [modified]).

[44] [Derrida puts the phrase "pas plus que l'historie de sa transmission ne fonde la valeur de l'or" in quotations. I have been unable to locate this phrase, and Professor Derrida himself does not remember from what it is taken. It might simply be an adaptation of the last phrase quoted from *Ideas I* on p. 43 above.]

for word from *Formal and Transcendental Logic* (Introduction, p. 6): "This return inquiry unavoidably remains within the sphere of generalities, but, as we shall soon see, these are generalities which can be richly explicated . . ." (158 [modified]).

Doubtless, as apriori determination, phenomenology will never be able to enrich these generalities, whose indigence is essential. And they will be "richly explicated" only in a prospective, regional, and, in a certain sense, *naive* style of work. But this naiveté would no longer have the sense it used to have *before* the sense-investigation of these generalities; a sense-investigation that Husserl terms a "criticism" and which will have a regulative and normative value for this work. Continually calling us back to the unnoticed presuppositions of ever recurring problems, sense-investigation will keep us from aberration, forgetfulness, and irresponsibility. "If science, with radical responsibility, has reached decisions, they can impress on life habitual norms as volitional bents, as predelineated forms within which the individual decisions ought in any case to confine themselves, and can confine themselves so far as those universal decisions have become actually appropriated. For a rational practice, theory a priori can be only a delimiting form; it can only plant fences, the crossing of which indicates absurdity or aberration" (*FTL*, p. 6).

The first of these radical generalities is precisely that which authorizes the return inquiry: the unity of geometry's sense is that of a tradition. Geometry's development is a *history* only because it is *a* history. However far its building up progresses, however generous the proliferation of its forms and metamorphoses may be, they do not call again into question the unified sense of what, in this development, is to be thought of as *the* geometrical science. The ground of this unity is the world itself: not as the finite totality of sentient beings, but as the infinite totality of possible experiences in space in general. The unity of *the* geometrical science, which is also its oneness, is not confined to the systematic coherence of *a* geometry whose axioms are already constituted; its unity is that of a traditional geometrical sense infinitely open to all *its own* revolutions. To pose the question of this traditional unity is to ask oneself: how, *historically,* have all geometries been, or will they be, geometries?

Furthermore, this unity of geometry's sense, such as it is *announced* in the *Origin,* is not a general concept that is extracted or abstracted from various known geometries. On the contrary, it is the primordial concrete essence of geometry that makes such a generalizing operation possible. Nor is this sense-unity to be confused with the concept that Husserl *in fact* determined as the ideal orienting geometrical practice in geometry's *objective* thematic field.[45] This concept (already marked by history) is, as we know, that of a *"definite"* nomology and an exhaustive deductivity.[46] Starting from a system of axioms which "governs" a multiplicity, every proposition is determinable *either* as analytic consequence *or* as analytic contradiction.[47] That would be an alternative we could not get beyond. Such confidence did not have long to wait before being contradicted; indeed its vulnerability has been well shown, particularly when Gödel discovered the rich possibility of *"undecidable"* propositions in 1931.

But all the questions about the possibility or impossibility of maintaining Husserl's demands—either as an essentially inaccessible regulative ideal or as a methodological rule and actual technique (which no longer in general seems possible)—are they not asked precisely *within* this unity of the geometrico-mathematical horizon in general, within the open unity of a science? And it is within the horizon that Husserl here questions that the preoccupation with decidability belongs. In its very negativity, the notion of the un-decidable—apart from the fact that it only has such a sense by some irreducible reference to the ideal of decidability[48]—also retains a mathematical value derived from some unique source of value vaster than the project of *definiteness* itself. This whole debate is only understandable within something like *the* geometrical or mathematical science, whose unity is still *to come* on the basis of what is announced in its origin. Whatever may be the responses contributed by the epistemologist or by the activity of the scientific inves-

[45] On the two "faces" of science's thematic and the objective character of the thematic on which the scientific researcher is exclusively focused in his activity as researcher, cf. *FTL*, §9, pp. 36–38. "Thus the geometer . . . will not think of exploring, besides geometrical shapes, geometrical thinking" (p. 36).

[46] On these questions, cf. in particular Jean Cavaillès, *Sur la Logique et la théorie de la science* (Paris: Presses Universitaires de France, 1947), pp. 70ff.; Trân-Dúc-Tháo, *Phénoménologie*, p. 35; and especially S. Bachelard, *A Study of Husserl's* Logic [Part I, Ch. 3], pp. 43–63.

[47] This ideal is clearly defined by Husserl, notably in the *LI*, I, Prol., §70, pp. 241 and 243, before a section in which the relations of the philosopher and the mathematician are defined; in *Ideas I*, §72, pp. 187–88; and in *FTL*, §31, pp. 94–97.

[48] Moreover, that the analyses of the *Origin* concerning the synthetic style of mathematical tradition serve as an example of tradition in general is thus confirmed. The very movement which enriches sense retains a sedimentary reference to the antecedent sense at the bottom of the new sense and cannot dispense with it. The intention which grasps the new sense is original insofar as the prior project still remains and the intention will simply not "give way" to it. Thus, undecidability has a revolutionary and disconcerting sense, it is *itself* only if it remains essentially and intrinsically haunted in its sense of origin by the *telos* of decidability—whose disruption it marks.

tigator to these important intra-mathematical questions of definiteness and completeness, they can only be integrated into this unity of the mathematical tradition which is questioned in the *Origin*. And they will never concern, in the "objective" thematic sphere of science where they must exclusively remain, anything but the determined nature of the axiomatic systems and of the deductive interconnections that they do or do not authorize. But the objective thematic field of mathematics must already be constituted in its mathematical sense, in order for the values of consequence and inconsistency to be rendered problematic, and in order to be able to say, against the classic affirmations of Husserl, *"tertium datur."*[49]

Consequently, if the origin of mathematics and the unity of its sense were in Husserl's eyes essentially tied to this ideal of exhaustive deductivity, and even if they were identical with this ideal, the *Origin's* question would be tainted at the outset by a certain historical relativity, no matter what Husserl himself may have thought about this relativity and despite whatever interest it may still hold as such. In other words, if the primordial act of grounding that Husserl wishes to elicit [*solliciter*] here was the institution of an axiomatic and deductive field or even the institution of axiomatics and the ideal of deductivity in general—and if this institution was described as that of mathematics itself—then the Husserlian project would be seriously threatened by the evolution of axiomatiziation toward a total formalization within which one necessarily comes up against the limits stated by Gödel's theorem (and related theorems). But that is not so! Even if Husserl at one time adopted the conception of grounding axiomatics and even proposed it as the ideal for "all 'exact' eidetic disciplines" (*Ideas I*, §7, p. 56), it seems he only considered this to be a *secondary* grounding. There is no doubt, in any case, that the kinds of primordial evidence he investigates here are for

[49] Husserl writes in *FTL*, §31, p. 96: "the idea of a '*nomological science*', or correlatively the idea of an *infinite province* (in mathematico-logical parlance, a multiplicity) governable by an explanatory nomology, includes the idea that there is no truth about such a province that is not deducibly included in the 'fundamental laws' of the corresponding nomological science—just as, in the *ideal Euclid*, there is no truth about space that is not deducibly included in the '*complete*' (*vollständigen*) system of space-axioms." Then, defining the "*multiplicity-form in the pregnant sense*," Husserl continues: "Such a multiplicity-form is defined, *not by just any formal axiom-system*, but by a '*complete*' one. . . . The axiom-system formally defining such a multiplicity is distinguished by the circumstance that any proposition (proposition-form, naturally) that can be constructed, in accordance with the grammar of pure logic, out of the concepts (concept-forms) occuring [*sic*] in that system, is either 'true'—that is to say: an analytic (purely deducible) consequence of the axioms—or 'false'—that is to say: an analytic contradiction—; *tertium non datur*."

him prior to those of axioms and serve as their ground. In fact, we can read in the *Origin* (168): "one must also take note of the constructive activities that operate with geometrical idealities which have been 'explicated' but not brought to primordial evidence. (Primordial evidence must not be confused with the evidence of 'axioms'; *for axioms are in principle the results of primordial sense-fashioning* (Sinnbildung) *and always have this behind them*)" [modified].[50]

Axiomatics in general (from which alone every ideal of exhaustive and exact deductivity can take its sense, from which alone every problem of decidability can then spring) already supposes, therefore, a sedimentation of sense: i.e., axiomatics supposes a primordial evidence, a radical ground which is already past. It is then already exiled from the origins to which Husserl now wishes to return.

Consequently, if Husserl (from the *Logical Investigations* to *Ideas I* and to *Formal and Transcendental Logic*) indeed assigned the narrow sense of decidability to the notion of geometrical determinability, this is because he let himself be guided in his nonhistorical investigations by the present state of a *ready-made* science. But as soon as the question of origin arises, geometrical determinability seems indeed to have the sense of geometrical determinability *in general,* as the infinite horizon of a science, whatever future forms develop.[51] When Husserl speaks in the

---

[50] Our emphasis. "Explication" *(Verdeutlichung)* is not to be confused either with clarification *(Klärung)* or reactivation: remaining within constituted sense, explication makes that sense *distinct* without restoring it to its full *clarity,* i.e., to its value as *present cognition,* and above all without reactivating its primordial intention. It is for reasons of grammatical construction (the use of past or present participles, of substantive or infinitive forms, etc.) that we have kept the classic translation of *Verdeutlichung* as explication. S. Bachelard comments more rigorously on the sense of this notion by translating it as "process of distinguishing" or "process which renders distinct." On all the problems concerning explication, clarification, and reactivation of propositions in general, problems to which allusion is made in the *Origin,* cf. notably *FTL,* §§16 and 17, pp. 56–63, and Appendix II, pp. 313–29; also S. Bachelard, *A Study of Husserl's* Logic, Ch. 1, pp. 14–23. In his formulation of the *Origin,* Fink specifies these distinctions. Instead of opposing "reactivation" and "explication," he distinguishes between two moments or types of reactivation in general: reactivation as "logical explication" and reactivation of the "tradition of sense-formation *(Sinnbildungstradition)* internally present in a thematic sense-formation." "When reactivation in the first sense is completed, when it comes to an end, only then does reactivation as return inquiry concerning the 'primal instituting' begin" ("Die Frage," p. 215). Thus, this formulation confirms and underscores the necessary anteriority of the *static* analysis and the *static* fixing of sense, both of which must control all *genetic* bearing [*démarche*].

[51] Geometrical determinability in the broad sense would only be the regional and abstract form of an infinite determinability of being in general, which Husserl so often called the ultimate horizon for every theoretical attitude and for all philosophy.

*Origin* of a "horizon of geometrical future in precisely this style" (159), this style is not that of deductivity, but of geometry or mathematics in general, from which as yet and always the undecidables or any other future mathematical formation will stem.

This means that from now on when investigating origins, the ideal itself of decidability, along with every factual stage of the history of mathematics as such, is *reduced;* so, too, is each determined factual tradition—by disclosing the purely mathematical tradition and pure traditionality in general. Thus we understand Husserl's repeated stipulation in the *Origin* that, concerning exact sciences, he is speaking about the "so-called 'deductive sciences'"; adding: "so called, although they by no means merely deduce" (168). There is thus a truth, or rather a geometrico-mathematical truth-sense in general, which does not permit itself to be bound by the alternative of *"true"* or "false," as prescribed by the ideal of a definite multiplicity, in which *"the concepts 'true' and 'formal implication of the axioms' are equivalent,* and likewise also the concepts 'false' and 'formally implied as the opposite of a formal implication of the axioms' " (*Ideas I,* §72, p. 188). The unity of geometrical truth's primordial sense, that unity which orients the *Origin,* could then be posed in a question of this kind: what is mathematical determinability in general, if the undecidability of a proposition, for example, is still a mathematical determination? Essentially, such a question cannot expect a determined response, it should only indicate the pure openness and unity of an infinite horizon.

Since a fact's opacity could be reduced from the very beginning by the production of ideal objects, historical interconnections are interconnections of sense and value, which—by capitalizing *ad infinitum* and according to an original mode—can never keep their sedimentary deposits out of circulation. That is a possibility, but not a necessity, since the interest and the difficulty of Husserl's analysis result from what this analysis accrues on both planes at once.

*Sometimes* Husserl considers geometry and science in general as certain forms among others of what he calls the cultural world. In effect they borrow all their characteristics from it. This world exists entirely "through tradition" (158). And the sciences are only some traditions among others. On the subject of tradition in general, we have some apriori evidence that no ignorance of factual history can undermine. On the one hand, we know with "a knowledge of unassailable evidence"—an "implicit knowledge" which inhabits this factual "lack of knowledge, everywhere and essentially" (158)—that cultural formations always refer to human productions; then, they refer to spiritual acts, as Husserl immediately concludes in a move which we will consider later. This reference to the productive act is inscribed in the formation itself, but it can pass unnoticed on account of the ideal formation's autonomy. Hence the necessity to recall the apriori banalities buried by science and culture.[52] In a similar fashion, we know that humanity has a past and that, from this fact, it is in the past that the "first inventors" (158) themselves are found; and although they have instituted new spiritual forms, they have been able to do so only by disposing of raw or already traditional, i.e., spiritually shaped, materials.

But on the other hand, traditional development, from which every culture acquires totality at each moment (in a mediate or immediate synchrony), does not have a causal style of genesis. In the world of natural reality subject to a causal type of development, sedimentation is not that of an acquired sense that is continually and internally recapitulated. There is no natural history for Husserl any more than for Hegel, and for the same reasons. The analogy will be even greater when we see that, for Husserl as for Hegel, culture itself in its finite empirical units is not sufficient to constitute the pure unity of a history. This will be the case for all anthropological cultures which do not participate in the European *eidos*.

Here the *Origin* repeats Husserl's critique of Dilthey in "Philosophy as Rigorous Science." While completely accepting Dilthey's criticism of the causalist naturalization of spirit and the principle of an original typo-morphology of cultural totalities, Husserl wishes to extract the idea of science (i.e., above all, philosophy) from the subjective immanence of the *Weltanschauung*.

As cultural form, the idea of science is undoubtedly also part of the *Weltanschauung,* and the content of science and philosophy is undoubtedly transmitted according to the same process as all other forms of culture and tradition in general. The process is analogous, if not identical, to that of internal time-consciousness described from the noematic viewpoint in the 1904–10 lectures. The present appears neither as the rupture nor the effect of a past, but as the retention of a present past, i.e., as the retention of a retention, and so forth. Since the retentional power of living consciousness is finite, this consciousness preserves significations, values, and past acts as habitualities *(habitus)* and sedimentations. Traditional sedimentation in the communal world will have the function of going beyond the retentional finitude of individual consciousness. Of course, sedimentary retention is not only the condi-

[52] This requirement of *Trivialität* is frequently justified by Husserl, notably in *C*, §9*h*, p. 50.

tion for the possibility of protention: it also belongs essentially to the general form of protention, which is itself conceived under the absolutely unique and universal form of the Living Present. The latter, which is the primordial absolute of temporality, is only the maintenance of what indeed must be called the *dialectic* of protention and retention, despite Husserl's repugnance for that word. In the movement of protention, the present is retained and gone beyond as past present, in order to constitute *another* primordial and original Absolute, another Living Present. Without this extraordinary absolute alteration of what always remains in the concrete and lived form of an absolute Present, without this always renewed originality of an absolute primordiality, always present and always lived as such, no history would be possible. Also, what is true of the Living Present is true of what supposes it as its ground, the historic present; the latter always refers more or less immediately to the totality of a past which inhabits it and which always appears under the general form of a *project*. At every moment each historic totality is a cultural structure animated by a project which is an "idea." Thus "*Weltanschauung,* too, is an 'idea' " ("PRS," p. 135).

But *at other times,* on the contrary, Husserl describes science as a unique and archetypal form of traditional culture. Besides all the characteristics that it has in common with other cultural formations, science claims an essential privilege: it does not permit itself to be enclosed in any historically determined culture as such, for it has the universal validity of *truth.* As a cultural form which is not proper to any de facto culture, the idea of science is the index of pure culture in general; it designates culture's *eidos par excellence.* In this sense, the cultural form "science" (of which geometry is one example) is itself "exemplary" in the double sense of this word, eidetic and teleological: it is the particular example which guides the eidetic reduction and intuition, but it also is the example and model which must orient culture as its ideal. Science is the idea of what, from the first moment of its production, must be true always and for everyone, beyond every given cultural area. It is the infinite *eidos* opposed to the finite ideal which animates the *Weltanschauung:*

> **Weltanschauung,** too, is an "idea," but of a goal lying in the finite, in principle to be realized in an individual life by way of constant approach. . . . The "idea" of **Weltanschauung** is consequently a different one for each time. . . . The "idea" of science, on the contrary, is a supratemporal one, and here that means limited by no relatedness to the spirit of one time. . . . Science is a title standing for absolute, timeless values. Every such value, once discovered, belongs

*thereafter to the treasure trove of **all** succeeding humanity and obviously determines likewise the material content of the idea of culture, wisdom, **Weltanschauung**, as well as of **Weltanschauung** philosophy. (**Ibid.**, pp. 135–36)*

In a non-descriptive pure science, the mode of sedimentation is such that no signification ceases to circulate at any moment and can always be reconceived and reawakened in its circulation. If it was necessary then to distinguish between natural reality and spiritual culture, we must now discriminate, in order to understand pure culture and traditionality in general, between empirical culture and that of truth. In other words, between de facto historical culture, on the one hand, in which sense-sedimentation does not exclude the fact that validity (which is rooted in a language, terrain, epoch, and so forth) can become dated [*péremption*], and on the other hand, the culture of truth, whose ideality is absolutely normative.[53] No doubt, the latter would be *in fact* impossible without the former. But on the one hand, the culture of truth is the highest and most irreducible possibility of empirical culture; on the other hand, the culture of truth is itself only the possibility of a *reduction* of empirical culture and is manifested to itself only through such a reduction, a reduction which has become possible by an irruption of the infinite as a revolution within empirical culture.

At the same time, the culture and tradition of the *truth* are characterized by a paradoxical historicity. In one sense, they can appear disengaged from all history, since they are not intrinsically affected by the empirical content of real history and by determined cultural interconnections. This emancipation can be confused with a breaking from history in general. For those who confine themselves to historical factuality, as well as for those who enclose themselves in the ideality of validity, the narration of the truth can only have the historic originality of myth.

But in another sense, one that corresponds to Husserl's intention, the tradition of truth is the most profound and purest history. Only the pure unity of such a tradition's sense is apt to establish this continuity. Indeed, without this no authentic history would be thought or projected as such; there would only be an empirical aggregate of finite and accidental units. As soon as phenomenology breaks from both conventional Platonism and historicist empiricism, the movement of

---

[53] As Husserl had already stressed in the *LI* (I, 1, §32, p. 331), ideality is not always normative. Validity is a higher ideality which can or cannot be attached to ideality in general. We will see this much later: the sense of error has its own particular ideality.

truth that it wishes to describe is really that of a concrete and specific history—the foundations of which are a temporal and creative subjectivity's acts based on the sensible world and the life-world as cultural world.

This progress is brought about by the permanent totalization and repetition of its acquisitions. Geometry is born "out of a *first* acquisition, out of first creative activities. We understand its persisting manner of being: it is not only a mobile forward process from one set of acquisitions to another but a continuous synthesis in which all acquisitions maintain their validity, all make up a totality such that, at every present stage, the total acquisition is, so to speak, the total premise for the acquisitions of the new level. . . . The same thing is true of every science" (159).

Let us understand this as true of every non-descriptive science. These syntheses do not occur in a psychological memory, however collective, but rather in that *"rational memory"* so profoundly described by Gaston Bachelard, a memory based on a *"recurrent fruitfulness,"* which alone is capable of constituting and retaining the *"events of reason."*[54] In his *Philosophy of Arithmetic,* Husserl already distinguished between psychological temporality as successiveness (what Hume described) and the temporality of the synthetic interconnections of sense. He continued to explicate this difference, and in the *Origin* (166) he emphasizes that a scientific stage is not only a sense which "in fact comes later," but the integration of the whole earlier sense in a new project.

Egological subjectivity cannot be responsible for this development, which is continually totalized in an absolute Present. Only a communal subjectivity can produce the historical system of truth and be wholly responsible for it. However, this total subjectivity, whose unity must be absolute and *a priori* (otherwise even the slightest truth would be unimaginable) is but the common place of all egological subjectivities, whether actually present or possible, whether past, present, or future, whether known or unknown. "Every science is related to an open chain of the generations of those who work for and with one another, researchers either known or unknown to one another who are the productive subjectivity of the total living science" (159 [modified]).

Since the totality of science is open, the universal community also has the unity of a horizon. Furthermore, the image of the "open chain" does not exhaust the depth of this communal subjectivity. For it not

[54] Cf. in particular *Le Rationalisme appliqué*, 4th ed. (Paris: Presses Universitaires de France, 1970), pp. 2 and 42–46.

only has the unity of interrelatedness and co-responsibility—each investigator not only feels himself *tied to* all the others by the unity of an object or task—but the investigator's own subjectivity is constituted by the idea or horizon of this total subjectivity which is made responsible in and through him for each of his acts as a scientific investigator. In and through him, that means without being substituted for him, because, at the same time, he remains the absolute origin, the constituting and present source of truth. Phenomenologically, the transcendental *we* is not *something other* than the transcendental *Ego*. The latter's acts, even when they seem mandated by an ideal community, do not cease to be irreducibly those of a monadic *"I think"*—to which it suffices to reduce the empirical egological content of the *ego* in order to discover the dimension of the *"we"* as a moment of the *eidos "ego."*[55] One would indeed be tempted to think that it is the *we* that makes possible the reduction of the empirical *ego* and the emergence of the *eidos "ego,"* if such an hypothesis did not lead, against Husserl's most explicit intentions, to placing the egological monad in abstract relation to the total subjectivity. In any case, if there is a history of truth, it can only be this concrete implication and this reciprocal envelopment of totalities and absolutes. This is possible only because we are dealing with ideal and spiritual implications. The description of these two characteristics, ideality and spirituality, so frequently evoked in the *Origin*, do not correspond, as we know, to any metaphysical assertion. In addition to which, they are *"founded"* in the sense of *Fundierung*.

The irreducible historicity of geometrical becoming is characterized by the fact that "the *total* sense of geometry" (and its necessary noetic correlate, total subjectivity) "could not have been present as a project and then as mobile fulfillment at the beginning" (159). If the history of geometry were only the development of a purpose wholly present from the beginning, we would have to deal only with an explication or a quasi-creation. We would have on one side a synchronic or timeless [*uchronique*][56] ground and, on the other side, a purely empirical diachrony with its indicative function but without any proper unity of its own. Neither pure diachrony nor pure synchrony make a history. The

---

[55] Then begins the formidable difficulties grappled with in the fifth of the *Cartesian Meditations*, and into which we do not want to enter here.

[56] [Derrida wants to suggest by the word *uchronie* a temporality akin to the spatiality of *utopia*. We should also note Derrida's use of the roots "temporalité" and "chronie" in various words: *panchronie* and *uchronie* versus *omnitemporalité* and *intemporalité* (as well as *synchronie*, *diachronie*, and *anachronie*). When *uchronie* occurs again on p. 73, it is translated as intemporality.]

rejected hypothesis is once more that of a complicity between "Platonism" and empiricism.

As a matter of fact, even before the possibility of the open project of geometry, "a more primitive formation of sense *(Sinnbildung)* necessarily went before it as a preliminary stage, undoubtedly in such a way that it appeared for the first time in the evidence of successful actualization" (159–60 [modified]).

## IV

Having reached this point, Husserl performs a detour which may seem disconcerting. Instead of describing this primitive genesis of sense in itself and in its *Erstmaligkeit,* he tacitly and provisionally considers it to be *already* done, its sense being already evident. He is content to recall that we know the general form of this evidence:[57] the latter must be—it cannot not be—like all evidence (whether perceptive or eidetic), the intuition of a natural reality or of an ideal object, i.e., "grasping an existent in the consciousness of its original being-itself-there" (160 [modified]). This recalls the *"principle of all principles"* defined in *Ideas I.* However little we may know about the first geometrical evidence, we do know *a priori* that it has had to assume this form. But even though applied to a historical origin in this case, this *a priori* knowledge concerning the form of evidence is nothing less than historical. Defining a *"source of authority"* [*Ideas I,* §24, p. 83] for the cognition of any object in general, it is one of those *formal a priori* supposed by every material science; here by geometry and history. Since the first geometrical evidence has had to conform to this pattern, we can have a first certainty about it in the absence of any other material knowledge. Hence the *content* of geometrical evidence (a content which is historical because created for the first time) is not defined for the moment. Husserl considers it already acquired.

This abstention before the content of the primordial act and evidence is provisional. It is a question of a methodological limitation and, once again, of the necessity to take one's starting point in the constituted. But this methodological necessity is only legitimate on the basis of a profound philosophical decision. Having cleared this stage, Husserl in effect continues his meditation (now protected by that formal legitimation) as if his theme were no longer the origin of geometrical sense, but

---

[57] This is done in terms which recall those of *Ideas I,* no doubt, but above all those of *FTL:* cf. notably *FTL,* §59, pp. 156–59.

the *genesis of the* absolute (i.e., ideal) *Objectivity* of sense, this sense being already present for any consciousness whatsoever. Husserl repeatedly and obstinately returns to a question which is at bottom the following: how can the subjective egological evidence of sense become objective and intersubjective? How can it give rise to an ideal and true object, with all the characteristics that we know it to have: omnitemporal validity, universal normativity, intelligibility for *"everyone,"* uprootedness out of all *"here and now"* factuality, and so forth? This is the historical repetition of the question of Objectivity so frequently asked in the five lectures of *The Idea of Phenomenology:* how can subjectivity go out of itself in order to encounter or constitute the object?[58]

Husserl has, then, provisionally abstained before the historical content of *Erstmaligkeit* only to ask the question of its objectification [*objectivation*], i.e., of its launching into history and its historicity. For a sense has entered into history only if it has become an absolute object,

---

[58] Husserl had posed this question in the same terms but in its most inclusive extension and with a more critical, but less historical, inflexion in *FTL*, §100, pp. 263–64. There, however, it is limited to the egological sphere of Objectivity. Here it is focused on the possibility of objective spirit as the condition for history and in this respect takes the opposite view to Dilthey's question. Dilthey, in effect, starts from the already constituted objective spirit. For him, what matters is knowing how the significations and the values of this objective milieu can be interiorized and assumed as such by individual subjects—first of all in the historian's work on the basis of testimonies which are individual in their origin or object. Moreover, this question led Dilthey to discover, like Husserl, a non-psychological dimension of the subject. Dilthey writes: "Now the following question arises: how a nexus which is not produced as such in a mind [*tête*], which consequently is not directly experienced and can no more be led back to the lived experience of a person, how can it be constituted as such in the historian on the basis of the statements of this person or of statements made about this matter? This presupposes that some logical subjects, who are not psychological subjects, can be constituted" (Part III: "Plan der Fortsetzung zum Aufbau der geschichtlichen Welt in den Geisteswissenschaften. Entwürfe zur Kritik der historischen Vernunft" ["Plan for the Continuation of the Formation of the Historical World in the Human Studies. Sketches for a Critique of Historical Reason"], in Dilthey's *Der Aufbau der geschichtlichen Welt in den Geisteswissenschaften,* ed. Bernard Groethuysen, 2nd ed. (Stuttgart: B. G. Teubner and Gottingen: Vandenhoeck and Ruprecht, 1958), Vol. 7 of *Gesammelte Schriften,* p. 282.

This question is "turned over" in the *Origin* in formulas which are strangely similar to those of Dilthey. This "reverse side" of the question concerns the radical origin and the conditions of possibility for the objective spirit itself. After the interconnections of sense and the evidences of a monadic *ego* from which we cannot not start, de facto as well as de jure, how can an objective spirit in general be constituted as the place of truth, tradition, co-responsibility, and so forth? We will see that, according to Husserl, a "logical" subject will no more be able to be responsible for such a possibility than could the psychological subject.

i.e., an ideal object which, paradoxically, must have broken all the moorings which secured it to the empirical ground of history. The conditions of Objectivity are then the conditions of historicity itself.

When Husserl farther on devotes a few lines to the production and evidence of geometrical sense as such and its own proper content, he will do so only *after* having determined the general conditions of its Objectivity and of the Objectivity of ideal objectivities. Thus, only *retroactively* and on the basis of its results can we illuminate the pure sense of the subjective praxis which has engendered geometry. The sense of the constituting act can only be deciphered in the web of the constituted object. And this necessity is not an external fate, but an essential necessity of intentionality. The *primordial* sense of every intentional act is *only* its *final* sense, i.e., the constitution of an object (in the broadest sense of these terms). That is why only a teleology can open up a passage, a way back toward the beginnings.

If the sense of geometrical sense is Objectivity or the intention of Objectivity, if geometry is here the exemplary index of being scientific, and if history is the highest and most revelatory possibility for a universal history (the concept of which would not exist without it), then the sense of sense in general is here determined as *object:* as some thing that is accessible and available in general and first for a regard or gaze. The worldly image of *gaze* would not be the unnoticed model of the theoretical attitude of pure consciousness but, on the contrary, would borrow its sense from that attitude. This is very much in accord with the initial direction of phenomenology: the object in general is the final category of everything that can appear, i.e., that can be for a pure consciousness in general. Objects in general join all regions to consciousness, the *Ur-Region.*[59]

Also, when Husserl affirms that a sense-production must have *first* presented itself as evidence in the personal consciousness of the inventor, and when he asks the question of its *subsequent* (in a factual chronological order) objectification, he elicits a kind of fiction destined to make the characteristics of ideal Objectivity problematic and to show that they are not a matter of course. Truly, there is not first a subjective geometrical evidence which would then become objective. Geometrical evidence only starts "the moment" there is evidence of an ideal objectivity. The latter is such only "after" having been put into intersubjective circulation. "Geometrical existence is not psychic existence; it does not exist as something personal within the personal sphere of consciousness; it is the existence of what is Objectively there for

---

[59] Cf. *Ideas I,* in particular §76, pp. 194–97.

'everyone' (for actual and possible geometers, or those who understand geometry). Indeed, it has, from its primal institution, an existence which is peculiarly supratemporal and which—of this we are certain—is accessible to all men, first of all to the actual and possible mathematicians of all peoples, all ages; and this is true of all its particular forms'' (160 [modified]).

"Before" and "after" must then be neutralized in their factuality and used in quotation marks. But can we simply replace them with the timeless "if" and "provided that" of the condition of possibility?

The language of genesis could well seem fictive at this point: the description of any real development (neutralized in principle) would not call for it, but bringing to light the formal conditions of possibility, the de jure implications, and eidetic stratifications does. Are we not then dealing with history? Does this not return us to a classic transcendental regression? And is not the interconnecting of transcendental necessities, even if *narrated* according to how it develops, at bottom the static, structural, and normative schema for the conditions of a history rather than history itself?

Questions of this kind might seriously impugn the whole originality of this attempt. But it seems they remain outside Husserl's intention. Undoubtedly there is not in this *account* the least grain of history if we understand by that the factual content of development. But the necessity of this reduction has been justified at the outset. And the annoyed letdown of those who would expect Husserl to tell them *what really happened,* to tell them a story [*leur raconte une histoire*], can be sharp and easily imaginable:[60] however, this disappointment is illegitimate. Husserl only wished to decipher in advance the text hidden under every empirical story about which we would be curious. Factual history can then be given free rein: no matter what its style, its method, or its *philosophy,* it will always more or less naively suppose the possibility and necessity of the interconnections described by Husserl. Undoubtedly these interconnections are always marked by a juridical and transcendental signification, but they refer to *concrete* acts *lived* in a *unique* system of instituting implications, i.e., in a system that has been originally produced only *once*—that remains de facto and de jure, *irreversible.* These then are the *interconnections-of* what is, in the fullest sense of the word, *history itself.* Thus, confronting what is through and through a historical adventure (the fact of which is irreplaceable), an

[60] Cf. in particular Trân-Dúc-Tháo, *Phénoménologie,* p. 221. Following this interpreter, "the subjectivist point of view" in *The Origin of Geometry* would have prohibited Husserl from "going beyond the level of common sense remarks."

apriori and eidetic reading and discourse should be possible. Husserl did not invent such a possibility; it was simply disclosed as what implicitly has always conditioned the existence of the ideal objects of a pure science and thus of a pure tradition, and consequently of a pure historicity, the model of history in general.

*Pure-interconnections-of* history, *apriori-thought-of* history, does this not mean that these possibilities are not in themselves historical? Not at all, for they are *nothing but* the possibilities *of* the appearance *of* history *as such,* outside which there is nothing. History itself establishes the possibility of its own appearing.

# V

This possibility is first called *"language."* If we ask ourselves about the manner in which the subjective evidence of geometrical sense gains its ideal Objectivity, we must first note that ideal Objectivity not only characterizes geometrical and scientific truths; it is the element of language in general. "It is proper to a whole class of spiritual products of the cultural world, to which not only all scientific formations and the sciences themselves belong but also, for example, the formations of literary art" (160 [modified]).

This movement is analogous to what we analyzed earlier: the ideal Objectivity of geometry is first presented as a characteristic common to all forms of language and culture, before its "exemplary" privilege is defined. In an important note, Husserl specifies that "the broadest concept of literature" (160) comprises all ideal formations, since, in order to be such, they must always be capable of being expressible in discourse and translatable, directly or not, from one language into another. In other words, ideal formations are rooted only in language in general, not in the factuality of languages and their particular linguistic incarnations.

It is through these themes, already present in the *Logical Investigations* and the first sections of *Formal and Transcendental Logic,* that the very subtle and specific character of the Husserlian question appears.

The ideal object is the absolute model for any object whatever, for objects in general.[61] It is always more objective than the real object,

---

[61] This ideality of the object, i.e., here, of the *mathematical thing itself,* is not the non-reality of the noema described in *Ideas I* (especially §§88, 97ff.). The latter characterizes the type of intentional inclusion of every noema in conscious lived experience, whatever the intended type of existent may be and however it may be intended (even if

than the natural existent. For if the latter resists or opposes anything, it would always be a de facto empirical subjectivity. Therefore, the real object can never attain that absolute Objectivity which can be proposed for all subjectivity in general in the intangible identity of its sense. The question *"how is any object in general possible?"* assumes its sharpest and most adequate form, then, in the *Origin,* when Husserl wonders: *"How is ideal Objectivity possible?"* Here the question also attains its greatest difficulty, since recourse to the natural Objectivity of a worldly existent is no longer possible. Besides, once having reached the level of ideal Objectivity, we still encounter several more degrees.

No doubt language is "thoroughly made up of ideal objectivities; for example, the word *Löwe* [lion] occurs only once in the German language; it is identical throughout its innumerable utterances by any given persons" (161 [modified]).

Thus, the word [*mot*] has an ideal Objectivity and identity, since it is not identical with any of its empirical, phonetic, or graphic materializations. It is always the *same* word which is meant and recognized through all possible linguistic gestures. Insofar as this ideal object confronts language as such, the latter supposes a spontaneous neutralization of the factual existence of the speaking subject, of words, and of the thing designated. Speech [*La parole*], then, is only the practice of an immediate eidetic.[62] André de Muralt notes very precisely that the

---

we are dealing with perception of a real thing). However, there is no doubt that this non-reality of the noema (a very difficult and decisive notion) may be what, in the last analysis, permits the repetition of sense as the "same" and makes the idealization of identity in general possible. Undoubtedly, we could show this in a precise way on the basis of §62 of *FTL,* devoted to "The Ideality of All Species of Objectivities Over Against the Constituting Consciousness" and the *"universal ideality of all intentional unities"* (pp. 165–66).

[62] The linguistic neutralization of existence is an original idea only in the technical and thematic signification that phenomenology gives it. Is not this idea the favorite of Mallarmé and Valéry? Hegel above all had amply explored it. In the *Encyclopedia* (one of the few Hegelian works that Husserl seems to have read), the lion already testifies to this neutralization as an exemplary martyr: "Confronting the name—Lion—we no longer have any need either of an intuition of such an animal or even an image, but the name (when we understand it) is its simple and imageless representation; in the name we think" (§462). (This passage is cited by Jean Hyppolite in his *Logique et existence: Essai sur la logique de Hegel* [Paris: Presses Universitaires de France, 1953], p. 39, a work which, on a great many points, lets the profound convergence of Hegelian and Husserlian thought appear.)

Hegel also writes: "The first act, by which Adam is made master of the animals, was to impose on them a name, i.e., he annihilated them in their existence (as existents)" ("System of 1803-1804"). Cited by Maurice Blanchot in *La Part du feu* (Paris: Gallimard, 1949), p. 325.

"*reduction is implicitly carried out*—simply performed and not yet made explicit—as soon as language is considered on its own account."[63]

Here we are concerned with the eidetic reduction. But, paradoxically, for this reason it seems more difficult to say that "a thought which moves solely on the level of language is necessarily in the attitude of the *phenomenological reduction* [our emphasis]; it is set squarely in the eidetic world of significations or pure lived experiences."[64]

For if the phenomenological reduction is taken in its fullest sense, it must also entail the reduction of constituted eidetics and then of its own language. The precaution of "quotation marks" only satisfies this imperative in an equivocal fashion. This transcendental reduction of eidetics, which in its most radical moment must still turn us back toward a new and irreducibly necessary eidetic, that of pure consciousness, creates in effect some considerable difficulties. Husserl is very conscious of this and he exposes these difficulties with the greatest clarity in *Ideas I*.[65]

Therefore, to the very extent that language is not "natural," it paradoxically offers the most dangerous resistance to the phenomenological reduction, and transcendental discourse will remain

---

[63] *The Idea of Phenomenology: Husserlian Exemplarism*, tr. Garry L. Breckon (Evanston: Northwestern University Press, 1974), p. 128.

[64] *Ibid.* [modified].

[65] "Meanwhile we cannot disconnect transcendents indefinitely, transcendental purification cannot mean the disconnection of *all* transcendents, since otherwise a pure consciousness might indeed remain over, but no possbility [*sic*] of a science of pure consciousness" (*Ideas I*, §59, p. 159). In this section, devoted to the necessary but difficult reduction of formal ontology and formal logic once all the transcendents of the material eidetics have been excluded, Husserl concludes in favor of the possibility of such a reduction, provided the "logical *axioms*" are maintained, axioms (like the principle of contradiction) "whose universal and absolute validity" the description of pure consciousness could "make transparent by the help of examples taken from the data of its own domain" (p. 160). But he says nothing about the language of this ultimate science of pure consciousness, about the language which *at least* seems to suppose the sphere of formal logic that we just excluded. For Husserl, the univocity of expression and certain precautions taken *within* and *with the help* of language itself (distinctions, quotation marks, neologisms, revaluation and reactivation of old words, and so on) will always be sufficient guarantees of rigor and nonworldliness.

That is why, despite the remarkable analyses which are devoted to it, despite the constant interest it bears (from the *Logical Investigations* to the *Origin*), the specific problem of language—its origin and its usage in a transcendental phenomenology—has always been excluded or deferred. This is explicitly so in *FTL* (§2, p. 21, and §5, p. 27) and in the *Origin*, where he has written: "we shall not go into the general problem which also arises here of the origin of language in its ideal existence and its existence in the real world" (161).

irreducibly obliterated by a certain ambiguous worldliness.[66] By imagining that the *Origin* will first indicate the possibility of history as the possibility of language, we are calculating how difficult is every attempt to reduce (in some ultimate and radical transcendental regression) a phenomenology of historicity. And so once more we see a certain nondependence confirmed in that phenomenology.

[66] This is a difficulty that Fink has frequently underscored (particularly in his famous article in *Kantstudien* of 1933 ["The Phenomenological Philosophy of Edmund Husserl and Contemporary Criticism"]). For him, the phenomenological reduction "cannot be presented by means of simple sentences of the natural attitude. It can be spoken of only by transforming the natural function of language" (Lettér of May 11, 1936, cited by Gaston Berger, *The* Cogito *in Husserl's Philosophy,* tr. Kathleen McLaughlin [Evanston: Northwestern University Press, 1972], p. 49).

And in his admirable lecture on "Les concepts opératoires dans la phénoménologie de Husserl," he attributes a certain equivocation in the usage of operative concepts (that of "constitution," for example) to the fact that "Husserl does not pose the problem of a 'transcendental language.' " He wonders if, after the reduction, one can still "have at his disposal a *Logos* in the same sense as before" (in *Husserl,* Cahiers de Royaumont, p. 229).

Similarly, concerning the expression "intentional *life,*" S. Bachelard evokes the danger of "a surreptitious return to psychologism," for "language does not know the phenomenological reduction and so holds us in the natural attitude" (*A Study of Husserl's* Logic, p. xxxi).

On the basis of the problems in the *Origin,* we can thus go on to ask ourselves, for example, what is the hidden sense, the nonthematic and dogmatically received sense of the word "history" or of the word "origin"—a sense which, as the common focus of these significations, permits us to distinguish between factual "history" and intentional "history," between "origin" in the ordinary sense and phenomenological "origin," and so on. What is the unitary ground starting from which this diffraction of sense is permitted and intelligible? What is *history,* what is the *origin,* about which we can say that we must understand them sometimes in one sense, sometimes in another? So long as the notion of origin *in general* is not *criticized* as such, the radical vocation is always threatened by this mythology of the *absolute beginning,* so remarkably denounced by Feuerbach in his "Contribution to the Critique of Hegel's Philosophy" (1839) (cf. *Manifestes philosophiques,* tr. L. Althusser [Paris: Presses Universitaires de France, 1960], pp. 18–21).

These questions can show the need for a certain renewed and rigorous philological or "etymological" thematic, which would precede the discourse of phenomenology. A formidable task, because it supposes that all the problems which it would have to precede are resolved, in particular, as a matter of fact: the interlocutory problem of history and that of the possibility of a historical philology. In any case, this task never seems to have appeared urgent to Husserl, even when the idea of linguistic "reactivation" takes on so much importance for him. Unlike Heidegger, he almost never indulges in etymological variations, and when he does so (cf. *FTL,* §1, pp. 18–19), it does not determine but follows the orientation of the investigation. For Husserl, it would be absurd for sense not to precede—de jure (and here the de jure is difficult to make clear [*une évidence difficile*])—the act of language whose own value will always be that of *expression.*

It is rather significant that every critical enterprise, juridical or transcendental, is made

But the word's degree of ideal Objectivity is only, we could say, *primary*. Only within a facto-historical language is the noun *"Löwe"* free, and therefore ideal, compared with its sensible, phonetic, or graphic incarnations. But it remains essentially tied, as a German word, to a real spatiotemporality; it remains interrelated in its very ideal Objectivity with the de facto existence of a given language and thus with the factual subjectivity of a certain speaking community. Its ideal Objectivity is then relative and distinguishable only as an empirical fact from that of the French or English word *"lion."*

Therefore we cross into a higher degree of ideal Objectivity—let us call it *secondary*—as soon as we pass from the word to the unity of the sense *"lion,"* from *"the expression"* to what Husserl calls in the *Logical Investigations* the *"intentional content"* or "the unity of its signification."[67] The *same* content can be intended starting from several

---

vulnerable by the irreducible factuality and the natural naiveté of its language. We become conscious of this vulnerability or of this vocation to silence in a *second* reflection on the possibility of the juridico-transcendental regression itself. Despite its necessarily speculative style, this reflection is always focused, without having to succumb to empiricism, on the world of culture and history. Attentiveness to the "fact" of language in which a juridical thought lets itself be transcribed, in which juridicalness would like to be completely transparent, is a return to factuality as the de jure character of the de jure itself. It is a reduction of the reduction and opens the way to an infinite discursiveness.

This explains why the return on itself of thought which has never wanted to prescribe anything but a turning back [*repli*] toward its own proper conditions remains more difficult for the "master" than for the "disciple." Did not Herder, in his *Verstand und Erfahrung: Eine Metakritik zur Kritik der reinen Vernunft* [Leipzig, 1799; rpt. Bruxelles: Culture et Civilisation, 1969, 2 vols.], already reproach Kant for not taking into consideration the intrinsic necessity of language and its immanence in the most apriori act of thought? Did not the author of the *Essay on the Origin of Language* [tr. Alexander Gode in *On the Origin of Language* (New York: Frederick Ungar, 1966)] also conclude that language, rooted in cultural experience and in history, made all aprioriness of synthetic judgments impossible or illusory? The inability of received language to be treated thematically, an inability which precedes every critical regression as its shadow—is not the unavowed dogmatism he thus denounces that *geschichtlose "Naivität"* about which Fink wonders whether it is not the basis for "phenomenology's methodological revolution" (cf. "L'Analyse intentionnelle et le problème de la pensée spéculative" [French tr. Walter Biemel and Jean Ladrière], in *Problèmes actuels de la phénoménologie*, ed. H. L. Van Breda [Paris: Desclée de Brouwer, 1952], pp. 64–65)? That is only one of the numerous analogies which could be taken up between the different futures of Kantian and Husserlian transcendental idealisms, such as they are already outlined. Thus, in any case, an irreducible proximity of language to primordial thought is signified in a zone which eludes by nature every phenomenal or thematic actuality. Is this immediacy the nearness of thought to itself? We would have to show why that cannot be *decided*.

[67] Vol. I, Introd. to Vol. II of the German ed., §5, and 1, §11, particularly pp. 259 and 284–85. Like those of *FTL*, the analyses concerning linguistic ideality in the *Origin*

languages, and its ideal identity assures its translatability. This ideal identity of sense expressed by lion, *leo, Löwe,* and so forth, is then freed from all factual *linguistic* subjectivity.

But the *"object" itself* is neither the expression nor the sense-content.[68] The flesh and blood lion, intended through two strata of idealities, is a natural, and therefore contingent, reality; as the perception of the immediately present sensible thing grounds idealities under those circumstances, so the contingency of the lion is going to reverberate in the ideality of the expression and in that of its sense. The translatability of the word *lion,* then, will not in principle be absolute and universal. It will be empirically conditioned by the contingent encounter in a receptive intuition of something like the lion. The latter is not an "objectivity of the understanding," but an "object of receptivity."[69] The ideality of its sense and of what it evokes irreducibly adheres to an empirical subjectivity. This would be true even if all men had been able to and could *in fact* encounter and designate the lion. Under those circumstances the tie to a de facto anthropological generality would not be reduced any further. This is because the ideality of sense, considered in itself and like that of language, is here a *"bound"*

---

directly suppose the subtle as well as indispensable distinctions found in the *LI* (nos. 1-5), especially in the first and fourth Investigations.

In the First Investigation, the notion of "intentional content" or "unity of its signification" announces in the linguistic sphere the notion of "noematic sense," or the *"nucleatic layer" (Kernschicht)* of the noema, a notion the former implies and which is fully elaborated only in *Ideas I* (in particular, cf. §90, pp. 241ff.). Just as the core unity of noematic sense (which is not the reality of the object itself) can be intended according to various intentional modes (the sense "tree" can be attained in a perception, a memory, an imagining, and so on) in order finally to constitute a "complete" noema with all its characteristics, so the ideal identity of signification is made accessible to several languages and allows itself to be "translated." In the Foreword to the 2nd edition of *LI* (1913; p. 48 of Vol. I of ET), Husserl recognizes that the notion of noema and of the noetic-noematic correlation lacks completion in the First Investigation.

[68] Husserl used a great number of examples when analyzing this distinction for the first time in the *LI* (I, 1, particularly §12, pp. 286–87).

[69] The difference between these two types of Objectivity, which comes back to the difference between ideal objectivity and real object, is amply described in *EJ* (§63, pp. 250ff.). The objectivities of the understanding are on a "higher level" than those of receptivity. They are not preconstituted, like the latter, in the pure passivity of sensible receptivity, but in predicative spontaneity. *"The mode of their original pregivenness is their production in the predicative activity of the Ego . . ."* [p. 251]. Another difference: that of their temporality (§64). Whereas the real object has its individual place in the objective time of the world, the irreal object is, with respect to this latter, totally free, i.e., "timeless." But its timelessness *(Zeitlosigkeit)* or its supratemporality *(Überzeitlichkeit)* is only a "mode" of temporality: omnitemporality *(Allzeitlichkeit).*

ideality and not a *"free"* one. This dissociation between *"free idealities"* and *"bound idealities,"* which is only implied in the *Origin*[70] (but indispensable for its understanding), enables us to comprehend what the absolute ideal Objectivity of, for example, the geometrical object can be and what distinguishes it from that of language *as such* and from that of the sense-content *as such*.

The ideal Objectivity of geometry is absolute and without any kind of limit. Its ideality—*tertiary*—is no longer only that of the expression or intentional content; it is that of the *object itself*. All adherence to any real contingency is removed. The possibility of translation, which is identical with that of tradition, is opened *ad infinitum:* "The Pythagorean theorem, indeed all of geometry, exists only once, no matter how often or even in what language it may be expressed. It is identically the same in the 'original language' of Euclid and in all 'translations'; and within each language it is again the same, no matter how many times it has been sensibly uttered, from the original expression and writing-down to the innumerable oral utterances or written and other documentations *(Dokumentierungen)*" (160).

The sense of "only once" or of "once and for all," which is the essential mode of the object's ideal existence and thus that which distinguishes the object from the multiplicity of related acts and lived experiences, seems to have been clearly defined in these very terms by Herbart (*Psychologie als Wissenschaft,* II, §120, p. 175) and taken up again by Husserl. The latter, recognizing that he owes much to Herbart and praising him for having distinguished better than Kant between the

---

[70] From the perspective of our text, this dissociation finds its most direct and illuminating explication in *EJ* (§65, p. 267). In particular, we can read there: "Thus it appears that even cultural systems are not always completely free idealities, and this reveals the *difference between free idealities* (such as logicomathematical systems and pure essential structures of every kind) and *bound idealities,* which in their being-sense carry reality with them and hence belong to the real world. All reality is here led back to spatiotemporality as the form of the individual. But originally, reality belongs to nature; the world as the world of realities receives its individuality from nature as its lowest stratum. When we speak of truths, true states of affairs in the sense of theoretical science, and of the fact that validity 'once and for all' and 'for everyone' belongs to their sense as the *telos* of judicative stipulation, then these are *free idealities.* They are bound to no territory, or rather, they have their territory in the totality of the [mundane] universe and in every possible universe. In what concerns their possible reactivation, they are omnispatial and omnitemporal. Bound realities [the German and Derrida's translation thereof reads: Bound idealities] are bound to Earth, to Mars, to particular territories, etc." (Husserl's emphasis). Husserl immediately specifies, however, that by their "occurrence," by their coming on the scene and their " 'being discovered' " in a historicially determined territory, free idealities are also factual and worldly. Thus he states the crucial difficulty of all his philosophy of history: what is the sense of this last factuality?

logical and the psychological, reproaches him, nonetheless, for having confused ideality and normativity (*LI*, I, Prol., §59, pp. 216–18).

This reproach is very enlightening, since absolutely objective, translatable, and traditional ideal identity is not just any geometrical objectivity, but *genuine* objectivity. Once we get beyond the bound idealities and reach ideal objectivity itself, we can still encounter a factual restriction: that of disvalue, falseness, or datedness [*péremption*]. No doubt the objective sense of a false judgment is also ideal. For this reason it can be indefinitely repeated and thus becomes omnitemporal.[71] But the origin and the possibility of this ideal omnitemporality remain marked by a factual contingency, that of the reality intended by the judgment or that of subjective acts. Thus, in descriptive judgments bearing on worldly realities, sense can lose its validity without simultaneously losing its omnitemporal ideality. For, to take up Husserl's example again, I can indefinitely repeat, as the *same,* the proposition: "The automobile is the fastest means of travel," whereas I know it to be false and out-of-date. The anachrony of validity in no way affects the intemporality [*uchronie*] or pantemporality [*pan-chronie*] of ideality. Likewise, in the interconnections of a non-descriptive science such as geometry, error also has a content which can become ideal and omnitemporal (error results either from the

---

[71] Once again it is in *Experience and Judgment* that the omnitemporality of simple ideality is scrupulously distinguished from the omnitemporality of validity: "Furthermore, it should be noted that this omnitemporality does not simply include within itself the omnitemporality of *validity*. We do not speak here of validity, of truth, but merely of objectivities of the understanding as suppositions [*Vermeinheiten*] and as possible, ideal-identical, intentional poles, which can be 'realized' anew at any time in individual acts of judgment—precisely as suppositions; whether they are realized in the self-evidence of truth is another question. A judgment which was once true can cease to be true, like the proposition 'The automobile is the fastest means of travel,' which lost its validity in the age of the airplane. Nevertheless, it can be constituted anew at any time as one and identical by any individual in the self-evidence of distinctness; and, as a supposition, it has its supratemporal, irreal identity" (§64 *c*, p. 261 [modified]). Also cf. *LI*, I, 1, §11, p. 285.

In the *Origin* Husserl also alludes to the ideal identity of judgments which not only would be anachronistic in their validity but also contradictory and absurd in their sense-content. These analyses, at the same time that they announce and orient a phenomenology of the specific ideality of negative validities (of the false, the absurd, the evil, the ugly, etc.), assign limits to the "freedom" of those idealities which will *always* be, as we will soon try to show, idealities "bound" to an empirical, determined temporality or to some factuality. For what *absolutely* frees and completes the ideality of sense (already endowed in itself with a certain degree of "freedom") is the ideality of *positive validity* (by which evidence is not only *distinct* but *clear* when it reaches judgment). It alone causes sense to attain infinite universality and infinite omnitemporality.

logico-deductive handling of symbols which are void of their sense and into which, unknown to us, a sensible factuality is reintroduced, or from some psychological contingency having no sense in comparison with geometrical truth). The content of error can become such even when (in error or assumption), once the strata of already defined idealities is traversed, we have not reached the truth of geometrical *Sachverhalt,*[72] and even when the very theme of the statement remains bound to factuality. The ideality of sense symbolically puts up with a deluded or inauthentically satisfied truth-intention.[73] It follows, then, that if the omnitemporality of disvalue is possible, it is always in the sense of empirical possibility, i.e., of contingent eventuality. Besides, omnitemporality is maintained in its *eventuality* only by a sense which always keeps up a certain essential relation with the absent or exceeded truth. This is because I know that such an outdated proposition *had been true* and still remains unified and animated by an intention of truth, authenticity, or "clarity" *(Klarheit)*—these terms are in certain respects synonyms for Husserl—that I can maintain and repeat the ideal unity of its sense. An eventually *absurd intention,* absurd in the sense of "nonsense" or "countersense," to be what it is, must continually point (in spite of itself) toward the *telos* of authenticity and let itself be guided symbolically by it in the very gesture in which the intention pretends to be disoriented. This intention must (in the Eurycleian language which the *Stranger* of the *Sophist* speaks) own up to [*dire*] the *telos* in order to disown [*dedire*] it.

This transgression of linguistic ideality, then, really describes a movement analogous to what we earlier described: science was a cultural form, but its pure possibility appeared as the pure possibility of

---

[72] A notion difficult to translate other than by the clumsy, strange, and less exact (but for so long accepted) expression "state-of-affairs."

[73] In the *LI,* I, 1, §11, pp. 285–86, these themes are already greatly explicated. For example, Husserl writes: "What my assertion asserts, the content that *the three perpendiculars of a triangle intersect in a point,* neither arises nor passes away. [The first German edition and the French translation continue: "Each time I (or whoever else it may be) pronounce with the same sense this same assertion, there is a new judgment. . . . But *what* they judge, *what* the assertion says, is all the same thing."] It is an identity in the strict sense, one and the same geometrical truth.

"It is the same in the case of all assertions, even if *what* they assert is false and absurd. Even in such cases we distinguish their ideal content from the transient acts [of] affirming or asserting it: it is the signification of the assertion, a unity in plurality. . . .

"If 'possibility' or 'truth' is lacking, an assertion's intention can only be carried out symbolically: it cannot derive any 'fulness' from intuition or from the categorial functions performed on the latter, in which 'fulness' its value for knowledge consists. It then lacks, as one says, a 'true', a 'genuine' signification. Later we shall look more closely into this distinction between intending and fulfilling signification" [modified].

culture only after a reduction of every de facto culture. So here science is, like languages and language in general, one of the forms of ideal Objectivity; but its pure possibility appears only through a reduction of all language—not only of every de facto language but of the fact of language in general. Thus Husserl specifies in an absolutely decisive sentence: "But the idealities of geometrical words, sentences, theories—considered purely as linguistic formations—are not the idealities that make up what is expressed and brought to validity as truth in geometry; the latter are ideal geometrical objects, states of affairs, etc. Wherever something is asserted, one can distinguish what is thematic, that about which it is said (its sense), from the assertion, which itself, during the asserting, is never and can never be thematic. And the theme here is precisely ideal objectivities, and quite different ones from those coming under the concept of language" (161 [modified]).[74]

Let us first note that in this sentence the sense of the assertion, the "theme" "about which [something] is said," and the object itself are identical, a fact which could never result in the case of real objects or of "bound" ideal objectivities. For the first time, with the absolute ideality of an object—the geometrical object which is through and through only the unity of its true sense—we pass beyond or rid ourselves of the ideal, but still bound, Objectivity of language. We simultaneously reach an Objectivity that is absolutely free with respect to all factual subjectivity. That is why the exemplary question of the origin of Objectivity could not be asked apropos linguistic ideality as such, but apropos what is intended across [*à travers*] and on the other side of [*au-delà de*] this ideality. But as the absolute ideal objectivity does not live in a *topos ouranios*, it follows that:

1. its freedom with respect to all factual subjectivity has only laid bare its legitimate [*de droit*] ties with a transcendental subjectivity;

2. its historicity is intrinsic and essential.

Thus the space for a *transcendental historicity* is prescribed in all its enigmatic depth. After having determined and provided access (with all its difficulties) to this space, Husserl can then ask the historico-

---

[74] By the distinction they propose, these sentences give the greatest and most exemplary sharpness to the central question of the *Origin*. Husserl added them after the fact to Fink's typed version of the manuscript. They do not appear in the published version of 1939.

At the end of a similar analysis, Husserl writes in *FTL:* locutions "are not thematic ends but theme-indicators" (§5, p. 27).

transcendental question which focuses all the disquietude of his text: "Our problem now concerns precisely the ideal objectivities which are thematic in geometry: how does geometrical ideality (just like that of all sciences) proceed from its primary intrapersonal origin, where it is a formation produced within the conscious space of the first inventor's soul, to its ideal Objectivity?" (161 [modified]).

## VI

Husserl's response is direct and comes very quickly. It has the style of a *turnabout* which can be surprising. Ideality comes to its Objectivity "by means of language, through which it receives, so to speak, its linguistic flesh" (161 [modified]). Husserl notes that "we see" this "in advance." The only question, then, is how *(Quomodo):* "how does linguistic incarnation make out of the merely intrasubjective formation the *Objective,* that which, for example, as geometrical concept or state of affairs, is in actual fact present, intelligible for all, now and always, already being valid in its linguistic expression as geometrical discourse, as geometrical proposition in its geometrical ideal sense?" (161 [modified]).

We might be surprised. After having so patiently extracted the thematic truth of *Sachverhalt* from linguistic ideality and from all "bound" idealities, Husserl then seems to *redescend* toward language as the indispensable medium and condition of possibility for absolute ideal Objectivity, for *truth* itself, which would be what it is only through its historical and intersubjective circulation. Thus, does Husserl not *come back* to language, culture, and history, all of which he reduced in order to have the pure possibility of truth emerge? Is he not "bound" again to lead into history that whose absolute "freedom" he just described? From then on, will he not be compelled to remove all the reductions step by step, in order to recover finally the *real* text of historical experience?

In reality—and we think it the most interesting difficulty of this text—Husserl does exactly the opposite. This *return* to language, as a *return home* to culture and history in general, brings to its final completion the purpose of the reduction itself. Going beyond "bound idealities" toward the theme of truth is itself a reduction which makes the independence of truth appear with respect to all de facto culture and language in general. But once more it is only a question of disclosing a juridical and transcendental dependence. No doubt geometrical truth is beyond every particular and factual linguistic hold as such, one for which every subject speaking a determined language and belonging to a determined cultural community is in fact responsible. But the Objectivity of this truth could *not* be constituted *without* the *pure possibility* of an inquiry into a pure language in general. Without this pure and essential possibility, the geometrical formation would remain ineffable and solitary. Then it would be *absolutely bound to the psychological life of a factual individual,* to that of a factual community, indeed to a particular moment of that life. It would become neither omnitemporal, nor intelligible for all: it would not be what it is.[75] Whether geometry can be spoken about is not, then, the extrinsic and accidental possibility of a fall into the body of speech or of a slip into a historical movement. Speech is no longer simply the expression *(Aüsserung)* of what, without it, would *already* be an object: caught again in its primordial purity, speech *constitutes* the object and is a concrete juridical condition of truth. The paradox is that, without the apparent fall back into language and thereby into history, a fall which would alienate the ideal purity of sense, sense would remain an empirical formation imprisoned as fact in a psychological subjectivity—*in the inventor's head.* Historical incarnation sets free the transcendental, instead of binding it. This last notion, the transcendental, must then be rethought.

Does this ultimate reduction, which opens onto a transcendental language, revolutionize Husserl's thought?[76] Does this return to the speaking subject as what constitutes the ideal object, and then absolute Objectivity, proceed to contradict a previous philosophy of language? Merleau-Ponty speaks of a "striking" contrast in this respect between the *Origin* on the one hand and the *Logical Investigations* on the other.[77]

[75] According to the same movement, omnitemporality and universal intelligibility (although they may be concrete and experienced as such) are only the reduction of factual historical temporality and factual geographical spatiality. "Supratemporality" *(Überzeitlichkeit)* and "timelessness" *(Zeitlosigkeit)* are defined in their transcendence or their negativity only *in relation* to worldly and factual temporality. Once the latter is reduced, they appear as omnitemporality *(Allzeitlichkeit),* the concrete mode of temporality in general.

[76] The expression "transcendental language" that we use here does not have the sense of "transcendental discourse." This latter notion, invoked earlier, has been utilized by Fink in the sense of discourse *adapted to* transcendental description. Here we are speaking of transcendental language insofar as, on the one hand, the latter is "constituting" compared with ideal Objectivity, and, on the other hand, insofar as it is not confused in its pure possibility with any de facto empirical language.

[77] Cf. "On the Phenomenology of Language," in Merleau-Ponty's *Signs,* tr. Richard C. McCleary (Evanston: Northwestern University Press, 1964), p. 84, or even "Phenomenology and the Sciences of Man," tr. John Wild in Merleau-Ponty's *The Primacy of Perception,* ed. James M. Edie (Evanston: Northwestern University Press, 1964), pp. 83–84.

Undoubtedly the *Logical Investigations* was more interested only in what corresponds to a first phase of description in the *Origin:* the autonomy of constituted ideal objects compared with a language that is itself constituted. But in reaction against a subjectivist psychologism, the question is above all to dissociate the ideal object from all subjectivity and all empirical language, both of which could only "confuse" the transparent, univocal, and objective significations of a pure logic. But the return to the primordiality of the speaking subject is no more in contrast with this first approach to language than the "idealism" of *Ideas I* is, as was thought, with the apparent "logicism" or "realism" of the *Logical Investigations.* The question is simply to parenthesize constituted language, which is what Husserl continues to do in *Formal and Transcendental Logic and* in the *Origin,* in order, subsequently, to let the originality of constitutive language come to light.

To *constitute* an ideal object is to put it at the permanent disposition of a pure gaze. Now, before being the constituted and exceeded auxiliary of an act which proceeds toward the truth of sense, linguistic ideality is the milieu in which the ideal object settles as what is sedimented or deposited. But here the act of primordial *depositing* is not the recording of a private thing, but the production of a *common* object, i.e., of an *object* whose original owner is thus dispossessed. Thus language preserves truth, so that truth can be regarded in the henceforth nonephemeral illumination of its sojourn; but also so that it can lengthen that stay. For there would be no truth without that word-hoarding [*thésaurisation*], which is not only what *deposits* and keeps hold of the truth, but also that without which a *project* of truth and the idea of an infinite task would be unimaginable. That is why language is the element of the only tradition in which (beyond individual finitude) sense-retention and sense-prospecting are possible.

In this respect there is so little discontinuity or contrast between Husserl's earliest and latest thought that we find pages in the *Logical Investigations* which could be inscribed without modification in the *Origin:* pages on the essential function of *Dokumentierung,* on the *"spiritual corporeality"* of language, and on the statement as the fulfilling of the truth-intention.[78] This is all the more so if we consider *Formal and*

[78] Thus, for example, Husserl writes: "All theoretical research, though by no means solely conducted in acts of verbal expression or complete statement, none the less terminates in such statement. Only in this form can truth, and in particular the truth of theory, become an abiding possession of science, a documented, ever available treasure for knowledge and advancing research. Whatever the connection of thought with speech may be, whether or not the appearance of our final judgements in the form of verbal

*Transcendental Logic* (particularly §§1–5, pp. 18–29) and the *Cartesian Meditations* (§4, p. 11). Each time, Husserl begins by uprooting thought from what it would be "solely . . . in the act of verbal expression," in order to specify then that it could not become "truth" without that *"stating"* and *"communicating . . . to others,"* of which he also spoke in the *Investigations* (*LI,* I, Intro. Vol. II of German Ed., §3, p. 255).

For, is the recognition in language of what *constitutes* absolute ideal Objectivity, as far as it *states* this Objectivity, not just another way of announcing or repeating that transcendental intersubjectivity is the condition of Objectivity? At bottom, the problem of geometry's origin puts the problem of the constitution of intersubjectivity on par with that of the phenomenological origin of language. Husserl is very conscious of this.[79] But he will not attempt this difficult regression in the *Origin,* although he says it "arises here" (161). For the moment it suffices to know, if not *how,* at least *that* language and consciousness of fellow humanity are interrelated possibilities and already given the moment the possibility of science is established. The horizon of fellow mankind supposes the horizon of the world: it stands out and articulates its unity against [*se détache et articule son unité sur*] the unity of the world. Of course, the world and fellow mankind here designate the all-inclusive, but infinitely open, unity of possible experiences and not this world right here, these fellow men right here, whose factuality for Husserl is never anything but a variable example. Consciousness of being-in-community in one and the same world establishes the possibility of a universal language. Mankind is first conscious of itself "as an immediate and mediate linguistic community" (162).

In connection with this we need to note three important points:

1. Within the horizon of this consciousness of fellow mankind, it is "mature, normal" mankind that is "privileged," both "as the horizon of civilization and as the linguistic community" (162). The theme of

---

pronouncements has a necessary grounding in essence, it is at least plain that judgements stemming from higher intellectual regions, and in particular from the regions of science, could barely arise without verbal expression" (*LI,* I, Introd. to Vol. II of German ed., §2, p. 250).

[79] Already in *FTL,* on the subject of the "idealizing presuppositions of logic" and tying the problem of *constitution* with that of *expression,* Husserl concluded: "The problem of constitution is again broadened when we recall that *verbal expression,* which we excluded from our considerations of logic, is an essential presupposition for intersubjective thinking and for an intersubjectivity of the theory accepted as ideally existing; and that accordingly an ideal identifiability of the expression, as expression, must likewise raise a problem of constitution" (§73, p. 188).

adult normality, which took up more and more room in Husserl's analyses, is here treated as a matter of course. We will not stress this,[80] despite the serious problems that it seems to have to pose for a transcendental philosophy: how can maturity and normality give rise to a rigorous transcendental-eidetic determination? Could adult normality ever be considered other than as an empirical and factual *modification* of universal transcendental norms in the classic sense, from which continually stem those other empirical "cases," madness and childhood? But here too Husserl has overthrown this classic notion of "transcendental," to the point of giving a sense to the idea of transcendental pathology.[81] The notion of (adult normality's) "privilege" denotes here a *telos'* meddling beforehand in the *eidos*. To have access to the *eidos* of mankind and of language, certain men and certain speaking subjects—madmen and children—are not *good* examples. And first, no doubt, because they do not possess in their own right a pure and rigorously determinable essence. But if this is so, does adult normality, which begins where childhood ends and stops when madness starts, have an essence? Because here the expression of adult normality is not a given eidetic determination, but the index of an ideal normativity which is *on the horizon* of de facto normal adults. In proportion to our advancement in the spiritual world and then in history, the *eidos* ceases to be an essence in order to become a norm, and the concept of horizon is progressively substituted for that of structure and essence.

2. The possibility of a mediate or immediate horizon of universal language risks running into essential difficulties and limits. This possibility first supposes that the hazardous problem concerning the possibility of a "pure grammar" and "*a priori* norms" of language is resolved, a possibility Husserl never ceased to take for granted.[82] It supposes, next, that everything "is namable in the broadest sense, i.e., linguisti-

---

[80] We propose to come back to this elsewhere. [Cf. Derrida's *Speech and Phenomena: And Other Essays on Husserl's Theory of Signs,* tr. David B. Allison (Evanston: Northwestern University Press, 1973), pp. 97–99.]

[81] In "Philosophy and the Crisis of European Humanity" (in *C*), the phenomenon of crisis is presented as a "sickness" of European society and culture, a sickness which is not "natural" and gets no relief from "something like nature doctors" (p. 270). This "pathology," moreover, has the profound ethical sense of a fall into "passivity," of an inability to be rendered "responsible" for sense in an authentic activity or authentic "reactivation." Technical activity (that of science also) as such is a passivity in comparison to sense; it is the agitation of the sick and, already, the tremors of delirium.

[82] Cf. *LI,* I, 4. On Husserl's faithfulness to this theme and the philosophical option that orients it, cf. in particular S. Bachelard, *A Study of Husserl's* Logic [Part I, Ch. 1], pp. 8–11.

cally expressible": "everyone can talk about what is within the sur-rounding world of his civilization as Objectively existing" (162 [modified]). In other words, as heterogeneous as the essential structures of several constituted languages or cultures may be, translation in prin-ciple is an always possible task: two *normal* men will always have *a priori*[83] consciousness of their belonging together to one and the same humanity, living in one and the same world. Linguistic differences—and what they imply—will appear to them at the bottom of an apriori horizon or structure: the linguistic community, i.e., the immediate cer-tainty of both being speaking subjects who can never designate any-thing but what belongs to the horizon of their world as the irreducibly common horizon of their experience. This implies that they can always, immediately or not, stand together before the same natural existent—which we can always strip of the cultural superstructures and categories founded *(fundiert)* on it, and whose unity would always fur-nish the ultimate arbitration for every *misunderstanding.* Consciousness of confronting the *same* thing, an object perceived as such,[84] is con-sciousness of a pure and precultural *we.* Here the return to preculture is not regression toward cultural *primitiveness* but the reduction of a de-termined culture, a theoretical operation which is one of the highest forms of culture in general. This purely natural objective existent is the existing sensible world, which becomes the first ground of communica-tion, the permanent chance for the reinvention of language. As the most universal, the most objectively exhibited element given to us, the earth itself is what furnishes the first matter of every sensible object. Insofar as it is the *exemplary* element (being more naturally objective, more permanent, more solid, more rigid, and so forth, than all other *elements;* and in a broader sense, it comprises them), it is normal that the earth has furnished the ground for the first idealities, then for the first abso-lutely universal and objective *identities,* those of calculus and geometry.

But preculturally *pure Nature* is always buried. So, as the ultimate

---

[83] But both still have to meet. The question here, then, is only that of a material, therefore in a certain sense contingent, *a priori* (cf. above).

[84] It is the "as such" of the object's substantial and objective unity which is decisive here. In particular it distinguishes human intersubjectivity from that which is created between animals, men and animals, children, etc. All those finite communities also rest on the sentiment of a presence to the same world whereby they confront the same things, and so on, but in a nonobjective, nontheoretical consciousness—which does not posit the object "as such" in its independence and as the pole of infinite determination. Those lower communities can also give rise to a specific phenomenology, and Husserl devoted important unpublished fragments to them.

possibility for communication, it is a kind of inaccessible infra-ideal. Can we not say, then, just the opposite of what Husserl said? Are not non-communication and misunderstanding the very horizon of culture and language? Undoubtedly misunderstanding is always a factual horizon and the finite index of the infinite pole of a sound intelligence. But although the latter is always announced so that language can begin, is not finitude the essential which we can never radically go beyond?

The above seems all the more true, especially since absolute translatability would be suspended starting the moment the signified could no longer be led back, either directly or indirectly, to the model of an objective and sensible existent. Every linguistic dimension that would escape this absolute translatability would remain marked by the empirical subjectivity of an individual or society. For Husserl, the model of language is the objective language of science. A poetic language, whose significations would not be *objects,* will never have any transcendental value for him. That fact would have no consequence *within* Husserlian thought, if his thought were not also the thorough investigation [*approfondissement*] of subjectivity. Now subjectivity in general, as much empirical as transcendental, appeared very early to Husserl as inaccessible to a direct, univocal, and rigorous language. Subjectivity is fundamentally ineffable. Already in *The Phenomenology of Internal Time-Consciousness,* Husserl referred to the ultimate identity of the constitutive flux of immanent time and absolute subjectivity and concluded: "For all this, names are lacking" (§36, p. 100).[85] And in the unpublished manuscripts of Group C on prototemporality, he wonders if pre-objective temporality, pretemporality *(Vorzeit),* is not beyond all discourse *(unsagbar)* for the "phenomenologizing Ego" (Ms C 13/15 II, 1934, p. 9). Therefore, language, tradition, and history exist only insofar as objects break the surface.

3. As the infinite horizon of every possible experience, the world is consequently "the universe of Objects which is linguistically expressible in its being and its being-such" (162). Thus, the signification of the world as horizon is clearly explicated, i.e., as the infinitely open common place for everything we can encounter in front of and for

[85] In the same sense, cf. all the subtle analyses in the *LI* devoted to expressions "lack[ing] an objective sense," such as personal pronouns which "indicate" mediately but can never give anything to be seen. "The word 'I' has not itself directly the power to arouse the specific I-presentation; this becomes fixed in the actual piece of talk. It does not work like the word 'lion' which can arouse the idea of a lion in and by itself. In its case, rather, an indicative function mediates, crying as it were, to the hearer 'Your *vis-à-vis* intends himself' " (I, 1, §26, p. 316).

ourselves. In front of and for ourselves implies, then, given as an object. The world, therefore, is essentially determined by the dative and horizontal dimension of being perceived [*l'être-perçu*] in a gaze whose object must always be able to be a *theorem*. Geometrical exemplariness undoubtedly results from the fact that, as an "abstract" material science, this exemplariness treats the spatiality of bodies (which is only one of the body's eidetic components), i.e., treats what confers sense on the notion of horizon and object. Despite all the antagonistic motifs which animate phenomenology, space's privilege therein is in certain respects remarkable. It testifies to that "objectivist" tendency which Husserl simultaneously opposes so vigorously, and yet which is only a *period*, an essential, and therefore irreducible, movement of thought. The profound rhythm of this tension between objectivism and the transcendental motif, a tension so remarkably described in the *Crisis*, is also imparted to phenomenology. In this respect, the problem of geometry is revealing.

Geometry, in effect, is the science of what is absolutely objective—i.e., spatiality—in the objects that the Earth, *our* common place, can indefinitely supply as our common ground with other men.[86] But if an objective science of earthly things is possible, an objective science of the Earth itself, the ground and foundation of these objects, is as radically impossible as that of transcendental subjectivity. The transcendental Earth is not an object and can never become one. And the possibility of a geometry strictly complements the impossibility of what could be called a *"geo-logy,"* the objective science of the Earth itself. This is the sense of the fragment[87] which *reduces*, rather than

---

[86] On the theme of *"our Earth"* as the "life-world" "in the most comprehensive sense" for a humanity which lives in community and where one can be "understood" in a communication which must always say and pass through the things of our Earth, cf. *EJ*, §38, pp. 162–67. This section effectively illuminates, especially by its degree of elaboration, the similarly inspired fragment on the Earth cited below. In this section, the unity of the Earth is grounded in the unity and oneness of temporality, the "fundamental form" *(Grundform)*, the "form of all forms" [*ibid.*, p. 164].

[87] This fragment, which is entitled "Grundlegende Untersuchungen zum Phänomenologischen Ursprung der Räumlichkeit der Natur" ["Fundamental Investigations on the Phenomenological Origin of the Spatiality of Nature"], dated May 1934, was published in 1940 by Marvin Farber in *Philosophical Essays in Memory of Edmund Husserl* [rpt. Greenwood Press, 1968], pp. 307–25. From the perspective of the science of space, it sketches a movement analogous to that of the *Origin*, but directed toward kinematics. In a certain sense, it completes the *Origin*, although in the *Origin* Husserl clearly specifies that geometry is only a title for all mathematics of pure spatiotemporality.

This text, very spontaneous and not greatly worked out in its writing, is presented as a

preface to a *"science of the origin of spatiality,"* of *"corporeality,"* of *"Nature in the sense of the natural sciences,"* and to a *"Transcendental Theory of Cognition in the Natural Sciences"* [p. 307]. Husserl first wonders about the sense of the world in the *infinite* openness of my surrounding world whose frontiers I can always go beyond. Over against a determined objectivation [*représentation*] of the world, that of the "Negroes" or "Greeks," he sets that of the Copernican world. "We Copernicans, we men of modern time, we say: the earth is not 'the whole of Nature,' it is one of the planets, in the infinite space of the world. The earth is a spherical body which certainly is not perceptible as a whole, by a single person and all at once, but in a primordial [*primordiale*] synthesis as the unity of singular experiences bound to each other. But nonetheless it is a body! Although for us it may be the experiential ground for all bodies in the experiential genesis of our world-objectivation" (p. 308).

Husserl then "reduces" the Copernican thesis by making the certainty of an Earth—as the origin of every objective kinetic determination—appear as the transcendental presupposition of this thesis. The question is to exhume, to unearth, the Earth, to lay bare the primordial ground buried under the sedimentary deposits of scientific culture and objectivism.

For the Earth cannot become a mobile body: "It is on the Earth, toward the Earth, starting from it, but still on it that motion occurs. The Earth itself, in conformity to the original idea of it, does not move, nor is it at rest; it is in relation to the Earth that motion and rest first have sense. But then the Earth does not 'move' nor is at rest—and it is entirely the same for the heavenly bodies and for the earth as one of them" (p. 309).

The Earth is the final ground of our co-humanity *(Mitmenscheit)*, for it is "the same Earth for us, on it, in it, above it, there are the same bodies existing on it—'on it,' etc., the same corporeal *(leiblichen)* subjects, subjects of bodies *(Leibern)*, who, for all, are bodies *(Körper)* in a modified sense. But for us all, the Earth is the ground and not a body in the full sense" (p. 315).

But toward the end of the text, the Earth takes on a more formal sense. No longer is it a question of this Earth here (the primordial *here* whose factuality would finally be irreducible), but of a *here* and a ground *in general* for the determination of body-objects *in general*. For if I reached another planet by flying, and if, Husserl then said, I could perceive the earth as a body, I would have "two Earths as ground-bodies." "But what does two Earths signify? Two pieces of a single Earth with one humanity" (pp. 317–18). From then on the unity of all humanity determines the unity of the ground as such. This unity of all humanity is correlative to the unity of the world as the infinite horizon of experience, and not to the unity of this earth here. The World, which is not the factuality of this historical world here, as Husserl often recalls, is the ground of grounds, the horizon of horizons, and it is to the World that the transcendental immutability attributed to the Earth returns, since the Earth then is only its factual index. Likewise—correlatively—humanity would then only be the facto-anthropological index of subjectivity and of intersubjectivity in general, starting from which every primordial *here* can appear on the foundation of the Living Present, the rest and absolute maintenance of the origin in which, by which, and for which all temporality and all motion appear.

Just as here he reduces the Copernican "relativity" of the earth, Husserl elsewhere reduces Einstein's "relativity": "Where is that huge piece of method subjected to critique and clarification—that method that leads from the intuitively given surrounding world to the idealization of mathematics and to the interpretation of these idealizations as Objective being? Einstein's revolutionary innovations concern the formulae through which the idealized and naively Objectified *physis* is dealt with. But how formulae in general, how mathematical Objectivation in general, receive sense on the substratum of

"refutes,"[88] the Copernican naiveté and shows that the Earth in its protoprimordiality does not move. Just as one's own body, as the primordial *here* and *zero-point* for every *objective* determination of space and spatial motion, is not itself in motion in this space as an object, so—analoguously—the Earth, as primordial body, as the ground-body *(Bodenkörper)* from which alone a Copernican determination of the earth as body-object becomes possible, is not itself one body among others in the mechanical system. Primordially, the Earth moves no more than our body moves and leaves the permanence of its *here*, grounded in a present. The Earth therefore knows the rest of an absolute *here;* a rest which is not the rest of the object (rest as "mode of motion"), but Rest starting from which motion and rest can appear and be thought as such, the Rest of a *ground* and a *horizon* in their common origin and end. The Earth is, in effect, both short of and beyond every body-object—in particular the Copernican earth—as the ground, as the here of its relative appearing. But the Earth exceeds every body-object as its infinite horizon, for it is never exhausted by the work of objectification that proceeds within it: "The Earth is a Whole whose parts . . . are bodies, but as a 'Whole' it is not a body" ["Grundlegende," p. 313]. There is then a science *of* space, insofar as its starting point is not *in* space.

If the possibility of language is already *given* to the primally instituting geometer, it suffices that the latter has produced in himself the identity and the ideal permanence of an object in order to be able to communicate it. Before the "same" is recognized and communicated among several individuals, it is recognized and communicated within the individual consciousness: after quick and transitory evidence, after a finite and passive retention vanishes, its sense can be re-produced as the "same" in the act of recollection; its sense has not returned to

---

life and the intuitively given surrounding world—of this we learn nothing; and thus Einstein does not reform *the* space and time in which our vital life *(unser lebendiges Leben)* runs its course" ("Philosophy and the Crisis of European Humanity," in *C*, p. 295 [modified]). In the *Crisis* (§34*b*, pp. 125ff.), a similarly oriented analysis also questions the objectivism of Einstein's relativity.

[88] In referring to this fragment, Trân-Dúc-Tháo *(Phénoménologie*, p. 222) speaks of an "undaunted refutation of the Copernican system." However, it is a matter of course that Husserl does not at any moment or on its own proper level contest the particular *truth* of the objective Copernican science. He only recalls that Copernican science presupposes a primordial Earth which this science will never be able to integrate into its objective system.

nothingness.[89] In this *coincidence of identity* [*recouvrement d'identité*], *ideality* is announced as such and in general in an egological subject. Consequently, what makes this ideality a *geometrical* ideality will only interest us later on. We will respect Husserl's order of description and in the meantime will define the conditions for ideality in an intersubjective community.

Thus, before being the ideality of an identical object for other subjects, sense is this ideality for *other* moments of the same subject. In a certain way, therefore, intersubjectivity is first the nonempirical relation of Ego to Ego, of my present present to other presents as such; i.e., as others and as presents (as past presents). Intersubjectivity is the relation of an absolute origin to other absolute origins, which are always my own, despite their radical alterity. Thanks to this circulation of primordial absolutes, the *same* thing can be thought through absolutely other moments and acts. We always come back to the final instance of this: the unique and essential form of temporalization. By its very dialecticalness, the absolute primordiality of the Living Present permits the reduction, without negation, of all alterity. The Living Present constitutes the other as other in itself and the same as same in the other.[90]

---

[89] These processes are abundantly described in *The Phenomenology of Internal Time-Consciousness, Ideas I,* and in *FTL.* The passage from passive retention to memory or to the activity of recollection, a passage which "produces" ideality and pure Objectivity as such and makes other absolute origins appear as such, is always described by Husserl as an already given essential possibility, as a structural ability whose source is not made a problem. Perhaps this source is not questioned by phenomenology because it is confused with the possibility of phenomenology itself. In its "factuality," this passage is also that of the lower forms of Nature and conscious life. It can also be the thematic site of what today is called an "overcoming." Here phenomenology would be "overcome" or completed in an interpretative philosophy. Thus Trân-Dúc-Tháo, after a remarkable interpretation of phenomenology, exposes the "Dialectic of Real Movement," starting from the concepts of retention and reproduction and from difficulties attached to them in phenomenology, which alone, however, can give them a rigorous sense.

[90] The possibility of constituting, within the unique and irreducible form of the Living Present (unchangeable in itself and always other in its "content"), *another* now and on its basis another *here,* another absolute origin of *my* absolutely absolute origin, this possibility is elsewhere presented by Husserl as the root of intersubjectivity. In the *Cartesian Meditations,* this dialectic of temporalization is invoked as an analogous example of the dialectic of intersubjectivity. In order to illuminate the extraordinary constitution of *"another monad . . . in mine,"* Husserl alludes to temporalization, in what he calls an "instructive comparison" (§52, p. 115).

But in some unpublished material, he seems to go much further: "Urhyle," i.e., temporal hyle, is defined there as the "core of the other than the Ego's own" (*Ichfremde Kern*). Cf. *Group C 6* (August 1930), p. 6. On the sense of this notion of *"alien to my*

## VII

A decisive step remains to be taken. By itself the speaking subject, in the strict sense of the term, is incapable of absolutely grounding the ideal Objectivity of sense. Oral communication (i.e., present, immediate, and synchronic communication) among the protogeometers is not sufficient to give ideal objectivities their "continuing to be" and *"persisting factual existence,"* thanks to which they perdure "even during periods in which the inventor and his fellows are no longer awake to such an exchange or even, more universally, no longer alive." To be absolutely ideal, the object must still be freed of *every* tie with an actually present subjectivity in general. Therefore, it must perdure "even when no one has actualized it in evidence" (164 [modified]). Speech [*langage oral*] has freed the object of *individual* subjectivity but leaves it bound to its beginning and to the synchrony of an exchange within the *institutive community.*

The possibility of *writing* will assure the absolute traditionalization of the object, its absolute ideal Objectivity—i.e., the purity of its relation to a universal transcendental subjectivity. Writing will do this by emancipating sense from its *actually present* evidence for a real subject and from its present circulation within a determined community. "The decisive function of written expression, of expression which documents, is that it makes communication possible without immediate or mediate address; it is, so to speak, communication become virtual" (164 [modified]).

That *virtuality,* moreover, is an ambiguous value: it simultaneously makes passivity, forgetfulness, and all the phenomena of *crisis* possible.

Far from having to fall again into a real [*réale*] history, a truth that we have gained from this history—scriptural spatiotemporality (whose originality we will soon need to determine)—sanctions and completes the existence of pure transcendental historicity. Without the ultimate objectification that writing permits, all language would as yet remain

---

Ego," "the intrinsically first other," or of "the first 'non-Ego' " in the constitution of the *alter ego,* see notably *CM*, §§48–49, pp. 105–08.

Preobjective and preexact temporality, which had to become the principal theme of the transcendental aesthetics projected by Husserl (cf. notably *FTL*, Conclusion, pp. 291–92; and *CM*, §61, p. 146), is then the root of transcendental intersubjectivity. All the *egos,* beyond all possible differences, can be encountered, recognized, and understood also in the identity of the *concrete* and universal form of the Living Present. In *EJ*, "time as the form of sensibility" is described as the "ground" of the "necessary connection . . . between the intentional objects of all perceptions and positional presentifications of an Ego and a community of Egos" (§38, p. 162 [modified]).

captive of the de facto and actual intentionality of a speaking subject or community of speaking subjects. By absolutely virtualizing dialogue, writing creates a kind of autonomous transcendental field from which every present subject can be absent.

In connection with the general signification of the *epochē*, Jean Hyppolite invokes the possibility of a "subjectless transcendental field," one in which "the conditions of subjectivity would appear and where the subject would be constituted starting from the transcendental field."[91] Writing, as the place of absolutely permanent ideal objectivities and therefore of absolute Objectivity, certainly constitutes such a transcendental field. And likewise, to be sure, transcendental subjectivity can be fully announced and appear on the basis of this field or its possibility. Thus a subjectless transcendental field is one of the "conditions" of transcendental subjectivity.

But all this can be said only on the basis of an intentional analysis which retains from writing nothing but writing's pure relation to a consciousness which grounds it as such, and not its factuality which, left to itself, is totally without signification [*insignifiante*]. For this absence of subjectivity from the transcendental field, an absence whose possibility frees absolute Objectivity, can be only a factual absence, even if it removed for all time the totality of actual subjects. The originality of the field of writing is its ability to dispense with, *due to its sense,* every present reading in general. But if the text does not announce its own pure dependence on a writer or reader in general (i.e., if it is not haunted by a virtual intentionality), and if there is no purely juridical possibility of it being intelligible for a transcendental subject in general, then there is no more in the vacuity of its soul than a chaotic literalness or the sensible opacity of a defunct designation, a designation deprived of its transcendental function. The silence of prehistoric arcana and buried civilizations, the entombment of lost intentions and guarded secrets, and the illegibility of the lapidary inscription disclose the transcendental sense of death as what unites these things to the absolute privilege of intentionality in the very instance of its essential juridical failure [*en ce qui l'unit à l'absolu du droit intentionnel dans l'instance même de son échec*].

When considering the de jure purity of intentional animation, Husserl always says that the linguistic or graphic body is a flesh, a proper body *(Leib),* or a spiritual corporeality *(geistige Leiblichkeit) (FTL,* §2, p. 21). From then on, writing is no longer only the worldly and

---

[91] We refer here to a comment by Jean Hyppolite during the discussion which followed the lecture of Fr. Van Breda on "La Réduction phénoménologique," in *Husserl,* Cahiers de Royaumont, p. 323.

mnemotechnical aid to a truth whose own being-sense would dispense with all writing-down. The possibility or necessity of being incarnated in a graphic sign is no longer simply extrinsic and factual in comparison with ideal Objectivity: it is the *sine qua non* condition of Objectivity's internal completion. As long as ideal Objectivity is not, or rather, *can* not be engraved in the world—as long as ideal Objectivity is not in a position to be party to an incarnation (which, in the purity of its sense, is more than a system of signals [*signalisation*] or an outer garment)— then ideal Objectivity is not fully constituted. Therefore, the act of writing is the highest possibility of all *"constitution,"* a fact against which the transcendental depth of ideal Objectivity's historicity is measured.

What Fink writes about speech in his excellent transcript of the *Origin* is *a fortiori* true for writing: "In sensible embodiment occurs the 'localization' and the 'temporalization' *(Temporalisation)* of what is, by its being-sense, unlocated and untemporal" ("Die Frage," p. 210).

Such a formulation remarkably sharpens the problem and awakens the peculiar virtue of language. It clearly translates Husserl's exacting effort to catch the ideality of thematic sense and of words [*mots*] in their relations with the linguistic event.[92] But does not this formulation per-

---

[92] This sensible embodiment has the peculiar qualities [*l'étrangeté*] of both sense's inhabitation of the word [*mot*] and the *here and now* use of the word's ideality. In the first case, embodiment is at its limit the inscription of an absolutely *"free"* and objective ideality (that of geometrical truth, for example) within the *"bound"* ideality of the word, or in general of a *more* free ideality within a *less* free ideality. In the second case, embodiment is that of a necessarily bound ideality, that of the word's identity within language, in a real-sensible event. But this last embodiment is still done through another step of mediate ideality which Husserl does not directly describe, but which we think can be located on the basis of strictly Husserlian concepts. It is a question of ideal forms or vague morphological types (a notion that we will have occasion to specify farther on), which are proper to the corporeality of graphic and vocal signs. The forms of graphic and vocal signs must have a certain identity which is imposed and recognized each time in the empirical fact of language. Without this always intended and approximate ideal identity (that of letters and phonemes, for example), no sensible language would be possible or intelligible as language, nor could it intend higher idealities. Naturally, this morphological ideality is still more "bound" than the word's ideality. The precise place of the properly termed realizing [*réalisante*] embodiment is ultimately therefore the union of the sensible form with sensible material, a union *traversed* by the linguistic intention which always intends, explicitly or not, the highest ideality. Linguistic incarnation and the constitution of written or scriptural space supposes, then, a closer and closer "interconnection" of ideality and reality through a series of less and less ideal mediations and in the synthetic unity of an intention. This intentional synthesis is an unceasing movement of going and returning that works to bind the ideality of sense and to free the reality of the sign. Each of the two operations is always haunted by the sense of the other: each operation is already announced in the other or still retained in it. Language frees the ideality of sense, then, in the very work of its "binding" ("interconnecting" [*enchainement*]).

mit linguistic embodiment to be understood as taking place outside the being-sense of ideal objectivity? As "occurring" or "unexpectedly happening" in addition to the being-sense? Does not this formulation give the impression that ideal objectivity is fully constituted as such *before* and *independently of* its embodiment, or rather, before and independently of its *ability to be embodied?*

But Husserl insists that truth is not fully objective, i.e., ideal, intelligible for everyone and indefinitely perdurable, as long as it cannot be said *and* written. Since this perdurability is truth's very sense, the conditions for its survival are included in those of its life. Undoubtedly, truth never keeps the ideal Objectivity or identity of any of its particular de facto linguistic incarnations; and compared to all linguistic factuality it remains "free." But this freedom is only possible precisely from the *moment* truth *can* in general be said or written, i.e., *on condition* that this *can* be done. Paradoxically, the possibility of being written [*possibilité graphique*] permits the ultimate freeing of ideality. Therefore, we could all but reverse the terms of Fink's formula: the *ability* of sense to be linguistically embodied is the only means by which sense becomes nonspatiotemporal.

Because ideal Objectivity can essentially inform or shape the body of speech and writing, and since it depends on a pure linguistic intention, it is radically independent of sensible spatiotemporality. This means that a specific spatiotemporality is prescribed for communication, and therefore for pure tradition and history, a spatiotemporality that escapes the alternative of the sensible and the intelligible, or the empirical and the metempirical. Consequently, truth is no longer *simply* exiled in the primordial event of its language. Its historical habitat authenticates this event, just as the protodocument *authenticates* whether it is the depository of an intention, whether it refers without falsification to an original and primordial act. In other words, whether the linguistic event refers to an *authentic* act (in the Husserlian sense of the word), because it establishes a truth-value, is made responsible for it, and can appeal to the universality of its testimony.

Husserl thus indicates the direction for a phenomenology of the written thing, specifically, describing the book in its unity as a chain of significations. This unity can be more or less ideal and necessary, and therefore universal, according to the book's sense-content.[93] And not

---

[93] In the *Origin*, Husserl distinguishes between literature in the broad sense, the realm of all written discourse, and literature as literary art. The literary work is often chosen by Husserl as the clue for analyzing the ideality of cultural objectivities. The ideal identity of the work will never be mistaken for its sensible embodiments. It does not derive its individual identity from the latter. The origin of identity, moreover, is the criterion which

only can that ideal unity be more or less "bound" to factuality, but also according to numerous and completely original forms and modalities. Moreover, the relation of the "exemplars" to their archetypal unity is undoubtedly unique among the reproductions of other cultural formations, especially those of the nonliterary arts. Finally, the book's proper volume and duration are neither purely sensible phenomena, nor purely intelligible noumena. Their specific character seems irreducible. This "being of the book," this "instance of *printed* thought" whose "language is not natural," Gaston Bachelard calls a *"bibliomenon."* [94]

---

permits us to distinguish between the real and the ideal. Husserl writes in *EJ* (§65, pp. 265–66): "We call *real* in a specific sense *all that which,* in real things in the broader sense, *is, according to its sense, essentially individualized by its spatiotemporal position; but we call irreal every determination which, indeed, is founded with regard to spatiotemporal appearance in a specifically real thing but which can appear in different realities as identical*—not merely as similar" (Husserl's emphasis).

Thus the relation between the ideal and the real in all cultural objectivities (and first in all the arts) can be explicated. That is relatively easy for the literary work. Thus, "Goethe's *Faust* is found in any number of real books ('book' denotes here what is produced by men and intended to be read: it is already a determination which is itself not purely material, but a determination of significance!), which are termed exemplars of *Faust*. This mental sense which determines the work of art, the mental structure as such, is certainly 'embodied' in the real world, but it is not individualized by this embodiment. Or again: the same geometrical proposition can be uttered as often as desired; every real utterance has . . . identically the same sense" (*ibid.,* p. 266).

But how can we determine the ideality of a work whose protoindividualization is tied to the work's single spatiotemporal embodiment? How can we make its ideality appear by varying factual exemplars, since the latter can only imitate a factuality and not express or "indicate" an ideal sense? Is it, in short, the same for the ideality of the plastic arts, of architecture? Or of music, whose case is even more ambiguous? Although repetition may be of a different nature here, which in each case requires an appropriate and prudent analysis, it is no less possible *in principle* and thus makes an incontestable ideality appear: "To be sure, an ideal object like Raphael's *Madonna* can *in fact* have only one mudane state *(Weltlichkeit)* and in fact is not repeatable in an adequate identity (of the complete ideal content). But *in principle* this ideal is indeed repeatable, as is Goethe's *Faust*" (*ibid.*).

From the first perception, then, of a work of plastic art as such (whose ideal value is primordially and intrinsically rooted in an *event*), there is a sort of immediate reduction of factuality which permits, next, the neutralization of the necessary imperfection of reproduction. Here is not the place to prolong these analyses of aesthetic perception and ideality. Husserl is content to situate their domain and to define preliminary, indispensable distinctions. He proposes some analogous distinctions in the cultural sphere of politics and strives to bring to light both the ideality of the constitution of the state (of the national will, for example) and the originality of its "boundness" to the factuality of a territory, a nation, etc., within which this constitution can be indefinitely repeated as its ideal validity (*ibid.,* pp. 266–67).

[94] *L'Activité rationaliste de la physique contemporaine* (Paris: Presses Universitaries de France, 1951), pp. 6–7.

In the *Origin,* Husserl illuminates more directly that milieu of writing whose difficult signification and importance he had already recognized in the *Logical Investigations.*[95] The difficulty of its description is due to the fact that writing defines and completes the ambiguity of all language. As the process of that essential and constitutive capacity for embodiment, language is also where every absolutely ideal object (i.e., where truth) is factually and contingently embodied. Conversely, truth has its origin in a pure and simple right to speech and writing, but once constituted, it conditions expression, in its turn, as an empirical fact. Truth depends on the pure possibility of speaking and writing, but is independent of what is spoken or written, insofar as they are in the world. If, therefore, truth suffers in and through its language from a certain changeableness, its downfall will be less a fall toward language than a degradation within language.

From then on, in effect, as is prescribed for it, sense is gathered into a sign,[96] and the sign becomes the worldly and exposed residence of an unthought truth. We have previously seen that truth can perdure in this way without being thought in act or in fact—and that is what radically emancipates truth from all empirical subjectivity, all factual life, and the whole real world. At the same time, man's communal being "is lifted to a new level" (164): it can appear, in effect, as a transcendental community. The authentic act of writing is a transcendental reduction performed by and toward the *we.* But since, in order to escape worldliness, sense *must* first *be able* to be set down in the world and be deposited in sensible spatiotemporality, it must put its pure intentional ideality, i.e., its truth-sense, in danger. Thus a possibility, which even here

[95] Cf. *LI,* I, Prol., §6, p. 60: "Science exists objectively only in its literature, only in written work has it a rich relational being limited to men and their intellectual activities: in this form it is propagated down the millennia, and survives individuals, generations and nations. It therefore represents a set of *external* arrangements, which, just as they arose out of the knowledge-acts of many individuals, can again pass over into just such acts of countless individuals, in a readily understandable manner, whose exact description would require much circumlocution" (our emphasis). On this level of analysis, which above all should disengage the objective autonomy of signification, the question is clearly that of "*external* arrangements": sensible exemplars on which neither the ideality of sense nor the *clear* intention of cognition depend. But this fact neither prohibits nor contradicts at all the subsequent theme of writing as the *intrinsic possibility* and *intrinsic condition* of acts of objective cognition. The *Origin maintains* these two themes. That is the difficulty we are striving to illuminate here.

[96] We take this word in the broad sense of sign-signifier or "sign-expression" (graphic or vocal), the meaning that Husserl gives this term by opposing it to the "indicative" sign (*LI,* I, 1, §§1–5, pp. 269–75). On the basis of this distinction, we could interpret the phenomenon of *crisis* (which, for Husserl, always refers to a disorder or illness of language) as a degradation of the sign-expression into a sign-indication, of a "clear" *(klar)* intention into an empty symbol.

accords only with empiricism and nonphilosophy, appears in a philosophy which is (at least because of certain motifs) the contrary of empiricism: the possibility of truth's *disappearance*. We purposely use the ambiguous word disappearance. What disappears is what is annihilated, but also what ceases, intermittently or definitely, to appear *in fact* yet without affecting its being or being-sense. To determine the sense of this "disappearance" of truth is the most difficult problem posed by the *Origin* and all of Husserl's philosophy of history. Furthermore, we were unable to find in Husserl an unequivocal response to a question which only makes that of phenomenology itself return: what is the sense of its appearing? That equivocation will presently reveal both how much the author of the *Crisis* was a stranger to history or how fundamentally incapable he was of taking it seriously, and at what point (in the same moment) he strives to respect historicity's own peculiar signification and possibility and truly to penetrate them.

What then is this possibility of disappearance?

1. In the first place, let us rule out the hypothesis of a *death of sense* in general within the individual consciousness. Husserl clearly specifies in the *Origin* and elsewhere that, once sense appeared in egological consciousness, its total annihilation becomes impossible.[97] A sense that is conserved as a sedimentary habituality and whose dormant potentiality can de jure be reanimated is not returned to nothingness by the vanishing of retentions of retentions. "Far from being a phenomenological nothing," "the so-called *'unconscious'* " or *"universal substratum"* where sense is deposited is "a limit-mode of consciousness" (*FTL,* p. 319).[98] Clearly in this type of analysis, upon which formidable difficulties already weigh, Husserl is only worried about the permanence and virtual presence of sense within the monadic subject, and not about the absolutely ideal Objectivity of sense gained through speech and writing from that subjectivity. Now this Objectivity is found threatened as truth in the world. Profound *forgetfulness* therefore extends into the spaces of intersubjectivity and the distance between communities. *Forgetfulness* is a historical category.[99]

[97] In *Ideas I;* in *EJ;* but above all in *FTL* (in terms which are literally taken up again in the *Origin*), cf. in particular Appendix II, §2c, pp. 318–19.

[98] On the *naiveté* of the classic problems of the Unconscious and on the question of knowing whether an intentional analysis can open a methodical access to the Unconscious, see "Fink's Appendix on the Problem of the 'Unbewussten,' " in *C,* pp. 385–87.

[99] *Forgetfulness* is a word that Husserl rarely employs in the *Crisis;* he never uses it in the first text of the *Origin,* perhaps because habit relates it very easily to individual consciousness or to its psychological sense; perhaps also because it can suggest an annihilation of sense.

2. The graphic sign, the guarantee of Objectivity, can also *in fact* be destroyed. This danger is inherent in the factual worldliness of inscription itself, and nothing can definitively protect inscription from this. In such a *case,* because Husserl considers sense neither an in-itself nor a pure spiritual interiority but an "object" through and through, we might first think that the forgetfulness which follows upon the destruction of Objectivity's custodial sign [*signe gardien*] would not affect (as in a "Platonism" or "Bergsonism") the surface of a sense without undermining the sense itself. Such a forgetfulness would not only suppress this sense but would annihilate it in the specific being-in-the-world to which its Objectivity is entrusted. For Husserl clearly said this: insofar as signs can be immediately perceptible by everyone in their *corporeality;* insofar as their bodies and corporeal forms are always already in an intersubjective horizon, then sense can be deposited there and communalized [*mettre en communauté*]. Corporeal exteriority undoubtedly does not *constitute* the sign as such but, in a sense that we must make clear, is *indispensable* to it.

Yet the hypothesis of such a factual destruction does not interest Husserl at all. While completely recognizing the terrifying *reality* of the current risk, he would deny it any thinkable, i.e., any philosophical significance. No doubt he would admit that a universal conflagration, a world-wide burning of libraries, or a catastrophe of monuments or "documents" in general would intrinsically ravage "bound" cultural idealities, whose notion we evoked above. By their adherence to some factuality, *the very sense of* these idealities would be vulnerable to that worldly accident. Death is possible for them alone and has the transcendental signification we just now granted it, but only insofar as the "bound" ideality is animated or traversed by a transcendental intention, only insofar as it is guided by the Telos of an absolute freeing which has not been fully attained. But like that which orients Husserl's reflection (specifically, the fully freed ideality and absolute Objectivity of sense, for which mathematics is the model), the threat of an intrinsic destruction by the body of the sign can be ruled out. All factual writings, in which truth could be sedimented, will never be anything in themselves but sensible "exemplars," individual events in space and time (which is only true to a certain degree for "bound" idealities). Since truth does *not* essentially depend on *any of them,* they could *all* be destroyed without overtaking *the very sense of* absolute ideality. Undoubtedly, absolute ideality would be changed, mutilated, and overthrown *in fact;* perhaps it would disappear in fact from the surface of the world, but its sense-of-being as truth, which is not in the world— neither in our world here, nor any other—would remain intact in itself.

Its being-sense would preserve its own *intrinsic* historicity, its own interconnections, and the catastrophe of worldly history would remain *exterior* to it.

That is what Husserl means when he opposes *internal* or intrinsic *(innere)* historicity to *external (aussere)* history. This distinction, which has only a phenomenological sense, is decisive.[100] It would be fruitless for him to object that historicity or being-in-history is precisely the possibility of being *intrinsically* exposed to the *extrinsic,* for then the historicity absolutely proper to any truth-sense would be missing, and Husserl's discourse would be plunged into a confusion of significations and regions. We would then be conceding that a pure ideality can be changed by a real cause, which is to lose sense. If geometry is true, its internal history must be saved integrally from all sensible aggression. Since geometry is tied neither to this moment here, nor to this territory here, nor to this world here, but to all the world *(Weltall)*, nothing will ever stand between the worldly experiences which incarnated geometry and what they have begun again: discovering afresh (without any traces and after the shrouding of this world here) the paths of an adventure buried in another real history. In comparison with *veritas aeterna,* whose proper historicity Husserl wishes to grasp and about which he speaks more and more often as his thought becomes allured by history, no real development other than that of the variable example interests him. Accordingly, the hypothesis of the world-wide catastrophe could even serve as a revelatory fiction.

Thus, we should be able to repeat *analogously* the famous analysis of Section 49 of *Ideas I.*[101] The analysis concluded that, after a certain eidetic-transcendental reduction, pure consciousness is intangible, even when the existing world is annihilated or factual experience dissolved "through internal conflict . . . into illusion" (*Ideas I,* §49, p. 137 [modified]). Husserl did not dispute that under those circumstances all consciousness would *in fact* be destroyed and that its worldly existence would be engulfed with the world. In addition, the clearest intention of

---

[100] The opposition between intrinsic penetration and extrinsic circumspection is already announced in *Ideas I,* precisely concerning the history of geometry. There Husserl shows how psychologistic or historicist empiricism remains *"outside"* [Derrida's emphasis] "geometrical thought and intuition," whereas "we should enter vitally into these activities and . . . determine their *immanent sense*" (§25, p. 85 [modified]). Once external history is "reduced," nothing is opposed to the fact that this immanent sense may have its own particular historicity. The opposition between the two histories is an explicit theme in the *Crisis* (see, for example, §7, pp. 17–18, and §15, p. 71), in "Philosophy as Mankind's Self-Reflection" (*C,* pp. 338–39), and above all in the *Origin.*

[101] P. 136. The movement is taken up again in *CM,* §7, pp. 17–18.

this analysis and fiction is to explicate a reduction which must reveal to the *Ur-Region*—transcendental consciousness—the essential relativity of the world's sense (the world being the totality of regions). Since transcendental consciousness can always and with complete freedom modify or suspend the thesis of *each* (therefore of *all*) contingent existence and of *each* (therefore of *all*) transcendence, its very sense is de jure and absolutely independent of the whole world. The situation of truth, particularly of geometrical truth, is analogous. It therefore provokes the same questions.

In fact, this eidetic independence, brought to light in a methodological idealism by a fiction, can be questioned as to its value beyond the moment of *Ideas I;* i.e., beyond the moment the eidetic-transcendental reduction has not yet attained its final radicality and is provisionally immobilized in one region. In effect, the region of pure consciousness is the "residue" of a "suspension" that still remains more eidetic than transcendental and is only the most profound of the eidetic reductions. Yet this suspension, which tends to discover the protoregion's essential structures and is certainly constitutive of the world, is constituted itself. And, as Husserl will say, it is not the "ultimate" transcendental regression (*ibid.*, §81, p. 216).[102] Would Husserl have judged this fiction valid the moment he studied (for example, in the *Cartesian Meditations*) the genetic constitution of the *ego* in the "unity" of its "history"?[103] In a certain sense we can say yes. Through the solipsistic hypothesis in which the *Cartesian Meditations* are first couched, pure consciousness is still considered as that which no worldly factuality can penetrate as such, as *"a self-contained nexus of being"* (*Ideas I,* §49, p. 139 [modified]). Undoubtedly, the intra-egological sedimentation, the potential evidence, the "residues," and the "references"[104] that this "history" makes necessary are only a network of sense. But by the irreplaceability, irreversibility, and invariability of their interconnections, are they not also "facts" or factual structures with respect to which pure consciousness would no longer be free? Could these sedimentary structures de jure survive the annihilation, the overthrow, in a word, the complete "variation" of factuality? As sense, would they not be marked by a certain order of the factual world to which *past* consciousness is tied—a consciousness tied there by its own interconnections and structurally implicated in every present consciousness?

---

[102] These first reductions lead us to "the very threshold of phenomenology" (*Ideas I,* §88, p. 237).

[103] Already cited [see note 7 above]. Also cf. on this *FTL,* Appendix II, §2*b,* pp. 316–17.

[104] Already cited [see note 7 above].

Husserl would probably reply that, in such a case, we are considering factual structures in the life of the *ego*—i.e., structures "bound" to some reducible contingency—and not essential ones reduced to their pure ideality. The "unity" of the *ego's* "*history*" is that of the *eidos* "*ego.*" Husserl's description means that the essential form of every interconnection, every sedimentation, and therefore every history for every *ego* is self-sufficient. Within this *form* of historicity that we wish to attain as an invariant, all facto-historical interconnections are variable at will.

Similarly, since the interconnections and sedimentations of geometrical truth are free of all factuality, no worldly catastrophe can put *truth* itself in danger. All factual peril, therefore, stops at the threshold of its internal historicity. Even if all geometrical "documents"—and as well, all actual geometers—had to come to ruin one day, to speak of this as an event "of" geometry would be to commit a very serious confusion of sense and to abdicate responsibility for all rigorous discourse. One cannot come back to all this evidence without making the sensible the ground of geometrical truth and, therefore, without questioning once more the sense of geometry constituted as an eidetic science. Now this sense was securely decided within the static analyses that, as we saw above, were the indispensable guard rails for all genetic or historical phenomenology.

3. We would be fully convinced, if here—as in his static analyses—Husserl had considered writing to be a sensible phenomenon. But did we not just find out that writing, inasmuch as it was grounding (or contributing to the grounding of) truth's absolute Objectivity, was not *merely* a constituted sensible body *(Körper)*, but was also a properly constituting body *(Leib)*—the intentional primordiality of a Here-and-Now of truth? If writing is *both* a factual event and the upsurging of sense, if it is both *Körper* and *Leib*, how would writing preserve its *Leiblichkeit* from corporeal disaster? Husserl is not going to immobilize his analysis within this *ambiguity*, which for him is only a provisional and factual confusion of regions. The phenomenologist must dissolve the ambiguity, if he does not want to be reduced to equivocation, to choose silence, or to precipitate phenomenology into *philosophy*. Husserl, therefore, maintains his dissociative analysis and disarticulates the ambiguity. In order to grasp the nature of the danger threatening truth *itself* in its constitutive speech or writing, in order not to leave "internal" historicity, he is going to track down the intention of writing (or of reading) in itself and in its purity; in a new reduction he is going to isolate the intentional act which constitutes *Körper* as *Leib* and maintain this act in its *Leiblichkeit*, in its living truth-sense. Such an analysis no longer has any need of *Körper* as such. Only in the intentional dimen-

sion of a properly animate body, of the *geistige Leiblichkeit,* more precisely, in the *Geistigkeit* of the *Leib* (to the exclusion of all factual corporeality), is sense intrinsically threatened. Although in a *word* [*mot*], *Körper* and *Leib,* body and flesh, are *in fact* numerically one and the same existent, their senses are definitively heterogeneous, and nothing can come to the latter through the former. *Forgetfulness* of truth itself will thus be nothing but the failure of an act and the abdication of a responsibility, a lapse more than a defeat—and this forgetfulness can be made to appear in person only on the basis of an intentional history.

From then on, whether it remains as the disappearance of intersubjective truth or, as we said above, a historical category, *forgetfulness* can nevertheless be described as a phenomenon of the *ego,* as one of its intentional "modifications." As intentional sense, everything can and should be described only as a modification of the pure *ego,* provided the sense of each modification is prudently respected, as Husserl tries to do, for example, concerning the difficult constitution of the *alter ego.* We also see that, for the same reason, forgetfulness will never be radical, however profound it may be, and sense can always, in principle and de jure, be reactivated.

In *Formal and Transcendental Logic* and then in the *Crisis,* linguistic objectification and mathematical symbolization were presented as the occasion of the technicist's and objectivist's alienation, which degraded science into a skill or game.[105] This accusation, taken up again in the *Origin,* is more particularly directed against the methodological and operative teaching of mathematics. One learns to use signs whose primordial sense (which is not always the logical sense that is sedimented and accessible to an *explication*) is concealed or potentialized under sedimentations. The latter, which are only intentions or intentional senses made dormant, are not only *superimposed* in the internal becoming of sense, but are more or less virtually *implicated* in their totality in each stage or step. (In the *Origin,* the notion of *Stufe* has both a structural and genetic sense and can be translated by "step" or by "stage.") The geological image of "sedimentation" translates remarkably well the style of that implication. It brings together, for all intents and purposes, the following images: The image of *level* or *stratum*—what is deposited by an inroad or a progression after the radical novelty of an irruption or *upsurge:* every advance, every proposition *(Satz)* of a new sense is *at the same time* a leap *(Satz)* and a

---

[105] Cf. in particular *C,* §9*f.* On "meaningless signs" [*signes dépourvus de signification*] and "games-meaning" [*signification de jeu*], cf. *LI,* I, 1, §20, pp. 304–06. On vocables and real signs as "bearers" of signified idealities, cf. *EJ,* §65, p. 268.

*sedimentary (satzartig)* fall back of sense. Also, the image of the substantial permanence of what is then *supposed* or *situated under* the surface of actually present evidence. And finally, the image of the concealed presence that an activity of excavation can always re-produce above ground as the foundation, that is itself grounded, of higher stratifications. It brings all this together in the structural and *internal* unity of a system, of a "region" in which all deposits, interrelated but distinct, are originally prescribed by an *archi-tectonics*.

Confronting sedimented sense, our first danger is *passivity*. In the *Origin,* Husserl dwells more on the receptive acceptance of signs—first in reading—than on the secondary technical or logical activity that is not only not contradictory to the first passivity but, on the contrary, supposes it. The synthesis which awakens the sign to signification is first, in fact, necessarily passive and associative.[106] The possibility of giving way to this first *expectation* of sense is a lasting danger. But only *freedom* can let itself be threatened in this way; we are always free to reawaken any passively received sense, to reanimate all its virtualities, and to "transform" them "back . . . into the corresponding activity." This freedom is the "capacity for reactivation that belongs originally to every human being as a speaking being" (164). By this reactivation, which, Husserl states, is not "in fact" the "norm" and without which a certain comprehension is always possible, I actively re-produce the primordial evidence; I make myself fully responsible for and conscious of the sense that I take up. *Reaktivierung* is, in the domain of ideal objectivities, the very act of all *Verantwortung* and of all *Besinnung,* in the senses defined earlier. *Reaktivierung* permits bringing to life, under the sedimentary surfaces of linguistic and cultural acquisitions, the sense arising from instituting evidence. This sense is reanimated by the fact that I restore it to its dependence on my act and reproduce it in myself such as it had been produced for the first time by another. Of course, the activity of reactivation is second. What it gives back to me

[106] This theme of passive synthesis is copiously explicated in *EJ* and *CM,* but once again it is in *FTL* that it is particularly focused (as in the *Origin*) by the problem of the sign and of the sedimentation of ideal objectivities. Cf. in particular Appendix II, pp. 313–29. On the sense of activities and passivities in a phenomenology of reading as outlined in the *Origin,* also see *FTL,* §16, pp. 56–60.

Of course, the themes of passivity and sedimentation, i.e., of the potentiality of sense, derive all their seriousness from the fact that they are imposed on a philosophy of *actually present evidence* whose "principle of all principles" is the *immediate and actual [en acte]* presence of sense itself. If *reactivation* is valuable and urgent, that is because it can bring back to present and active evidence a sense which is thus retrieved out of historical virtuality. If, on the surface, phenomenology allows itself to be summoned outside of itself by history, it thus has found in *reactivation* the medium of its fidelity.

is the originally presentive intuition (that of the geometrical formation, for example) which is both an activity and a passivity. If this activity is especially illuminated here, it is no doubt because the evidence considered is that of created and established ideal formations.[107]

Responsibility for reactivation is a co-responsibility. It engages the one who recieves, but also and first of all the one who creates and then expresses the sense. For sedimentations obliterate sense only insofar as there are surfaces available for this. The *equivocity* of expression is the chosen field of sedimentary deposits. That is why the primally instituting geometer and those who follow after him must be concerned about "the univocity of linguistic expression and about securing, by a very careful coining of words, propositions, and complexes of propositions, the results which are to be univocally expressed" (165 [modified]).

Husserl never ceased to appeal to the imperative of univocity. Equivocity is the path of all philosophical aberration. It is all the more difficult not to be hasty here, as the sense of equivocity in general is itself equivocal. There is a *contingent* plurivocity or multisignificance and an *essential* one. These are already distinguished in the *Investigations* (*LI,* I, 1, §26, p. 314). The first depends on an objective convention; thus the word "dog" signifies both "a type of animal" and (in German) "a type of wagon (used in mines)." This plurivocity does not mislead anyone and we are always free to reduce it.[108] The second is of

---

[107] To try to illuminate this point, we first would have to approach directly and for itself the difficult and decisive problem in phenomenology of activity and passivity in general on the basis of texts directly devoted to this *(EJ, FTL, CM).* Such a study would perhaps have to conclude that phenomenology has only argued with the arbitrary sense [*exigence du sens*] of this couple of concepts, or indefinitely struggled with them, namely, with the most "irreducible" heritage (and indeed thereby perhaps the most obscuring heritage) of Western philosophy. In one of the finest analyses where he works with the concepts of passivity, activity, and passivity in activity, Husserl notes that the distinction between these two notions cannot be "inflexible," and that in each case their sense must be "recreated" according to "the concrete situation of the analysis," as "for every description of intentional phenomena" *(EJ,* §23, p. 108).

[108] *LI,* I, 1, §26, p. 314: "The class of ambiguous expressions illustrated by this last example are what one usually has in mind when one speaks of 'equivocation'. Ambiguity in such cases does not tend to shake our faith in the ideality and objectivity of significations. We are free, in fact, to limit our expression to *a single* signification. The ideal unity of each of the differing significations will not be affected by their attachment to a common designation" [modified].

The purpose of univocity supposes, then, a decisive rupture with spontaneous language, with the "civil language" of which Leibniz used to speak; after that, "philosophical" or "scholarly [*savant*]" language can freely be given its own particular conventions. Does not the sentence just cited sound like the faithful echo of another sentence of the *Nouveaux Essais sur l'Entendement Humain,* well known to Husserl and where

subjective origin, and it depends on original intentions, on always new experiences which animate the identity of objective sense and make it enter into unforeseeable configurations. This plurivocity is an "unavoidable rather than chance ambiguity [*plurivocité*], one that cannot be removed from our language by an artificial device or convention" (*LI*, p. 314).

However, this last equivocity is what science and philosophy must overcome. It is "unavoidable" only in natural language, i.e., in the facto-cultural phenomenon preceding the reduction. That Husserl is so anxious to reduce the equivocal sense of cultural naiveté reveals a concern that once more could be interpreted both as a refusal of history and as a deep fidelity to the pure sense of historicity. *On the one hand,* in effect, univocity removes truth out of history's reach. Univocal expression completely breaks the surface and offers no turning back [*repli*] to the more or less virtual significations that the intentions could deposit all along the advances of a language or culture. Thus Husserl's constant association of equivocal proceedings with a criticism of *profundity* is understandable.[109] Because it brings everything to view within a present act of evidence, because nothing is hidden or announced in the penumbra of potential intentions, because it has mastered all the dynamics of sense, univocal language remains *the same.* It thus keeps its ideal identity throughout all cultural development. It is the condition that allows communication among generations of investigators no matter how distant and assures the exactitude of translation and the

---

Theophilus says: "it depends upon us to fix their meanings [*significations*], at least in any scholarly language, and to agree to destroy this tower of Babel" (Book II, Ch. ix, §9 [ET: *New Essays Concerning Human Understanding,* tr. Alfred Gideon Langley (Chicago: Open Court, 1916), p. 373])? This optimism is only one of the affinities between Leibniz's and Husserl's philosophies of language. More broadly speaking, Husserl also very early felt himself the heir to the Leibnizian conception of logic in general. Cf. notably *LI,* I, Prol., §60, pp. 218ff.

[109] On this, cf. above all "PRS," p. 144: "Profundity [*Tiefsinn*] is a mark of the chaos that genuine science wants to transform into a cosmos, into a simple, completely clear, lucid order. Genuine science, so far as its real doctrine extends, knows no profundity." Husserl then proposes to re-strike (*umprägen*), as in the case of a currency revaluation, "the conjectures of profundity into unequivocal [German: *eindeutige;* French: *univoques*] rational forms" and thus to "constitut[e] anew the rigorous sciences." Likewise, Husserl's criticisms written in the margins of [Heidegger's] *Sein und Zeit* attribute to a *Tiefsinnigkeit* the responsibility for the Heideggerian "displacement" toward what Husserl defines as a facto-anthropological plane. Husserl prefers the value of *interiority* to that of *profundity* or depth, interiority being related to the penetration of internal, intrinsic *(inner),* i.e., essential *(wesentlich)* sense.

purity of tradition.[110] In other words—*on the other hand*—the very moment univocity removes sense beyond the reach of historical modification, it alone makes pure history possible, i.e., as the transmission and recollection [*recueillement*] of sense. Univocity only indicates the limpidity of the historical ether. Once again, Husserl's demand for univocity (which he formulated before the practice of the reduction) is therefore only the reduction of empirical history toward a pure history. Such a reduction must be recommenced indefinitely, for language neither can nor should be maintained under the protection of univocity.

If a radical equivocity precludes history, in effect, by plunging it into the nocturnal and ill-transmissible riches of "bound" idealities, absolute univocity would itself have no other consequence than to sterilize or paralyze history in the indigence of an indefinite iteration. Since equivocity always evidences a certain depth of development and concealment of a past, and when one wishes to assume and *interiorize* the memory of a culture in a kind of *recollection (Erinnerung)* in the Hegelian sense, one has, facing this equivocity, the choice of two endeavors. One would resemble that of James Joyce: to repeat and take responsibility for all equivocation itself, utilizing a language that could equalize the greatest possible synchrony with the greatest potential for buried, accumulated, and interwoven intentions within each linguistic atom, each vocable, each word, each simple proposition, in all wordly cultures and their most ingenious forms (mythology, religion, sciences, arts, literature, politics, philosophy, and so forth). And, like Joyce, this endeavor would try to make the structural unity of all empirical culture appear in the generalized equivocation of a writing that, no longer translating one language into another on the basis of their common cores of sense, circulates throughout all languages at once, accumulates their energies, actualizes their most secret consonances, discloses their furthermost common horizons, cultivates their associative syntheses instead of avoiding them, and rediscovers the poetic value of passivity. In short, rather than put it out of play with quotation marks, rather than "reduce" it, this writing resolutely settles itself *within* the *labyrinthian* field of culture "bound" by its own equivocations, in order to travel through and explore the vastest possible historical distance that is now at all possible.

---

[110] Exactitude and univocity are overlapping notions for Husserl. Moreover, the exactitude of expression will have as its condition the exactitude of sense. Geometry, the model of the sciences whose objects are exact, will therefore more easily attain univocity than will the other sciences, phenomenology in particular. We will return to this later. About the relations between exactitude and univocity in geometry, also cf. *Ideas I*, §73, pp. 189–90.

The other endeavor is Husserl's: to reduce or impoverish empirical language methodically to the point where its univocal and translatable elements are actually transparent, in order to reach back and grasp again at its pure source a historicity or traditionality that no de facto historical totality will yield of itself. This historicity or traditionality is always already presupposed by every Odyssean repetition of Joyce's type, as by all *philosophy of history* (in the current sense) and by every *phenomenology of the spirit*. The essences of finite totalities and the typology of figures of the spirit will always be idealities that are bound to empirical history. Only by means of historicism is it possible to remain there and confuse them with the movement of truth.[111]

But Husserl's project, as the transcendental "parallel" to Joyce's, knows the same relativity. Joyce's project, which also proceeded from a certain anti-historicism and a will "to awake" from the "nightmare" of "history,"[112] a will to master that nightmare in a total and present resumption, could only succeed by allotting its share to univocity, whether it might draw from a given univocity or try to produce another. Otherwise, the very text of its repetition would have been unintelligible; at least it would have remained so forever and for everyone. Likewise, Husserl had to admit an irreducible, enriching, and always renascent equivocity into pure historicity. In effect, absolute univocity is imaginable only in two limiting cases. *First:* suppose the designated thing is not only an absolutely singular, immutable, and natural object, but also an existent whose unity, identity, and Objectivity would in themselves be prior to all culture. Now if we suppose that such a thing or perception exists, linguistic ideality and its project of univocity— i.e., the act of language itself—intervene and from the outset place that supposition in a culture, in a network of linguistic relations and oppositions, which would load a word with intentions or with lateral and virtual reminscences. Equivocity is the congential mark of every culture. This first hypothesis of a univocal and natural language is, therefore, absurd and contradictory.

*Second:* is not the result the same if, at the other pole of language, an absolutely ideal object must be designated? This time, the chance for

[111] Husserl has always associated "Hegelianism" with "romanticism" and with "historicism," to which romanticism is led when "belief" in its "metaphysics of history" has been lost. (Cf. especially "PRS," pp. 76–77.) Was not the expression *Weltanschauung* first Hegelian? (Cf. on this J. Hyppolite, *Genesis and Structure of Hegel's Phenomenology of Spirit,* tr. Samuel Cherniak and John Heckman [Evanston: Northwestern University Press, 1974], pp. 469–70.)

[112] James Joyce, *Ulysses* (New York: Random, 1961), p. 34 ["History, Stephen said, is a nightmare from which I am trying to awake."].

univocity would not be offered by a precultural, but by a transcultural object, for example, the geometrical object. In any case, univocity corresponds to the very vocation of science. Husserl writes in the *Origin:* "In accord with the essence of science, then, its functionaries maintain the constant claim, the personal certainty, that everything they put into scientific assertions has been said 'once and for all,' that it 'stands fast,' forever identically repeatable, usable in evidence and for further theoretical or practical ends—as indubitably able to be reactivated with the identity of its genuine sense" (165–66 [modified]).

But this identity of sense, the ground of univocity and the condition for reactivation, is always relative, because it is always inscribed within a mobile system of relations and takes its source in an infinitely open project of acquisition. Even if those relations are, within a science, relations of pure idealities and "truths," they do not therein give rise any less to some singular placings in perspective [*mises en perspectives*], some multiple interconnections of sense, and therefore some mediate and potential aims. If, in fact, equivocity is always irreducible, that is because words and language in general are not and can never be absolute *objects*.[113] They do not possess any resistant and permanent identity that is absolutely their own. They have their linguistic being from an intention which traverses them as mediations. The "same" word is always "other" according to the always different intentional acts which thereby make a word significative [*signifiant*]. There is a sort of *pure* equivocity here, which grows in the very rhythm of science. Consequently, Husserl specifies in a note that the scientific statement, without being questioned again as to its truth, always remains provisional, and that "Objective, absolutely firm knowledge of truth is an infinite idea" (166). Absolute univocity is inaccessible, but only as an Idea in the Kantian sense can be. If the univocity investigated by Husserl and the equivocation generalized by Joyce are in fact *relative*, they are, therefore, not so *symmetrically*. For their common *telos,* the positive value of univocity, is *immediately* revealed only within the relativity that Husserl defined. Univocity is also the absolute horizon of equivocity. In giving it the sense of an infinite task, Husserl does not make univocity, as could be feared, the value for a language impoverished and thus removed out of history's reach. Rather, univocity is both the apriori and the teleological condition for all historicity; it is that

---

[113] That is why, as we noted above, Husserl could not inquire as to the *absolute* ideal Objectivity concerning language itself, whose ideality is always that of a "thematic index" and not a theme. This irreducible *mediacy* thus makes illusory all the safety promised by speech or writing *themselves*.

without which the very equivocations of empirical culture and history would not be possible.

The problem of univocity echoes immediately upon that of reactivation. Its schema is the same, for, without a minimal linguistic transparency, no reactivation would be imaginable. But if univocity is in fact always relative, and if it alone permits the reduction of all empirical culture and of all sedimentation, is the possibility of a pure history of sense to be doubted de jure? More particularly since, after having presented the capacity for reactivation, Husserl does not fail to ask the serious question of its *finitude*. In a science like geometry, whose potentiality for growth is extraordinary, it is impossible for every geometer, at every instant and every time he resumes his task after necessary interruptions, to perform a total and immediate reactivation of the "immense chain of foundings back to the original premises" (166 [modified]). The necessity of those interruptions is a factual one (sleep, professional breaks, and so forth), which has no sense compared with geometrical truth but is no less irreducible to it.

A *total* reactivation, even if that were possible, would paralyze the internal history of geometry just as surely as would the radical impossibility of all reactivation. Husserl is not worried about that: at this point a total recuperation of origins is still only a teleological horizon. For under the extrinsic necessity that geometrical activity be intermittent is also hidden an essential and internal necessity: since no piece of the geometrical edifice is self-sufficient, no *immediate* reactivation is possible, on any level. That is why, Husserl remarks, the "individual and even the social capacity" for reactivation is of an "obvious finitude" (168). It will always be denied immediate totality.

The obviousness [*évidence*] of that finitude and of that necessary mediacy could stamp Husserl's whole purpose as nonsense. Since that finitude is in fact irreducible, should it not furnish the true starting point for reflecting on history? Without that essential concealment of origins and within the hypothesis of an all-powerful reactivation, what would consciousness of historicity be? Also, no doubt, that consciousness would be nothing, if it was radically prohibited access to origins. But, so that history may have its proper density, must not then the darkness which engulfs the "original premises" (it can be penetrated but never dissipated) not only hide the fact but also the instituting sense? And must not the "critical" forgetfulness of origins be the faithful shadow in truth's advance rather than an accidental aberration? This distinction between fact and sense (or the de facto and the de jure) would be effaced in the sense-investigation of a primordial finitude.

But for Husserl, as we know, that finitude can *appear* precisely in its primordiality only given the Idea of an infinite history. Thus, faced with the finitude of reactivation, Husserl does not give up, as we suspect, the first direction of his investigation. He postpones the problem until later and invites us, with a slightly enigmatic brevity, to "notice" that there exists "an idealization: namely, the removal of limits from our capacity, in a certain sense its infinitization" (168). A secondary idealizing operation then comes to relieve the reactivative ability of its finitude and lets it get beyond itself. This movement is analogous to the constitution, for example, of the unity of the world's infinite horizon or (beyond the finite interconnection of retentions and protentions) to the constitution of the evidence for a total unity of the immanent flux as an Idea in the Kantian sense.[114] But above all, this movement is analogous to the production of geometry's exactitude: the passage to the infinite limit of a finite and qualitative sensible intuition. Strictly speaking, even here it is geometrical idealization which permits infinitizing the reactivative ability. Working in the diaphanousness of pure ideality, this ability easily and de jure transgresses its limits, which are then no more than the nominal limits of pure factuality. This idealization, which has for its correlate an infinite Idea, always decisively intervenes in the difficult moments of Husserl's description. The phenomenological status of its evidence remains rather mysterious. The impossibility of adequately determining the content of this Idea does not undermine, Husserl says in *Ideas I,* the rational transparency of its insightful evidence *(Einsichtigkeit).*[115] However, the certainty of what can never immediately and as such present itself in an intuition should pose some serious problems for phenomenology (problems similar to those, for example, of the constitution of the *alter ego* by an irreducibly mediate intentionality). We will come directly back to this later, when the production of geometrical exactitude by idealization will be our concern. At the present juncture, Husserl provisionally averts this difficulty. He writes: "The peculiar sort of evidence belonging to such idealizations will concern us later" (168 [modified]).

The capacity of reactivation must then be transmitted, in order that science not decay into a "tradition emptied of sense." As long as

---

[114] Cf. *Ideas I,* especially §83, pp. 220–22.

[115] *Ibid.,* p. 221. [In his translation of the *Origin,* Derrida translates *Einsicht* by "evidence rationnelle." In this he follows, as he says, the justification and practice of S. Bachelard (see *A Study of Husserl's* Logic, p. 106). This helps elucidate the phrase "la transparence rationnelle de son évidence" as a "translation" of "Einsichtigkeit." In his *Guide for Translating Husserl,* Dorion Cairns suggests the following: insight, insightfulness, intellectual seenness, apodictic evidentness, evidentness. Note adapted by Tr.]

science moves away from its beginnings and its logical superstructures are accumulated, the chances for such a transmission decrease until the day when the ability happens to fail. "Unfortunately . . . this is our situation, and that of the whole modern age" (169). The advancements of science can be pursued, even when the sense of its origin has been lost. But then the very logicality of the scientific gestures, imprisoned in mediacy, breaks down into a sort of oneiric and inhuman absurdity. Did not Plato describe this situation? Was not the eternity of essences for him perhaps only another name for a nonempirical historicity? "Geometry and the studies [*sciences*] that accompany it" are exiled far from their fundamental intuitions. They are incapable of "vision" *(idein)* and riveted to the hypotheses held as their principles. Confusing symbol with truth, they seem to us to dream *(orōmen ōs oneirottousi)* *(Republic* VII, 533c).[116] The return inquiry is therefore urgent: through us and for us it will reawaken science to its primordial sense, i.e., as we know, its final sense.

## VIII

Thus the method and the sense of the question concerning origins are illuminated at the same time as the conditions for the tradition of science in general. In closing these preliminary considerations, Husserl recalls their exemplary and fully "historical" character (in the sense of *Historie*): "Everywhere the problems, the clarifying investigations, the insights into principles are *historical (historisch)*. . . . We stand, then, within the historical horizon in which everything is historical, however little we may know about determined things. But this horizon has its essential structure that can be disclosed through methodical inquiry" (171–72 [modified]).

With respect to other sciences, as with respect to the world of prescientific culture, other returns to their origins are therefore prescribed. They are always possible, although as problems they still remain "unasked." This field of inquiry has no limits, since historicity embraces the infinite totality of being and sense: "Naturally, problems of this particular sort immediately awaken the total problem of the universal historicity of the correlative manners of being of humanity and the cultural world and the a priori structure contained in this historicity" (172).

[116] Plato, *The Collected Dialogues,* ed. Hamilton and Cairns (Princeton: Princeton University Press, 1961), p. 765. The translation is that of Paul Shorey.

After having opened his question about geometry to its broadest horizon, but before coming back to the determined origin of that science, Husserl responds (as a sort of complementary clarification) to two diametrically opposed methodological objections.

Certainly, the first would proceed from a standard epistemologism for which the return to primordial evidence and to its instituting concepts is an indispensable task. But there is nothing historical to that. The illusion of history can be given to this first objection only by verbal or symbolic allusions to some "undiscoverable" [172] but hardly mythical Thales. Husserl himself had handled this classic objection when, concerning the origin of science and geometry in particular, he attacked empiricism and external history.[117] He now rejects it because it misconstrues its own style of historical investigation, which is as *internal* and nonempirical as possible. Is it useful to recall that never has it been a question of returning to Thales or the factual beginnings of geometry? But to renounce factual history is not at all to cut oneself off from history in general. On the contrary, it is to open oneself to the sense of historicity. And in a sentence whose stress, at least, contrasts with that of his early phenomenology (but which only confirms and deepens, with an admirable fidelity, the initial distrust with regard to conventional history), Husserl specifies (172–73):

> *The ruling dogma of the separation in principle between epistemo-logical elucidation and historical, even humanistic-psychological explanation, between epistemological and genetic origin, is fundamentally mistaken* [is fundamentally turned upside down: Derrida's translation], *unless one inadmissibly limits, in the usual way, the concepts of 'history,' 'historical explanation,' and 'genesis.' Or rather, what is fundamentally mistaken is the limitation through which precisely the deepest and most genuine problems of history are concealed.*

To investigate the sense of a science as tradition and as cultural form is to investigate the sense of its complete historicity. From this fact, every intrascientific explication, every return to first axioms, to primordial evidences and instituting concepts, is at the same time "historical disclosure" [173]. Whatever our ignorance on the subject of

---

[117] In *Ideas I*, §25, pp. 84–86, will be found a long passage in which Husserl develops on his own, and in curiously similar terms, the objection that he pretends to address here. The confrontation of this text with that of the *Origin* can be remarkably illuminating as to the sense and fidelity of Husserl's itinerary.

actual history, we know *a priori* that every cultural present, therefore every scientific present, implicates in its totality the totality of the past. The unity of this unceasing totalization which is always brought about in the form of the historic Present (the "Primordial in itself"-*[Primordial en soi]*) leads us, if correctly inquired of, to the universal Apriori of history. As the Absolute unchangeable-in-itself of the Living Present in which it is grounded, the historic Present is at first sight only the irreducible and pure place and movement of that totalization and that traditionalization.[118] The historic Present is the historical Absolute— "the vital movement of the coexistence and the interweaving (*des Miteinander und Ineinander*) of primordial formations and sedimentations of sense (*Sinnbildung* [*und Sinnsedimentierung*])" (174 [modified]).

Every particular historical investigation must de jure note its more or less immediate dependence on that insight into apodictic principles [*évidence absolument principielle*]. All habitual factual history "remains incomprehensible" (174) as long as these a priori have not been explicated and as long as factual history has not adapted its method to the notion of intrinsic history, to the notion of the intentional history of sense.

This leads us to the second riposte, this time directed against historicism rather than empirical history. The schema of this criticism is analogous to that which underlies "Philosophy as Rigorous Science." But the historicism Husserl now attacks, despite affinities connecting it to Dilthey's theory of the *Weltanschauung*, seems to have a more ethnosociological, a more *modern* style. And here what Husserl wants to wrest from historical relativism is less the truth or ideal norms of science and philosophy than the a priori of historical science itself.

In effect, ethnologism sets the abundant multiplicity of testimonies attesting that each people, each tribe, each human group has its world, its a priori, its order, its logic, its history, over against the universal a priori, the unconditioned and apodictic structures, the unitary ground of history, such as Husserl means to describe them.

Now, *on the one hand,* these unimpeachable testimonies do not belie but, on the contrary, presuppose the structure of the universal horizon and the a priori of history that Husserl designates; these pre-

---

[118] Naturally, it is a question, as Husserl clearly states, of the historic Present *in general* as the ultimate universal form of every possible historical experience, an experience which itself is grounded in the Living Present of egological consciousness. Moreover, Husserl emphasizes in a footnote [174] that all of intrinsic history passes through the intrinsic history of the totality of individual persons.

suppositions only cause singular and determined a priori to be articulated therein. It suffices, then, to respect those articulations and the
complicated hierarchy which submits more or less determined material
a priori to the apriori form of universal historicity. *On the other hand,*
the "facts," which are thus invoked to support this relativism, can be
determined as certain historical facts only if something like historical
truth is determinable in general.[119] Ranke's " 'how it really was' "
[176], the ultimate reference for all factual history, presupposes as its
horizon a historical determinability that every empirical science, by
itself alone and as such, is powerless to ground. "Accordingly, we need
not first enter into some kind of critical discussion of the facts set out by
historicism; it is enough that the claim of their factuality already presupposes the historical a priori if this claim is to have any sense" (176
[modified]).

In order to be able "to establish" facts as facts *of* history, we must
always already know what history is and under what conditions—
concrete conditions—it is possible. We must already be engaged in a
precomprehension of historicity, i.e., of the invariants of history that
language, tradition, community, and so forth are. In order for the
ethnological "fact" to appear, ethnological communication must already be started within the horizon of universal humanity; two men or
two groups of men must have been able to be understood starting from
the possibilities, however poor, of a universal language. The ethnologist
must be sure, apodictically, that *other* men also necessarily live within a
community of language and tradition, within the horizon of a history;
sure, also, of what the fact means in general. In the ultimate recourse, it
is necessary to know that the historic Present in general—the irreducible form of every historical experience—is the ground of all historicity,
and that I could always come to terms in this Present with the most
distant, the most different "other." However strange to each other two
men may be, they always are understandable—at the limit—in the
commonalty of their Living Present in which the historic Present is
rooted. That each of their fundamental Presents is, *also,* materially
determined by its insertion within the factual content of a tradition,
social structure, language, and so forth, that each does not have the
same sense-content, this in no way affects the commonalty of their
form. This universal form, which is the most *primordial* and *concrete*
lived experience, is supposed by all being-together. This form also
seems to be the final retrenchment, therefore the most *responsible* secu-

[119] Some analogous developments will be found in the Vienna Lecture, "Philosophy
and the Crisis of European Humanity," in *C,* p. 296.

rity, of every phenomenological reduction. In this ultimate *juridical instant* [*instance*] is announced the most radical unity of the world.

Thus every problem of historical facts involves historical invariants the very moment the problem authorizes a certain *relativism*.[120] The latter retains all its value, provided its level of *materiality* and its apriori conditions are appropriately determined. The part devoted to relativism in the celebrated Letter to Lévy-Bruhl can be interpreted in this way. From that letter, written a year earlier than the *Origin*,[121] we might think, on the contrary, that Husserl renounced the historical a priori discovered by imaginary variation and recognized that the pure phenomenology of history had to expect something other than examples from the content of the empirical sciences, ethnology in particular. This is notably the reading that Merleau-Ponty proposed: "In a letter to Lévy-Bruhl which has been preserved, Husserl seems to admit that the facts go beyond what we imagine and that this point bears a real significance. It is as if the imagination, left to itself, is unable to represent the possibilities of existence which are realized in different cultures. . . . [Husserl] saw that it is perhaps not possible for us, who live in certain historical traditions, to conceive of the historical possibility of these primitive men by a mere variation of our imagination."[122]

Or again:

*Historical relativism is now no longer dominated at one stroke by a mode of thought which would have all the keys of history and would be in a position to draw up a table of all historical possibles before any factual experimental inquiry. On the contrary, the thinker who wishes*

---

[120] Is it necessary to underscore that the question here is not that of a criticism of historical or socio-ethnological science as such? Husserl simply wants to call the problem back to its presuppositions. Phenomenology, which alone can bring them to light as such, at times has been, moreover, taken up by the researchers themselves with various degrees of explication.

This precaution had been formulated as an hommage to history as human science in "PRS," p. 129.

[121] Letter of March 11, 1935. Husserl there speaks notably of the "indubitable legitimacy" that "historical relativism" involves *"as anthropological fact"* (our emphasis) and of the possible and necessary task of a comprehensive *Einfühlung* with respect to primitive societies that are "without history" *(geschichtlos)*. [A great deal of this letter is available in Merleau-Ponty's articles cited below. See notes 122–125—tr.] He insists vigorously on the fact that the rights of relativism thus understood are preserved and "conserved" by "the intentional analysis" of transcendental phenomenology.

[122] Cf. "Phenomenology and the Sciences of Man," pp. 90–91. The same interpretation is presented in Merleau-Ponty's article, "The Philosopher and Sociology," in *Signs,* pp. 98–113.

*to dominate history in this way must learn from the facts and must enter into them. . . . The eidetic of history cannot dispense with factual historical investigation. In the eyes of Husserl, philosophy, as a coherent thought which leads to a classification of facts according to their value and truth, continues to have its final importance. **But it must begin by understanding all lived experiences.** (Our emphasis)*[123]

Is such an interpretation justified?

The only relativism Husserl acknowledges as valid is that attached to historico-anthropological "facts" as such and in their factuality. Husserl never contested this validity even in "Philosophy as Rigorous Science." The historical a priori to which he had always appealed (and more and more, as a matter of fact) were never presented, it seems, as "keys of history" or as a "table of all historical possibles before any factual experimental inquiry." And since history and the historical possibles about which Merleau-Ponty speaks represent the material and determined content of historical modifications (i.e., the factual possible realized in such and such a society, culture, epoch, and so forth), to interpret Husserl in the above manner is to ascribe to him the pretension of deducing factuality itself *a priori*. We cannot stop with such a hypothesis, which contradicts the very premises of phenomenology. Husserl undoubtedly thought that all of history's determined possibles had to conform to the apriori essences of historicity concerning every possible culture, every possible language, every possible tradition. But never did he dream to foresee, by some eidetic deduction, all the facts, all the particular possibles which must conform to these a priori of universal historicity.

But not to deduce factuality *a priori,* is that to "learn from the facts"? Not any more, if that signifies that eidetic intuition will have to be abandoned—even provisionally—and facts used otherwise than as examples in an imaginary variation. The purpose of the variation technique in eidetic reading had never been to exhaust the multiplicity of possible facts: on the contrary, the technique even has the privilege of being able to work on only one of those possibles in an exemplary consciousness [*conscience d'exemple*]. Thus, this technique has never had the mission of "dispens[ing] with factual historical investigation"; or at least, if it does this, it is not by pretending to substitute for the historical inquiry (in anticipating the facts) the "solitary reflection of a historian";[124] it simply *de jure* precedes every material historical investigation and has no need of facts as such to reveal to the historian the apriori sense of his activity and objects. To determine this sense is, for

[123] *Ibid.*, pp. 91–92 [modified].

[124] *Ibid.*, p. 92.

Husserl, so little a question of "begin[ning] by understanding all lived experiences," of abandoning or limiting the technique of imaginary variation, that the latter is explicitly and frequently prescribed in the *Origin,* a writing that can be considered one of Husserl's last. For him, this technique remains the "method" according to which we obtain "a universal and also fixed a priori of the historical world which is always originally genuine" (177).

Farther on, he says: "we also have, and know that we have, the capacity of complete freedom to transform, in thought and phantasy, our human historical existence. . . . And precisely in this activity of free variation, and in running through the conceivable possibilities for the life-world, there arises, with apodictic self-evidence, an essentially general set of elements going through all the variants. . . . Thereby we have removed every bond to the factually valid historical world and have regarded this world itself merely as one of the conceptual possibilities" (177).

Here again, no doubt, imaginary variation and the reduction *de facto* take their starting point in factuality. But again they retain from fact only its exemplarity and its essential structure, its "possibility" and not its factuality.

If the discovery of the apriori structures and the invariants of universal historicity is methodologically and juridically first, this discovery teaches us nothing—this is evident, and first to Husserl—about each real society's or each real historical moment's own specific character proposed for the sociologist's or historian's activity. Therefore, it has never been a question of that, nor of "construct[ing] what makes sense of other experiences and civilizations by a purely imaginary variation of [one's] own experiences."[125]

Nevertheless, if I were able to "construct" the "sense of other experiences and civilizations" in that manner, I would discover in what way they are *also* experiences and civilizations, and not how they are *different.* In order to attain this sense of *every* civilization or *every* experience,

---

[125] Merleau-Ponty, "The Philosopher and Sociology," p. 107 [modified]. Always commenting on the same letter, Merleau-Ponty writes: "Here he [Husserl] seems to admit that the philosopher could not possibly have immediate access to the universal by reflection alone—that he is in no position to do without anthropological experience or to construct what constitutes the meaning of other experiences and civilizations by a purely imaginary variation of his own experiences" (p. 107).

In Merleau-Ponty's *Phenomenology of Perception* [tr. Colin Smith (New York: Humanities Press, 1962)], the whole last period of Husserl's thought was already interpreted as "tacitly [breaking] with the philosophy of essences," a rupture by which Husserl was "merely explicitly laying down analytic procedures which he had long been applying" (p. 49).

I will first have to reduce what there is of *my own* (in the factual sense, of course) in the experience and civilization from which I in fact start. Once that sense of the experience or civilization in general has been made clear, I could legitimately try to determine the *difference* between the various facts of civilization and experience. This does not mean that I should abandon every eidetic attitude from that moment on. Within a much greater factual determination, other reductions are still possible and necessary, reductions that must be prudently articulated according to their degree of generality, dependence, and so forth, yet always respecting, as Husserl specifies in the *Origin*, the rule of the strict "subsumption" [159] of the singular under the universal. In proportion to the increase of material determination, "relativism" extends its rights, but, since it is dependent to the highest degree, it will never be, as Husserl notes in the same letter, "the last word of scientific knowledge."

Certainly the work of the historian, sociologist, ethnologist, and so forth constitutes a kind of realized imaginary variation in the encounter with factual difference; this kind of variation can be used directly for access to the concrete and universal components of sociality or historicity. Since these invariants will teach us nothing about the specific character of a particular society or epoch, I will—especially—have to "empathize" *(einzufühlen)*, as Husserl said to Lévy-Bruhl. But this empathizing *(Einfühlung)*, as the factual determination of difference, cannot exactly institute science de jure. *Einfühlung* itself is possible only *within* and *by virtue* of the apriori universal structures of sociality and historicity. It supposes an immediate transcendental community of all historical civilizations and the possibility of an *Einfühlung* in general. In the material determination of historicities, *Einfühlung*, moreover, strictly conforms with the method of all historical phenomenology, since it penetrates historical significations from within and makes the *external* inquiry depend on *internal* intuition.

But, then, how do we reconcile the affirmation according to which historicity is an essential structure of the horizon for all humanity (as well as for every community) and the allusion to the "nonhistoricity" *(Geschichtlosigkeit)* of certain archaic societies?[126] This nonhistoricity seems not to have any pure and absolute signification for Husserl. It would only *modify* the apriori structure of mankind's universal historicity empirically or materially. It would be the form of historicity that is only proper to finite societies enclosed in their "locked horizons"— societies as yet removed from the irruption of the "European" Idea of

[126] Letter already cited.

the infinite task and tradition. Their "stagnation" would not be the mere absence of historicity but a kind of finitude in the project and recollection of sense. Therefore, and only in comparison with the infinite and pure historicity of the European *eidos,* do archaic societies seem "without history." In the *Crisis,* moreover, Husserl only recognizes an *empirical* type in those societies which do not participate in the European Idea. Nonhistoricity, then, would only be the lower limit-mode of empirical historicity. The ambiguity of an *example* which is at once an undistinguished *sample* and a teleological *model* is still found here. In the first sense, in fact, we could say with Husserl that every community is in history, that historicity is the essential horizon of humanity, insofar as there is no humanity without sociality and culture. From this perspective, any society at all, European, archaic, or some other, can serve as an example in an eidetic recognition. But on the other hand, Europe has the privilege of being the *good example,* for it incarnates in its purity the Telos of all historicity: universality, omnitemporality, infinite traditionality, and so forth; by investigating the sense of the pure and infinite possibility of historicity, Europe has awakened history to its own proper end. Therefore, in this second sense, pure historicity is reserved for the European *eidos.* The empirical types of non-European societies, then, are only *more or less* historical; at the lower limit, they *tend toward* nonhistoricity.

Thus Husserl is led to distinguish the originality of various levels *within* the most universal *eidos* of historicity. In a very brief fragment, whose inspiration is very similar to that of the *Origin,* Husserl determines three stages or steps of historicity. In proportion to the advancement in that hierarchy or to the progression in that development, historicity assumes greater possession of its own essence. First, there would be historicity in the most general sense, as the essence of all human existence, inasmuch as human existence necessarily moves in the spiritual space of a culture or tradition. The immediately higher level would be that of European culture, the theoretical project, and philosophy. The third level, finally, would be characterized by the "conversion of philosophy into phenomenology."[127] Thus, at each

---

[127] "Stufen der Geschichtlichkeit. Erste Geschichtlichkeit," 1934, Beilage XXVI, in *K,* pp. 502–03. Elsewhere Husserl writes in the same vein: "Human life is necessarily, in the main and as cultural life, historical in the strictest sense. But scientific life, life as the life of a man of science in a horizon of a community of men of science, signifies a new kind of historicity" (Beilage XXVII, 1935, in *K,* p. 507). Also see "Philosophy and the Crisis of European Humanity," in *C,* p. 279. Husserl speaks there of a "revolutionization of historicity." [In the version that Paul Ricoeur translates (see note 149 below), the line is rendered: "revolution *in the heart* of historicity," the emphasis by Derrida.]

stage, the revolution which overthrows the previous project by an infinitization is only the sense-investigation of a hidden intention. (Moreover, the equivalence of every sense-investigation to an infinitization can be posited as a phenomenological rule.) On the other hand, since these three moments are stratifying structures of different heights, they are not in fact mutually exclusive: not only do they coexist in the world, but one and the same society can make them cohabit within itself, in the differentiated unity of an organic simultaneity.

It is then straight toward the eidetic invariants and the teleological absolutes of historicity that Husserl's reflection is directed. The *internal* and *dynamic* differentiation of those invariants must not lose sight of that fact; this differentiation is precisely the sign that the invariants *of* historicity, the essences *of* becoming are really in question here. We could then be tempted by an interpretation diametrically opposed to that of Merleau-Ponty and maintain that Husserl, far from opening the phenomenological parentheses to historical factuality under all its forms, leaves history more than ever *outside* them. We could always say that, by definition and like all conditions of possibility, the invariants of history thus tracked down by Husserl are not *historical* in themselves. We would then conclude, like Walter Biemel, that "Husserl's essays which try to grasp historicity thematically can be considered as failures."[128]

But what would historicity and discourse about history be, if none of those invariants were possible? In order to speak of failure in the thematization of historicity, must we not already have access to an invariant and more or less thematic sense of historicity? And is not that sense precisely what is announced in Husserl's last meditations, incomplete as they are?

If the thematization of the apodictic invariants and of the historical a priori was at fault, would not that be in comparison with *history* rather than with *historicity?* The failure would then be flagrant if, at some moment, Husserl was to become interested in something like history.

---

[128] "Les Phases décisives dans le développement de la philosophie de Husserl" (already cited [see note 5], in *Husserl,* Cahiers de Royaumont, p. 58). [This comment is only found in the French version of this essay.] Walter Biemel very accurately sees the *Crisis* as a work of old age too easily interpreted as a turning point in Husserl's thought, despite the profound continuity which unites it to his previous investigations. At the end of this valuable lecture—while underscoring Husserl's fidelity—the author recalls the discomfort of Husserl who, in "an entire series of manuscripts from group K III," "asks himself why philosophy should need history" (in *The Phenomenology of Husserl*, ed. Elveton, p. 167). And in Beilagen XXV and XXVIII of the *Krisis,* Husserl asks himself in particular: "Why does philosophy need the history of philosophy?" (in *K,* p. 495), and: *"How* is History Required?" (in *K,* p. 508; in *C,* Appendix IX, p. 389).

He never seems to have done that. Would not, then, his original merit be to have described, in a properly *transcendental* step (in a sense of that word which Kantianism cannot exhaust), the conditions of possibility for history which were at the same time *concrete?* Concrete, because they are experienced [*vécues*] under the form of *horizon.*

The notion of horizon is decisive here: "horizon-consciousness," "horizon-certainty," "horizon-knowledge," such are the key concepts of the *Origin.* Horizon is given to a *lived* evidence, to a *concrete* knowledge which, Husserl says, is never "learned" [176], which no empirical moment can then hand over, since it always presupposes the horizon. Therefore, we are clearly dealing with a primordial knowledge concerning the totality of possible historical experiences. Horizon is the always-already-there of a future which keeps the indetermination of its infinite openness intact (even though this future was *announced* to consciousness). As the structural determination of every material indeterminacy, a horizon is always virtually present in every experience; for it is at once the unity and the incompletion for that experience—the anticipated unity in every incompletion. The notion of horizon converts critical philosophy's state of abstract possibility into the concrete infinite potentiality secretly presupposed therein. The notion of horizon thus makes the a priori and the teleological coincide.

## IX

After broadening his reflection to include the problems of universal historicity, Husserl narrows the field of his analysis and comes back to the origin of geometry. In a few pages, he puts forward the most concrete descriptions of this text. Commentators have most often retained these descriptions because, in short, as Husserl himself underscores, they go beyond "formal generalities" [177] and (starting from human praxis) draw near to the constitution of geometrical protoidealities in the prescientific sphere of the cultural world.

The posture [*situation*] of this analysis seems rigorously prescribed by the bearing of the meditation, despite its rather free style. As we are going to see, its content is less novel in Husserl's work than at first apparent. After having determined the conditions for traditionality *in general,* we have the right to return to *one* of those traditions which (serving just a moment ago as an exemplary guide) is now studied in itself. After having fixed the sense and the method for *all* questioning of origins, we ask *a* question about a single origin. On the other hand, geometry has been recognized as a traditional system of ideal objectivities. Now in ideal objectivity, both Objectivity and ideality must be

accounted for; despite their deep-rooted interrelatedness and their reciprocal conditioning, they can be separated. Analyzed *in general* and
not as geometrical (as in the first part of the text), ideality effectively
enters into tradition by its objectification and thus can be freed, can be
handed over. We ought, then, to begin (as Husserl does) by accounting
for Objectivity, i.e., the historicity of ideal objectivity in general. The
apriori structures of historicity could be questioned only by recourse to
language, writing, the capacity of reactivation, and finally to method.
Thanks to this method, which alone enables comprehension of the invariants of historicity *in general* with an apodictic certainty, we can now
return (this side of science) to the invariants *of* the prescientific world
on the basis of which geometrical protoidealities have been produced
and established. Thus, after having defined the conditions for the Objectivity of ideal objects, we can try to describe the conditions for
geometrical ideality itself, by a new reduction of constituted scientific
Objectivity and all its specific historicity. Earlier, it will be recalled,
Husserl asked himself: how could ideal sense, *already constituted* in
subjective immanence, be objective and engaged in history and in the
movement of intersubjectivity? He now asks himself: how, in a "previous" moment, could ideality itself be constituted?

The necessity of this way of going back [*récursion*] through a series of
"zigzags" seems to guide Husserl when he writes: "Through this
method, going beyond the formal generalities we exhibited earlier, we
can also make thematic that apodictic aspect of the prescientific world
that the original founder of geometry had at his disposal, that which
must have served as the material for his idealizations" (177).

First, we must delimit those structures of the prescientific world
which could institute a geometry. This description is always possible,
since the stratum of the prescientific world is never destroyed, nor
definitively concealed. This stratum remains intact under the universe
determined by the ideal exactitude of science. And, according to an
image which Husserl uses at least twice, it is "nothing more than a garb
of ideas thrown over the world of immediate intuition and experience,
[over] the life-world; for each of the results of science has its foundation
of sense in this immediate experience and its corresponding world and
refers back to it. 'It is through the garb of ideas that we take for true
Being what is actually a method'. . . ."[129]

---

[129] *EJ*, pp. 44–45, in a paragraph which concerns precisely geometry's ideal exactitude.
The same image is used in *C* (§9*h* : "The life-world as the forgotten meaning-fundament of
natural science," p. 51). Husserl's ambiguous attitude before science—which he valued
utmost as project and least in its superstructural precariousness and ability to conceal—
reflects the very movement of the "historical" constitution of sense: creation which
discloses and sedimentation which covers over imply each other.

Therefore, it is proper to reduce the ideal sedimentations of science, in order to discover the nakedness of the pregeometrical world. This new *"epochē"* of the objective sciences, the problem of which is developed in the *Crisis,* is difficult for several reasons:[130]

1. The first difficulty is that of every reduction: it must be kept from being a forgetfulness and a negation, a subtraction or devaluation of what it methodically de-sediments or neutralizes.

2. As the reduction of objective-exact science, this new *epochē* must not cause us to renounce all scientificness. The thematization of the *Lebenswelt* must be "scientific" and attain to the a priori which are no longer the habitual ones of logic and objective science.[131] Husserl often presents this as a "paradox": the *Lebenswelt,* the preobjective sphere of "subjective-relative" significations, has a universal, unconditioned structure, a structure prescribed for its very relativity.[132] The a priori of logic and objective science are also "rooted" and "grounded" in the a priori of the *Lebenswelt* (*C, §34 e,* p. 130). We are confined by naiveté to the former and kept ignorant of their "sense-relation" *(Sinnbeziehung)* to the life-world. Without this grounding relation, they are "in mid-air" *(ibid.,* §36, p. 141).

3. Finally, it is not sufficient to dissolve what Husserl calls, in the language of Bolzano, the truths of science, " 'truths in themselves' " *(ibid.,* p. 130); we must continually make problematic the relation of the *Lebenswelt's* subjective-relative truths and science's objective-exact truths. The paradox of their mutual interrelation makes both truths "enigmatic" at once *(ibid.,* p. 131). In the insecurity of this enigma, in the instability of the space between these two truths, the *epochē* must be stretched between the *archē* and the *telos* of a passage. Two *truths,* that of *doxa* and that of *epistēmē,* whose sense and a priori are heterogeneous in themselves, remain interrelated *(Aufeinanderbezogenheit)* *(ibid.).* Science's truth "in itself" is not any less truth-*of* the subjective-relative world, in which it has its bases. No doubt there exists a naively superficial baselessness *(Bodenlosigkeit):* that of the rationalists and the traditional scientific investigators who move unconstrained in the atmosphere of the logical and objective a priori and do

---

[130] Cf. notably §§33 to 39, pp. 121–48, and the related texts appended there.

[131] *Ibid.* On the difficulty and necessity for a scientific thematization of the *Lebenswelt,* cf. [§33], p. 122. On the distinction between the two *a priori,* cf. above all [§36], pp. 137–41. In the *Origin,* "logic" always has the sense of the "sedimented."

[132] *Ibid.* [§37], pp. 142–43. On the structural permanence of the prescientific life-world, also cf. [§9h], p. 51.

not relate them to their historical ground in the life-world. They neither worry about their own *responsibility* nor ask themselves: *what am I in the process of doing?* Nor: *from where does that come?* But there is another naiveté just as serious, but with a more modern style: naiveté of profundity or depth and not of superficiality, it consists in redescending toward the prescientific perception without making problematic the "transgression" *(Überschreitung)* *(ibid.,* §36, p. 139 [ET: "surpassing"]) of the life-world's truth toward the world of truths "in themselves." The return to the structures of prescientific experience must continually keep alive the *question: How can the a priori of scientific Objectivity be constituted starting from those of the life-world?* Without this question, any return, however penetrating, risks abdicating all scientific quality *in general* and all philosophical dignity, even if it might have tried precipitating a legitimate reaction to what Husserl calls "intellectualistic hypertrophy" *(ibid.,* §34*f*, p. 133). If we consider this question to be *at once* historical and transcendental, we see to what irresponsible empiricism all the "phenomenologies" of prescientific perception are condemned, phenomenologies which would not let themselves be beset by that question.

We must also beware of forgetting that the prescientific world— which the protogeometer has at his disposal and which we thus recover—does not have the radicality of the prepredicative world to which Husserl tries to return, above all, in *Experience and Judgment.* [133] The prescientific world is a cultural world already informed by predication, values, empirical techniques, and the practice of measurement and inductiveness which themselves have their own style of certainty.

The above enables us to point out again the dependent status of Husserl's text, the status of every starting point and every clue guiding reflection on universal historicity. Certainly, the essential structures of the prescientific world are discovered by a double reduction: that of all determined factual culture and that of the scientific superstructures which extend beyond particular cultural areas in order to be free of them. But this should not make us forget that the prescientific cultural world can be reduced, in its turn, in a radical *"epochē"* which wants to cut a path toward what is already supposed: the transcendental constitution of the object in general (before the ideal object which serves, however, as example and model for Objectivity), the prepredicative stratum of experience, the static and genetic constitution of the *ego* and

---

[133] This work does not attain the prepredicative world in its first radicality. It supposes, like *Ideas I,* an *already constituted* temporality. Cf. on this *Ideas I,* notably §81, pp. 216–17, and *EJ,* §14, p. 68.

*alter ego*, primordial temporality, and so forth. These reductions, moreover, are done in texts earlier than the *Crisis*. In *Ideas I*, the broadening of the transcendental reduction already extends *by anticipation* as far as the eidetic of history, which Husserl thought still remained to be done. After having justified his suspension of "all transcendent-eidetic domains," "actual physical Nature," and the empirical or eidetic sciences of Nature (geometry, kinematics, pure physics, and so forth), Husserl wrote:

> *Similarly, just as we have suspended all experiential sciences dealing with the nature of animate beings and all empirical human sciences concerning personal beings in personal relationships, concerning men as subjects of history, as bearers of culture, and treating also the cultural formations themselves, and so forth, we also suspend now the eidetic sciences which correspond to these objectivities. We do so, in advance and in idea; for, as everyone knows, these ontological-eidetic sciences (rational psychology, sociology, for instance) have not as yet received a proper grounding, at any rate none that is pure and free from all objection. (Ideas I, § 60, p. 162 [modified]; our emphasis)*

We could then say that Husserl in advance subjected history's eidetic to the authentic transcendental reduction—an eidetic he will try to constitute starting in the *Crisis*. That is why, no doubt, the word "transcendental," which Husserl nearly always reserves for the *ego*'s pure constituting activity, is never utilized in the *Origin*. If I myself have spoken of transcendental historicity, I do so in order to distinguish at once empirical history and a simple eidetic of history parallel to the other eidetics of Nature and spirit. The *eidos* of historicity, as explicated after the *Crisis*, seems to exceed the limits assigned to it beforehand by *Ideas I*. Its science is no longer *merely* one human science among others. It is that of an activity constituting the whole sphere of absolute ideal Objectivity and all the eidetic sciences. That this constituting history may be more profoundly constituted itself, such is, no doubt, one of the most permanent motifs of Husserl's thought; also, one of the most difficult, for it accords badly with that of a historicity which (as Husserl said more and more often) traverses everything through and through, and first of all the *ego* itself.[134]

---

[134] All these difficulties seem concentrated to us in the sense that Husserl gives to the expression *"transcendental history,"* which he utilizes (to our knowledge) only once, in an unpublished manuscript of Group C (C 8 II, October 29, p. 3): thus, the question concerns the intermonadic relation (always considered in itself, of course, as an intentional modification of the monad in general in its primordial temporality), a relation thanks to which the constitution of a common world becomes possible. This relation structurally implies the horizon of the history of the spirit, past and future; the latter discovers for us what perception cannot give us.

## X

What, then, are the essential and general components of the prescientific cultural world? Or rather, what are, in that world, the invariant structures which have conditioned the advent of geometry? However profound our ignorance concerning historical facts, we know with an immediate and apodictic knowledge—the sense of which can always be investigated—the following:

1. That this pregeometrical world was a world of *things* disposed of according to an anexact space and time.[135]

2. That these things must have been "corporeal." Corporeality is a particular determination of thinghood *(Dinglichkeit)* in general; but since culture already had to have left its mark on the world (because language and intersubjectivity must have preceded geometry),[136] corporeality does not exhaustively overlap thinghood: "since the necessarily coexisting human beings are not thinkable as mere bodies and, like even the cultural Objects which belong with them structurally, are not exhausted in corporeal being" (177).

3. That these pure bodies had to have spatial shapes, shapes of motion, and "alterations of deformation" [177].

4. That material qualities (color, weight, hardness, and so forth) must necessarily be "related" to these pregeometrical, spatiotemporal shapes by a supplementary eidetic determination.

In *Ideas I,* while explicating the principles of regional articulation and internal structure, Husserl treated these eidetic characteristics as an index, whereas they are a direct theme in the *Origin:* "The construction of the highest concrete genus (the region) out of genera that are partly disjunctive, partly founded in one another (and in this mutually inclusive), corresponds to the construction of the concreta that belong to it out of lowest differences that are partly disjunctive, partly founded in one another; *as obtains with temporal, spatial, and material determinations, for instance, in the case of the thing*" (§72, p. 186 [modified]; our emphasis).[137]

Pure geometry and kinematics (and all the associated sciences for

---

[135] This idea, already developed in §9a of the *Crisis,* is more directly inscribed within an analysis of the *Lebenswelt,* in §36, p. 139, an analysis identical to that in the *Origin.*

[136] This justifies (at least on a specific point) the anteriority of the *Origin*'s analyses concerning language and being-in-community.

[137] Also cf. §149, pp. 382–83 et passim.

which they are the example here), then, will be *material* eidetics, since their purpose is the thingly, and thus the corporeal, determination of objects in general. But they are *abstract* material sciences, because they only treat certain eidetic components of corporeal things in general, disregarding their independent and concrete totality, which also comprises the "material" *(stofflich)*, sensible qualities and the totality of their predicates. Spatial shapes, temporal shapes, and shapes of motion are always *singled out from* the totality of the perceived body.

By itself alone, then, a static analysis could *a priori* and rigorously recall for us that the protogeometer always already had at his disposal anexact spatiotemporal shapes and essentially "vague" morphological types, which can always give rise to a pregeometrical *descriptive* science. This could be called *geography*. For such a subject, the rigor of eidetic assertions (like that for determining vague essences) is not at all undermined by the necessary anexactitude of the perceived object. We must indeed beware of scientific naiveté, which causes this anexactitude of the object or concept to be considered as a "defect," as an inexactitude. Husserl writes (we are still quoting from *Ideas I*): "The most perfect geometry and its most perfect practical control cannot help the descriptive scientific investigator of Nature to express precisely (in exact geometrical concepts) that which in so plain, so understandable, and so entirely suitable a way he expresses in the words: notched, indented, lens-shaped, umbilliform, and the like—simple concepts which are *essentially and not accidentally inexact,* and are *therefore* also unmathematical" (§74, p. 190 [modified]).[138]

5. That, by a practical necessity of daily life, certain shapes and certain processes of transformation could be perceived, restored, and progressively perfected; for example, rigid lines, even surfaces, and so forth. Every morphological, i.e., pregeometrical, determination works according to the qualitative gradations of sensible intuition: *more or less smooth* surfaces, sides, lines, or *more or less rough* angles, and so on. This does not prohibit a rigorous and univocal eidetic fixing of vague morphological types. In the *Origin*, Husserl writes (parenthetically and somewhat enigmatically) that before exactitude emerges, "proceeding from the factual, an essential form becomes recognizable through a method of variation" (178). The sense of this remark becomes clearer on the basis of *Ideas I* and the *Crisis*. By imaginary variation we can obtain inexact but pure morphological types: "roundness," for exam-

---

[138] This whole section, devoted to "Descriptive and Exact Sciences," is very important for understanding the *Origin*.

ple, *under* which is *constructed* the geometrical ideality of the "circle."[139] The notion of this operation of "substruction" is also repeated in the *Crisis*. But the type "roundness" is no less already furnished with a certain ideality; it is not to be confused with the multiplicity of natural shapes which more or less correspond to it in perception. Only an imaginative intending can attain that ideality in its pregeometrical purity. But this pure ideality is of a sensible order and must be distinguished carefully from pure geometrical ideality, which in itself is released from all sensible or imaginative intuitiveness. The imagination is what gives me the pure morphological type, and it "can transform sensible shapes only into other sensible shapes" (*C*, §9*a*, p. 25). According to Husserl, then, pure sensible ideality is situated on a premathematical level. *Once constituted,* pure mathematics will thus be accessible only to "understanding" (whose notion has no precise technical sense in Husserl); in any case, to an activity conceivable in the sense of Cartesian intellectualism, since this activity is at once freed from two homogeneous faculties, from imagination and sensibility. In some very enlightening lines concerning this in the *Crisis,* the precise content of which does not seem to be found in any other of Husserl's texts, he has written:

> *In the intuitively given surrounding world, by abstractively directing our regard to the mere spatiotemporal shapes, we experience "bodies"—not geometrical-ideal bodies but **precisely those bodies that we actually experience, with the content which is the actual content of experience**. No matter how arbitrarily we may transform these bodies in phantasy, the free and in a certain sense "ideal" possibilities we thus obtain are anything but geometrical-ideal possibilities: they are not the geometrically "pure" shapes which can be inscribed in ideal space—"pure" bodies, "pure" straight lines, "pure" planes, other "pure" figures, and the movements and deformations which occur in "pure" figures. **Thus geometrical space does not signify anything like imaginary space**. . . . (Ibid., [modified]; our emphasis)*[140]

[139] Cf. on this *Ideas I*, §75; and Notes 3 and 4 of Ricoeur in *Idées*, p. 238. We would find anticipated in the *Philosophy of Arithmetic* the principle for an analogous distinction between perceptive plurality and arithmetical plurality. On the other hand, a distinction of the same type between a certain "style" of causality or of premathematical inductivity and those of pure physics is invoked in the *Crisis* and appended texts, notably in passages devoted to Galileo.

[140] An essential difference remains, even if here he outwardly echoes Kant ("the propositions of geometry are not the results of a mere creation of our poetic imagination," *Prologomena to Any Future Metaphysics,* §13 [ET: ed. Lewis White Beck (New York: The Liberal Arts Press, 1950), p. 34]). According to Kant, geometry is not imaginary [*fantastique*] because it is grounded on the universal forms of pure sensibility, on the

Although geometrical ideality may be produced *starting* from sensible morphological ideality, this facto-historical departure point is nullified as a ground within constituted geometry. Undoubtedly, in its turn, imaginative-sensible idealization (without which geometry could not have arisen) poses some delicate problems of origin, of which Husserl is very conscious. Although this origin is the origin of what precedes and conditions geometry, it is not to be confused with the origin of geometry itself and all of its related possibilities; it only authorizes what we earlier called a *"geography."* In every phenomenological regression to beginnings, the notion of an *internal* or *intrinsic* history and sense lets us delineate some safety-catches [*crans d'arrêt*], as well as articulate, if not avoid, all *"regressus ad infinitum."* The internal sense of geometry, which provides us with a static analysis, prescribes that the question of geometry's origin stop at the *constituted* sense of what has *immediately* conditioned geometry. The source of pregeometrical idealities can be left provisionally in the dark.[141] Thus, Husserl writes: "Still, questions like that of the clarification of the origin of geometry have a closed character, such that one need not inquire beyond those prescientific materials" (172).

The problems of origin posed outside that enclosure and concerning the sense of preexact or preobjective spatiotemporality would find their

---

ideality of sensible space. But according to Husserl, on the contrary, geometrical ideality is not imaginary [*imaginaire*] because it is uprooted from *all* sensible ground in general. In accordance with Kant, it was sufficient for Husserl to be purified of empirical and material sensibility to escape empirical imagination. As for what concerns at least the *structure* of mathematical truth and cognition, if not their *origin*, Husserl remains then nearer to Descartes than to Kant. It is true for the latter, as has been sufficiently emphasized, that the concept of sensibility is no longer derived from a "sensualist" definition. We could not say this is always the case for Descartes or Husserl.

[141] Access to the origin of sensible ideality, a product of the *imagination*, would also require, then, a direct thematization of imagination as such. Now the latter, whose operative role is nevertheless so decisive, never seems to have been sufficiently inquired into by Husserl. It retains [*garde*] an ambiguous status: a derived and founded reproductive ability on the one hand, it is, on the other, the manifestation of a radical theoretical freedom. It especially makes the exemplariness of the fact emerge and hands over the sense of the fact outside of the factuality of the fact. Presented in the *Crisis* as a faculty that is homogeneous with sensibility, it simultaneously uproots morphological ideality from pure sensible reality.

It is by beginning with the direct thematization of imagination in its situation as an original *lived experience* (utilizing imagination as the operative *instrument* of all eidetics), by freely describing the phenomenological conditions for fiction, therefore for the phenomenological method, that Sartre's breakthrough [*trouée*] has so profoundly unbalanced—and then overthrown—the landscape of Husserl's phenomenology and abandoned its horizon.

place inside the new *transcendental aesthetics* which Husserl particularly contemplated in the Conclusion of *Formal and Transcendental Logic* (pp. 291–93).[142]

Paradoxically, because ideal geometrical space is not imaginary (and therefore not sensible), its ideality can be related to the total unity of the sensible world. And, for the same reason, applied geometry remains possible, going so far as to be confused in our eyes with the "true nature" that applied geometry at the same time conceals.[143] In effect, a sensible ideality, which always springs from imagination, could only give rise to an imaginary *[fantastique]* space and an imaginary *[fantastique]* science of space, to an unforeseeable and inorganic proliferation of morphological types. In that case, we could not affirm, as we legitimately and with complete security did, that "we have *not two but only one universal form of the world:* not two but only *one geometry* . . ." (*C*, §9 *c*, p. 34).

This sensible and, to a certain degree, empirical anticipation (although in comparison with facts submitted to variation, imaginative ideality of the morphological type can no longer be merely empirical) is true not only for geometrical *forms* but also for geometrical measurement. The latter comes to the fore in and through praxis: for example, "where just distribution is intended" (178). An empirical technique of measurement (in surveying, in architecture, and so forth) must necessarily belong to every prescientific culture. Husserl does not elaborate on that in the *Origin*. In the *Crisis* he seems to consider empirical measure as a stage further than sensible morphology on the path towards pure geometrical ideality. Measure initiates an advance in the sense of the univocal, intersubjective, therefore ideal-objective determination of the geometrical thing (*C*, §9*c*, p. 34).[144] Moreover, on a clearly higher or subsequent level, the arithmetization of geometry will be evoked as a new revolution within geometry. However, the origin of this science will only be more deeply buried, and its sense "emptied."[145]

[142] These few pages are very important, here in particular, for determining the architectonic situation of the *Origin*. On the sense of this "transcendental aesthetics," also cf. *CM*, §61, p. 146.

[143] "So familiar to us is the shift between a priori theory and empirical inquiry in everyday life that we usually tend not to separate the space and the spatial shapes geometry talks about from the space and spatial shapes of experiential actuality, as if they were one and the same" (*C*, §9*a*, p. 24).

[144] On surveying, see notably §9*a*, pp. 27–28. On surveying as "pregeometrical achievement," which is also "a meaning-fundament for geometry," see §9*h*, p. 49.

[145] Cf. *C*, §9*f*, pp. 44–45. Husserl speaks there of an "arithmetization of geometry" which "leads almost automatically, in a certain way, to the *emptying of its sense*"

We know, then, *a priori* that the physical thing, the body, the vague morphological and phoronomic types, the art of measure, the possibility of imaginary variation, and preexact spatiotemporality already had to be located in the cultural field that was offered "to the philosopher who did not yet know geometry but who should be conceivable as its inventor" (178).

Thus the institution of geometry could only be a *philosophical* act. Husserl, who often speaks of "Platonizing geometry" (*FTL*, Conclusion, p. 292), always assigned to this instituting act a contemporaneity of *sense* with "the school of Plato" (*Ideas I*, §9, p. 58), "Platonism" (*C*, §9, p. 23), the Greeks "guided by the Platonic doctrine of Ideas" (*ibid.*, §8, p. 21),[146] "Platonic idealism,"[147] and so forth. The philosopher is a man who inaugurates the theoretical attitude; the latter is only the spirit's radical freedom, which authorizes a move beyond finitude and opens the horizon of knowledge as that of a prehaving, i.e., of an infinite project or task *(Vorhaben)*. Thereby, the theoretical attitude makes idealization's decisive "passage to the limit" possible, as well as the constitution of the mathematical field in general. Naturally, this passage to the limit is only the going beyond every sensible and factual limit. It concerns the ideal limit of an infinite transgression, not the factual limit of the transgressed finitude.

Starting from this inaugural infinitization, mathematics cognizes new infinitizations which are so many interior revolutions. For, if the primordial infinitization opens the mathematical field to infinite fecundities for the Greeks, it no less *first* limits the apriori system of that productivity. The very content of an infinite production will be confined within an apriori system which, for the Greeks, will always be *closed*.

---

[modified]. Formal algebrization was already presented as a threat for primordial sense and the "clarity" of geometry in *Ideas I*, where the " 'pure' geometer" was defined as the one "who dispenses with the methods of algebra" (§70, p. 182).

[146] As Husserl often remarked, the allusion to Greece, to the Greek origin of philosophy and mathematics, has no external historico-empirical sense. It is the factual [*événementiel*] index of an internal *sense* of origin. Cf. on this particularly "Philosophy and the Crisis of European Humanity" (in *C*, pp. 279–80). Of course, the whole problem of a phenomenology of history supposes that the "indicative" character of such language is resolved.

[147] "Idealization and the Science of Reality—The Mathematization of Nature" (Before 1928), Abhandlung in *Krisis*, p. 291; Appendix II in *Crisis*, p. 313. In addition to this text, one of the most specific sketches from the historical perspective concerning the relation between Plato's philosophy and the advent of pure mathematics by idealization and passage to the limit has been published by R. Boehm in Beilage VII of *Erste Philosophie (1923/24)*, Vol. 1 (in *Husserliana*, Vol. 7 [The Hague: Nijhoff, 1956], pp. 327–28).

The guide here is Euclidean geometry, or rather the *"ideal Euclid,"* according to Husserl's expression, which is restricted to sense, not historical fact. Later, at the dawn of modern times, the apriori system will itself be overthrown by a new infinitization. But the latter will only take place *within* infinity as the possibility of a mathematical a priori in general. Perhaps, then, we need to distinguish between, on the one hand, infinitization as the instituting act of mathematics, i.e., as the disclosure of mathematical aprioriness itself—the possibility of mathematization in general—and, on the other hand, infinitizations as the enlargements of apriori systems. These latter would only have had to add dimensions of infinity to the a priori, but they would not concern aprioriness itself. In the *Origin,* Husserl is interested in infinitization in the first sense. That is why he *reduced* all the apriori systems of past or present geometry, in order to reach back and grasp again the origin of aprioriness itself at its source, i.e., the institutive infinitization.

Perhaps such a distinction accounts for a contradiction, pointed out by Paul Ricoeur, between the Vienna Lecture ("Philosophy and the Crisis of European Humanity") and the *Crisis* itself, which, Ricoeur notes, "goes back to Greek thought and in particular to Euclidean geometry, to assign the glory of having conceived of an infinite task of knowing. . . ."[148]

Moreover, the difference we propose to observe between the two kinds of infinity would not at all completely efface what, in the literalness of the texts, remains a flagrant opposition. Let us place side by side the two most apparently irreconcilable passages:

A)

> *Only Greek philosophy leads, by a specific development, to a science in the form of infinite theory, of which Greek geometry supplied us, for some millennia, the example and sovereign model.*
> *Mathematics—the idea of the infinite, of infinite tasks—is like a Babylonian tower: although unfinished, it remains a task full of sense, opened onto the infinite. This infinity has for its correlate the new man of infinite ends.*

And farther on:

> *Infinity is discovered, first in the form of the idealization of magnitudes, of measures, of numbers, figures, straight lines, poles, surfaces, etc. . . . . Now without its being advanced explicitly as a*

[148] Paul Ricoeur, "Husserl and the Sense of History," in *Husserl: An Analysis,* p. 161, n. 15.

*hypothesis, intutitively given nature and world are transformed into a mathematical world, the world of the mathematical natural sciences. Antiquity led the way: in its mathematics was accomplished the first discovery of both infinite ideals and infinite tasks. This becomes for all later times the guiding star of the sciences.*[149]

B)

*Of course the ancients, guided by the Platonic doctrine of Ideas, had already idealized empirical numbers, units of measurement, empirical figures in space, points, lines, surfaces, bodies; and they had transformed the propositions and proofs of geometry into ideal-geometrical propositions and proofs. What is more, with Euclidean geometry had grown up the highly impressive idea of a systemically coherent deductive theory, aimed at a most broadly and highly conceived ideal goal, resting on "axiomatic" fundamental concepts and principles, proceeding according to apodictic arguments—a totality formed of pure rationality, a totality whose unconditioned truth is available to insight and which consists exclusively of unconditioned truths recognized through immediate and mediate insight. But Euclidean geometry, and ancient mathematics in general, knows only finite tasks, a **finitely closed a priori**. Aristotelian syllogistics belongs here also, as an a priori which takes precedence over all others. Antiquity goes this far, but never far enough to grasp the possibility of the infinite task which, for us, is linked as a matter of course with the concept of geometrical space and with the concept of geometry as the science belonging to it. (C, § 8, pp. 21–22; Husserl's emphasis)*

We can note that the first of the above texts only attributes infinitization in the first sense to Greek philosophy and geometry,[150] i.e., the creative idealization of mathematics in general—a fact they will not be denied in the *Crisis*. There exists an infinity which equalizes

---

[149] [The first part of this passage is taken from "La Crise de l'humanité européenne et la philosophie," translated by Paul Ricoeur. This version (translated from Ms M III 5 II b) differs in places from the version (Ms M III 5 II a) published in the *Krisis* and translated into English (Lauer's translation of this text in the same volume that contains his translation of "PRS," *Phenomenology and the Crisis of Philosophy*, also follows the latter version). I have always cited the version in *C*, since here occurs the only significant divergence between the two texts in Derrida's use of them. The second part of the above quoted passage is found on p. 293 of *C*. Note adapted by tr.]

[150] In this respect, it can be said that, by their intention, the Vienna Lecture and the *Origin* are nearer each other than they both are to the *Crisis*. Both are interested in a proto-origin prior to the "Galilean" origin of modern times. Cf. what we said above about the reduction of the Galilean attitude.

the discovery of the aprioriness of mathematics in general and the transgression of sensible finitudes, even if the first apriori system is in itself *closed,* as the second passage states. On the basis of a finite apriori system, an infinite number of mathematical operations and transformations is already possible in that system, even if they are not infinitely creative. Above all, despite the closedness of the system, we are *within* mathematical infinity because we have definitively idealized and gone beyond the factual and sensible finitudes. The infinite infinity of the modern revolution can then be announced in the finite infinity of Antiquity's creation. While investigating the sense of what they created—mathematical aprioriness—the Greeks simply would not have investigated the sense of all the powers of infinity which were enclosed in that aprioriness and, therefore, to be sure, of the pure and infinite historicity of mathematics. That will be done only progressively and later on, by interconnecting revolutionary developments conforming to the profound historicity of mathematics and to a creativity which always proceeds by disclosure.[151]

If that were so, the contrast between the two texts would be less abrupt: one would thematize mathematical *aprioriness* and the other the apriori system or systems, or rather mathematical *systematicity.* Within the infinity opened by the Greeks, a new infinitization is produced, one which will make the previous closure appear, not as the closure paralyzing the Greeks *on the threshold* of mathematical infinity itself, but as the closure secondarily limiting them *within* the mathematical field in general. Even in the spirit of the *Crisis,* the modern infinitization will mark less an authentic upsurging than a kind of resurrection of geometry. Moreover, this self-rebirth [*renaissance à soi*] will be at the same time only a new *obliteration* of the first birth certificate. And, it must be added, the process of intra-mathematical infinitization can then be generalized *ad infinitum* and according to an accelerated rhythm.[152]

But if each infinitization is a new birth of geometry in its authentic primordial intention (which we notice still remained hidden to a certain

---

[151] On this cf. the *Crisis,* notably §8, p. 22, and §9*h*, pp. 51–52, and §71, pp. 245–46.

[152] The text taken from the *Crisis,* which does not seem to put into question ever again the "Greek" origin of mathematics as an infinite task, poses thus the difficult intra-mathematical problem of *closure,* a notion which can have multiple senses according to the contexts in which it is employed. On all these questions, we refer particularly to S. Bachelard, *A Study of Husserl's Logic,* Part I, Ch. 3, pp. 43–63. Moreover, there is also a closure of the mathematical domain in general in its ideal unity as mathematical sense, a closure within which all infinitization will have to be maintained, simply because this infinitization still concerns ideal-mathematical objectivities. About *the* mathematical system in general, Husserl speaks of "an infinite and yet self-enclosed world of ideal objectivities as a field for study" (*C,* §9*a,* p. 26 [modified]).

extent by the closure of the previous system), we may wonder if it is still legitimate to speak of *an* origin of geometry. Does not geometry have an infinite number of births (or birth certificates) in which, each time, another birth is announced, while still being concealed? Must we not say that geometry is on the way toward its origin, instead of pro- ceeding from it?

Husserl undoubtedly would agree. Telelogical sense and the sense of origin were always mutually implicated for him. Being announced in each other, they will be revealed fully only through each other at the infinite pole of history. But, then, why have geometry begin with pure idealization and exactitude? Why not have it begin with imaginative-sensible idealization and morphological typology, since exactitude is *already* anticipated there? Or, conversely, why *still* call the systems which were totally rid of concrete geometry geometrical? This type of questioning undoubtedly *relativizes* the specificity of geometrical sense as such but does not question it in itself. The geometrical *telos* is no doubt only the fragment or particular segment of a universal Telos which traverses, precedes, and goes beyond the geometrical one; but geometry's adventure is rigorously articulated or deployed in [*s'articule en*] that Telos: the adventure did not begin *as such* before the emergence of absolutely pure and nonsensible ideality; it remains the adventure–*of* geometry as long as pure ideal objectivities are confined within the field of aprioriness opened by the Greeks.[153] Then Husserl can *at one and the same time* speak of a pure sense and an internal historicity of geometry and can say, as he often does, that a universal teleology of Reason was at work in human history before the Greco-European coming to con- sciousness [*prise de conscience*], that pure ideality is announced in bound ideality, and so on. Thus, at the same time he saves the *abso- lutely* original sense or *internal* historicity of each traditional line and its "relativity" within universal historicity. In this manner he is assured of penetrating universal historicity only from within, especially if, by preference, he turns his regard to a tradition as "exemplary" as that of mathematics.

Far from being the access to some possibility that is itself ahistoric yet discovered within a history (which would in turn be transfigured by it), the openness of the infinite is only, on the contrary, the openness of history *itself,* in the utmost depths and purity of its essence. Without

---

[153] This is true, of course, only insofar as these objectivities are related, immediately or not, to spatiality in general, if geometry is considered in itself and in the strict sense; to movement in general, if kinematics is considered in itself and in the strict sense. (But Husserl often says that "geometry" is an "abbreviation" for all the objective and exact sciences of pure spatiotemporality.) But if geometry is considered in its exemplariness, this is generally true for every absolutely pure and "free" ideal objectivity.

this rift in the finite, historical humanity, or rather historical civilizations, would only claim an empirical type of socio-anthropological unity. But, as we have clearly seen: empirical history is essentially undis-
tinguishable from nonhistory.

Also, Husserl judges it no more necessary in the *Origin* than in the
Vienna Lecture or the *Crisis* to account, *historically,* for the birth of
philosophy which has conditioned that of geometry. This was the birth
of pure history. The origin of historicity *(Geschichtlichkeit)* will never be
dependent on a history *(Historie).* Although the theoretical attitude may
be secondary and intermittent on the order of factuality,[154] it would be
fruitless to describe the phenomenological and intrinsic genesis of what
precisely establishes the possibility for such a description. This does
not mean, moreover, that it is impossible or useless to try an extrinsic
and "parallel" historical approach to this subject, utilizing all the possible factual givens (geographical, economic, cultural, sociological,
psychological, and so forth) with the finest competence, the utmost
methodological security, and without yielding to causalism, atomism,
and so on. Likewise, a facto-genetic description of the most ambitious
transcendental reduction can be tried, with the help of all available
empirical tools. Such attempts would have their full value only insofar
as they would be conducted with the certainty that everything is spoken
of then *except* the reduction *itself, except* the origin of philosophy and
history *themselves* and as such. In the best of cases, we speak of what is
strictly "parallel" to them.

From the moment Husserl is given both the prescientific cultural
world *and* the philosopher as conditions for geometry's origin, the absence of all concrete description of the institutor's acts should not be
surprising. Nor disappointing. Those conditions were indispensable,
but also sufficient. Also, in some very allusive lines which add nothing
to the previous static descriptions, the sense of the inaugural operation
is exhausted. The finitudes, which the protogeometer philosopher has
at his disposal (among the highest are "bound" idealities) and which he
perceives on an infinite horizon, "as formations developed out of praxis
and thought of in terms of perfection, clearly serve only as bases for a
new sort of praxis out of which similarly named new formations grow.
It is evident in advance that this new sort of formation will be a product
arising out of an idealizing, spiritual act, one of 'pure' thinking, which
has its materials in the designated universal pregivens of this factual
humanity and human surrounding world and creates 'ideal objectivities'
out of them" (179 [modified]).

[154] On this cf. notably *EJ* §14, p. 65.

Here we are, then, as a last recourse, before an idealizing operation whose activity has never been studied for itself and whose conditions are never to be so studied, since we are dealing with a radically institutive operation. This idealization is that which, on the basis of a sensible ideality (the morphological type of "roundness," for example), makes a higher, absolutely objective, exact, and nonsensible ideality occur—the "circle," a "similarly named [but] new" formation.[155] In order to reach back and grasp again the *species* (i.e., the original aspect of sensible morphological ideality), we must constantly get free from geometrical *habits* which tend to obfuscate it. In *The Poetics of Space,* concerning the chapter entitled: "The Phenomenology of Roundness," Gaston Bachelard evokes this troublesome but necessary *deception:* "The difficulty that had to be overcome in writing this chapter was to avoid all geometrical evidence."[156]

Unlike morphological ideality, exact ideality has been produced without the essential aid of sensibility or imagination; it broke away by a leap from every descriptive mooring. Undoubtedly this leap drew its support or appeal from sensible ideality; Husserl always speaks of geometry's sensible "support," "substrate," or "basis" (*Ideas I,* §70, p. 183).[157] But these foundations are not the fundamentals ones, al-

---

[155] The same principle and notion of *substructive idealization,* but without substantial supplementary explication, is found again and again from one end to the other of Husserl's work. In particular: a) in the *LI,* I, 1, §18, p. 302. There we read among others those lines devoted to idealization and to which the *Origin* will add nothing: "The image . . . provides only a foothold for *intellectio*. It offers no genuine instance of our intended pattern, only an instance of the sort of sensuous form which is the natural starting-point for geometrical 'idealization'. In these intellectual thought-processes of geometry, the ideal of a geometrical figure is constituted, which is then expressed in the fixed meaning of the definitory expression. Actually to perform this intellectual process may be presupposed by our first formation of primitive geometrical expressions and by our application of them in knowledge, but not for their revived understanding and their continued significant use"; b) in *Ideas I,* §74, pp. 190–91; c) in "Idealization and the Science of Reality—The Mathematization of Nature" (Before 1928), Appendix II, in *C,* pp. 301–14; d) in *EJ,* §10, pp. 41–46; e) in *FTL,* §96*c,* and Conclusion, pp. 243 and 291–93; f) in *C,* §9*a* naturally, but also in §36, where in summary is said: "These categorical features of the life-world have *the same names* but are not concerned, so to speak, with the theoretical idealizations and the hypothetical substructions of the geometrician and the physicist" (p. 140; our emphasis); and g) in Appendix V: "Objectivity and the World of Experience," in *C,* pp. 343–51.

[156] *The Poetics of Space,* tr. Maria Jolas (Boston: Beacon, 1964), p. xxxv.

[157] All these formulas are also encountered in the texts we just cited. The sensible type serves as the foundation for geometry in the process of being constituted. Next, it will only serve as an illustrative "auxiliary" or "adjunct" to a geometrical activity which goes through it toward pure ideality.

though the latter ought not to make the former be forgotten. It is "pure thinking" that is responsible for the leaping advance of idealization and for geometrical truth as such. The inaugural character of the idealizing act, the radical and irruptive freedom which that act manifests, and the decisive discontinuity which uproots the act from its past conditions, all this hides the idealizing act from a genealogical description.[158]

If the earlier texts do not teach us any more about the *process* of idealization, are they more precise as to the *origin of the ability* to idealize? It does not seem so. In its most concrete determinations, the operation is always presented as a "passage to the limit." Starting from an *anticipatory* structure of intentionality, we go beyond morphological ideality toward the ideal and invariant pole of an infinite approximation.[159]

But for the intentional anticipation to leap to the infinite, it must *already* be ideal. What this idealization of anticipation at once au-

---

[158] In the same sense Gonseth notes: "The passage from the intuitive notion: *the intended line,* to the ideal notion: *the straight line,* is something completely indescribable" *(Les Mathématiques et la réalité: Essai sur la méthode axiomatique* [Paris: Librairie Felix Alcan, 1936], p. 76).

[159] To us the most specific passages concerning this seem to be the following:

A) "Geometrical concepts are *'ideal' concepts,* they express something which one cannot 'see'; their 'origin,' and therefore their content also, is essentially other than that of the *descriptive concepts* as concepts which express the essential nature of things as drawn directly from simple intuition, and not anything 'ideal.' Exact concepts have their correlates in essences, which have the character of *'Ideas' in the Kantian sense.* Over against these Ideas or ideal essences stand the *morphological essences,* as correlates of descriptive concepts.

"That ideation . . . gives ideal essences as *ideal 'limits,'* which cannot on principle be found in any sensory intuition, to which on occasion morphological essences 'approximate' more or less, without ever reaching them . . ." *(Ideas I,* §74, pp. 190–91; Husserl's emphasis).

B) The text which follows, taken from the *Crisis* (§9*a*, p. 26), is of a more genetic style. Here Husserl also shows himself more sensitive to the difficulty of a description which, he thinks, still remains to be done: "Without going more deeply into the essential interconnections involved here (which has never been done systematically and is by no means easy), we can understand that, out of the praxis of perfecting, of freely pressing toward the horizons of *conceivable (erdenklicher)* perfecting 'again and again' *(Immer-wieder),* *limit-shapes* emerge toward which the particular series of perfectings tend, as toward invariant and never attainable poles. If we are interested in these ideal shapes and are consistently engaged in determining them and in constructing new ones out of those already determined, we are 'geometers.' The same is true of the broader sphere which includes the dimension of time: we are mathematicians of the 'pure' shapes whose universal form is the coidealized form of space-time. In place of real praxis . . . we now have an *ideal praxis* of 'pure thinking' which remains exclusively within the *realm of pure limit-shapes."* Husserl's emphasis.

thorizes and prescribes is the presence for consciousness of an *Idea in the Kantian sense*. The latter is the object of an *ideation,* a name Husserl often gives to idealization and which must be distinguished from ideation as the intuition of an essence *(Wesensschau).*[160] The difference between these two ideations is: one can constitute an object as a creation, the other can determine it in an intuition. Primordial geometrical ideation, for example, brings about an essence which did not exist before the ideation. This ideation is therefore more *historical*. But once the ideal object is constituted within ready-made geometry, the *Wesensschau* regains its rights. It is not by chance that the same word designates two different operations: in both cases, the object is an irreal essence, although not at all imaginary *[fantastique]*. In constituted geometry, the *Wesensschau* only repeats the productive idealization. If the geometrical *Wesensschau* is possible only because idealizing ideation has *already* produced the geometrical object, conversely, the primordial passage-to-the-limit is possible only if guided by an essence which can always be anticipated and then "recognized," because a *truth* of pure space is in question. That is why passages to the limit are not to be done arbitrarily or aimlessly. That is why geometry is this extraordinary operation: the creation of an eidetic. It follows that geometry's infinite history will always see its unity prescribed by the eidetic structure of a region, or more precisely, by the unity of an abstract "moment" (spatiality) of a region. This unity certainly is not historical, it is empirically unchangeable. But it is only the unity *of* the infinite historical development of the eidetic called geometry. It *is nothing* outside the history of geometry itself.

Essence-limits suppose then an open horizon and the breakthrough toward the infinite of an *"immer wieder"* or an *"und so weiter,"* which is the very movement of mathematical idealization in general. If the structure of the *"again and again"* is fundamental here,[161] the privileged position of the protentional dimension of intentionality and of that of the future in the constitution of space in general must be acknowledged.

---

[160] Cf. *Idées,* §74, pp. 235–36, n. 1 of translator.

[161] On the "again and again," the iterative "over and over again," or the "and so forth" as fundamental forms of idealization, "since de facto no one can always again" [take *all* the idealizations into consideration] (*FTL,* p. 188), cf. *FTL,* §74, pp. 188–89; and S. Bachelard, *A Study of Husserl's* Logic [Part II, Ch. 3], pp. 119ff. The "and so forth," inasmuch as it belongs to the evident structure of the noema of the thing in general, had been copiously described in *Ideas I* (cf. particularly §149, pp. 379–83, which sketches on this a comparison between ideation, intuition of the Idea and of the "and so forth," and *pure intuition* in the Kantian sense, whose ideation would only be phenomenological clarification).

But in opposition to the lived space in which the indefiniteness of the adumbrations is a transcendence that essentially can never be mastered, the idealized space of mathematics allows us to go immediately to the infinite limit of what is in fact an unfinished movement. Thus, the transcendence of every lived future can be absolutely appropriated and reduced in the very gesture which frees that future for an infinite development. Mathematical space no longer knows what Sartre calls "transphenomenality." The developments of mathematical space will never *de jure* escape us; that is why it might seem more reassuring, more *our own*. But is that not also because it has become more foreign to us?

Were we to respect and to repeat these numerous mediations once again, we would thus be led back once more toward primordial temporality. The "again and again" which hands over exactitude inscribes the advent of mathematics within the ethico-teleological prescription of the infinite task. And the latter is grounded, then, in the movement of primordial phenomenological temporalization, in which the Living Present of consciousness holds itself as the primordial Absolute only in an indefinite protention, animated and unified by the Idea *(in the Kantian sense)* of the total flux of lived experience.[162] As we have seen, the Living Present is the phenomenological absolute out of which I cannot go because it is that in which, toward which, and starting from which every going out is effected. The Living Present has the irreducible originality of a Now, the ground of a Here, only if it retains (in order to be distinguishable from it) the past Now *as such,* i.e., as the past pre-

---

[162] Cf. the important §83 of *Ideas I*: "Apprehension of the Unitary Stream of Experience as 'Idea,'" pp. 220–22. This Idea is the common root of the theoretical and the ethical. Finite and objective ethical values are undoubtedly constituted and grounded, according to Husserl, by a theoretical subject. This point has been very accurately brought to light by Emmanuel Levinas (*The Theory of Intuition in Husserl's Phenomenology,* tr. André Orianne [Evanston: Northwestern University Press, 1973], pp. 133–34) and by Gaston Berger (*The* Cogito *in Husserl's Philosophy*, pp. 80–82). But on a deeper level, theoretical consciousness is nothing other, in itself and thoroughly understood, than a practical consciousness, the consciousness of an infinite task and the site of absolute value for itself and for humanity as rational subjectivity. Cf., for example: "Philosophy as Mankind's Self-Reflection," Appendix IV in *C*, pp. 335–41. There we read: mankind "is rational in seeking to be rational . . . reason allows for no differentiation into 'theoretical,' 'practical,' 'aesthetic' . . . being human is teleological being and an ought-to-be . . ." (p. 341). Also cf. *CM*, §41, p. 88. The unity of Reason in all its usages would manifest *itself* fully for Husserl in the theoretical project (rather than in the practical function, as would be the case for Kant). On this point, a systematic confrontation between Husserl and Kant on the one hand and Husserl and Fichte on the other would be necessary.

sent of an absolute origin, instead of purely and simply succeeding it in an objective time. But this retention will not be possible without a protention which is its very form: first, because it retains a Now which was itself an original project, itself retaining another project, and so on; next, because the retention is always the essential modification of a Now always in suspense, always tending toward a next Now. The Absolute of the Living Present, then, is only the indefinite Maintenance [the Nowness] of this double enveloping. But this Maintenance itself appears *as such,* it is the *Living* Present, and it has the *phenomenological* sense of a *consciousness* only if the unity of this movement is given as *indefinite* and if its sense of indefiniteness is *announced* in the Present (i.e., if the openness of the infinite future is, as such, a possibility *experienced* [*vécue*] as sense and right). Death will not be comprehended as sense but as a fact extrinsic to the movement of temporalization. The unity of infinity, the condition for that temporalization, must then be *thought,* since it is announced without appearing and without being contained in a Present. This thought unity, which makes the phenomenalization of time as such possible, is therefore always the Idea in the Kantian sense which never phenomenalizes itself.

The unfinishedness of Husserl's reflections on primordial temporality—their richness, but also, as is said, the dissatisfaction they left their author—have long been underscored. If the manuscripts of *Group C* thus justly fascinate Husserl's commentators, is that not because these manuscripts touch on the most profound region of phenomenological reflection, where darkness risks being no longer the provision of appearing or the field which offers itself to phenomenal light, but the forever nocturnal source of the light itself? Are not the Idea and the idealizing ability, which exemplarily occupy us here as the origin of mathematics, kept back in this essential darkness?

The Idea in the Kantian sense, the regulative pole for every infinite task, assumes diverse but analogous functions that are decisive at several points along Husserl's itinerary. Paul Ricoeur very precisely recognizes in the Idea "the mediating role between consciousness and history."[163] Now, while completely marking it with the highest and most constant teleological dignity, while completely granting a believing attention to what it conditions, Husserl never made the Idea *itself* the *theme* of a phenomenological description. He never directly defined its type of evidence within phenomenology, whose *"principle of all principles"* and archetypal form of evidence is the immediate presence of the

---

[163] "Husserl and the Sense of History," in *Husserl: An Analysis,* p. 145.

thing itself "in person." Implicitly that means: of the phenomenally defined or definable thing, therefore the *finite* thing. (The motif of finitude has perhaps more affinity with the latter implication than it first seems to have with phenomenology's principle of principles.[164] Phenomenology would thus be *stretched* between the *finitizing* consciousness of its *principle* and the *infinitizing* consciousness of its final *institution,* the *Endstiftung* indefinitely deferred [*différée*] in its content but always evident in its regulative value.)

It is not by chance that there is no phenomenology of the Idea. The latter cannot be given in person, nor determined in an evidence, for it is only the possibility of evidence and the openness of "seeing" itself; it is only *determinability* as the horizon for every intuition in general, the invisible milieu of seeing analogous to the diaphaneity of the Aristotelian Diaphanous, an elemental third, but the one source of the seen and the visible: "by diaphanous I mean what is visible, and yet not visible in itself, but rather owing its visibility to the colour of something else." It is thanks to this alone "that the colour of a thing is seen" (*De Anima,* 418b).[165] If there is nothing to say about the Idea *itself,* it is because the

---

[164] An essential finitude can appear in phenomenology in another sense: to recognize that the transcendental reduction must remain an eidetic reduction in order to avoid empirical idealism is to recognize that transcendental idealism does not proceed, even in the Kantian tradition itself, without the affirmation of the philosopher's radical finitude. This necessity for the transcendental reduction to remain so is the necessity to make the absolute and primordial ground of the sense of being appear in a region (the region "consciousness" unified by an *ego* and an Idea), i.e., in a region which, even were it the *Ur-Region,* is no less a domain of determined existents. The unitary ground of all regions can only appear in one region; it can only then be concealed under a type of stanchion [*étance*] determined the very moment it appears as the ground. Without this occultation, philosophical discourse would renounce all eidetic rigor, i.e., all sense. The eidetic limitation is then indispensable, and the reduction receives its true sense which, contrary to appearances, is that of prudence and critical humility. Without this disappearing of the ground necessary for appearing itself, without this limitation within a certain regionalness, without this reduction that Heidegger implicitly reproaches him with, Husserl thinks that philosophy even more surely falls back into regionalness; better still, into empirical regionalness—here, for example, under the form of anthropological factuality, Husserl thinks, that of *Dasein.* On this point, the dialogue between Husserl and Heidegger could go on indefinitely, except considering that the reduction is always already supposed as the essential possibility of *Dasein,* and that, conversely, consciousness as transcendental source is not a "region" in the strict sense, even if the necessity of an eidetic language has to consider it as such. For both Husserl and Heidegger, the complicity of appearing and of concealing seems in any case primordial, essential, and definitive.

[165] [ET: *On the Soul,* tr. J. A. Smith, in *The Basic Works of Aristotle,* ed. Richard McKeon (New York: Random House, 1941), p. 568 (modified).]

Idea is that starting from which something in general can be said. Its own particular presence, then, cannot depend on a phenomenological type of evidence. Despite the multiplicity of references to the Idea in Husserl's last writings, the most precise text concerning its type of evidence is found, it seems, in the chapter of *Ideas I* devoted to the phenomenology of Reason (§143, pp. 366–67). Concerning the adequate givenness of the transcendent thing, we find there a problem analogous to that of the total unity of the immanent flux in which, this time, each lived experience is adequately given. Although the transcendent thing belonging to Nature cannot be given "with complete determinancy and with similarly complete intuitability in any limited finite consciousness," "*as Idea* (in the Kantian sense), [*its*] *complete givenness is . . . prescribed . . .*" (*ibid.*, p. 366).

This Idea of the infinite determinability of the same X—moreover, as well, that of the world in general—"designat[es] through its essential nature a *type of evidence that is its own*" (*ibid.*, p. 367 [modified]).[166] But this evidence of the Idea as regulative possibility is absolutely exceptional in phenomenology: it has no proper content, or rather it is not evidence of the Idea's content. It is evidence only insofar as it is *finite*, i.e., here, *formal*, since the content of the infinite Idea is absent and is denied to every intuition. "The idea of an infinity essentially motivated is not itself an infinity; the evidence that this infinity is intrinsically incapable of being given does not exclude but rather demands the transparent givenness of the *Idea* of this infinity" (*ibid.* [modified]).

In the Idea of infinity, there is determined evidence only of the Idea, but not of that of which it is the Idea. The Idea is the pole of a pure intention, empty of every determined object. It alone reveals, then, the being of the intention: *intentionality* itself.

Thus, for once, nothing appears in a specific evidence. What does appear is only the regulative possibility of appearing and the finite certainty of infinite phenomenological determinability, i.e., a certainty without a corresponding evidence. By definition, nothing can be added to this formal determination of the Idea. The latter, as the infinite determinability of X, is only *relation with an object*. It is, in the broadest sense, *Objectivity* itself.

In his article on "Kant and Husserl," Paul Ricoeur writes: "the

---

[166] In *FTL,* Husserl also evokes "this phenomenologically clarifiable infinite anticipation (which, *as* an infinite anticipation, has an evidence of its own)" (§16*c*, n. 1, p. 62). But, at that point, Husserl no longer goes beyond the promise or suggestion made in the passage. Moreover, at the end of this note he refers to *Ideas I.*

distinction, fundamental in Kant . . . between *intention* and *intuition*"
is "totally unknown in Husserl."[167] In fact, such a distinction is never
thematic in Husserl. No doubt, an intention in which nothing is given
cannot have, as such, a phenomenological character, and Husserl cannot concretely describe it; at least not in its content, for the intention's
form is a concrete and lived evidence, which is not the case in Kant.
Accordingly, *phenomenology* cannot be grounded as such in itself, nor
can it *itself* indicate its own proper limits. But is not the certainty
(without a materially determined evidence) of the infinite determinability of X or of the object in general an intention without intuition, an
empty intention which both grounds and is distinguished from every
determined phenomenological intuition? Is not the same true for any
consciousness of the infinite task and for teleological certainty under all
its forms? Assuredly, then, this intentional pure sense [*sens pur d'intention*], this *intentionality,* in itself is the last thing that a phenomenology
can directly describe otherwise than in its finite acts, intuitions, results,
or objects; but, without wanting or being able to describe it, Husserl
nevertheless recognizes, distinguishes, and *posits* this intentionality as
the highest source of value. He locates the *space* where consciousness
notifies itself of the Idea's prescription and thus is recognized as
transcendental consciousness through the sign of the infinite: this space
is the *interval* between the Idea of infinity in its formal and finite (yet
concrete) evidence and the infinity itself of which there is the Idea. It is
on the basis of this horizon-certainty that the historicity of sense and the
development of Reason are set free.

[167] "Kant and Husserl," in *Husserl: An Analysis,* pp. 175–201. In this very dense
article, Ricoeur defines Husserlianism as the completion of a latent phenomenology and
the reduction of an ontological disquietude, both of which animate Kantianism; of these
he has said that "Husserl *did* phenomenology, but Kant *limited* and *founded* it" (p. 201).
In this way the formidable and decisive problems of the Fifth Cartesian Meditation are
taken up again in a Kantian reading: the *practical* determination of the person by *respect*
must precede and condition a theoretical constitution which, by itself alone, cannot have
access to the *alter ego* as such. Also cf. on this *Fallible Man,* tr. Charles Kelbley
(Chicago: Henry Regnery, 1965), pp. 105–21. As for the relation with an object which
preoccupies us here, Ricoeur writes more particularly: "The key to the problem is the
distinction, fundamental in Kant but totally unknown in Husserl, between *intention* and
*intuition*. Kant radically separates from one another the relation to something and the
intuition of something. An object = X is an intention without intuition. This distinction
subtends that of thinking and knowing and maintains the agreement as well as the tension
between them" (p. 189).
   Here we naturally leave aside those various possibilities, so often invoked by Husserl,
of empty intentions, like the symbolic intentions that are deceived or not fulfilled, and so
on. They could not be said to be deprived of intuition in *general*. Their emptiness is
circumscribed, in that they always bear reference to a determined but absent intuition.

Perhaps this helps us to comprehend why the Idea in the Kantian sense and, here, the mathematical idealization which supposes it could only be *operative* and *not thematic* concepts.[168] This phenomenological nonthematization obeys a profound and irreducible necessity. The Idea is the basis on which a phenomenology is set up in order to achieve the final intention of philosophy. That a phenomenological determination of the Idea itself may be radically impossible from then on signifies perhaps that phenomenology cannot be reflected in a phenomenology of phenomenology, and that its *Logos* can never appear as such, can never be given in a philosophy of seeing, but (like all Speech) can only be heard or understood through the visible. The *Endstiftung* of phenomenology (phenomenology's ultimate critical legitimation: i.e., what its sense, value, and right tell us about it), then, never directly measures up to a phenomenology. At least this *Endstiftung* can give access to itself in a philosophy, insofar as it is *announced* in a concrete phenomenological evidence, in a concrete *consciousness* which is made *responsible* for it despite the finitude of that consciousness, and insofar as it grounds transcendental historicity and transcendental intersubjectivity. Husserl's phenomenology starts from this *lived anticipation* as a radical responsibility (something which, when considered literally, does not seem to be the case with the Kantian critique).

## XI

The presence of the Idea alone, therefore, authorizes the leap to pure ideality by the figure-limit and the advent of mathematics, a fact that could give rise to doubts about that origin's specific historicity. Are we not confronted with an ahistorical Idea on the one hand and its insertion in the event or historical fact on the other? In which case, we would strike the snags that Husserl precisely wants to avoid and would miss our target—phenomenological history. What we truly need is to investigate the sense of the Idea's profound historicity.

Undoubtedly the Idea and the Reason hidden in history and in man as *"animal rationale"* are eternal. Husserl often says this. But this eternity is *only* a historicity. It is the *possibility of* history itself. Its supratemporality—compared with empirical temporality—is only an omnitemporality. The Idea, like Reason, is *nothing* outside the history

[168] We refer here to the very enlightening distinction proposed by Fink in his lecture, already cited, on "Les Concepts opératoires dans la phénoménologie de Husserl." [See note 66 above.]

in which it *displays* itself, i.e., in which (in one and the same movement) it discloses and lets itself be threatened.

Since the Idea is nothing outside history but is the *sense of* all history, only a historico-transcendental subjectivity can be made responsible for it. Thus, in the *Cartesian Meditations* (I, §4), Husserl speaks of disclosing the final sense *(Zwecksinn)* of science as a *"noematic phenomenon."* In transcendental subjectivity's disclosure of the Idea, *progressiveness* is not an extrinsic contingency that affects the Idea but the imperative prescription of its essence.[169] The Idea is not an Absolute that *first* exists in the plenitude of its essence and then descends into history or becomes disclosed in a subjectivity whose acts would not be intrinsically indispensable to it.[170] If that were true, all transcendental historicity could be said to be only an "empirical history . . . utilized as what reveals essential interconnections."[171] But these essential interconnections would be impossible, they would be nothing without a transcendental subjectivity and its transcendental historicity. The Absolute of the Idea as the Telos of an infinite determinability is the Absolute *of* intentional historicity. The *of* designates neither a merely objective nor a merely subjective genitive: the "of" concerns neither an independent, objective Absolute that is disclosed in an intention which is relative to that Absolute, waits for it, and conforms to it; nor does the "of" concern a subjective Absolute which creates and assimilates sense into its own interiority. Rather, this "of" concerns the intentional Absolute of *Objectivity,* the pure relation with an object—a relation in which subject and object are reciprocally engendered and governed. If the *of* announces neither an objective nor a subjective genitive, that is because it concerns the Absolute *of genitivity* itself as

[169] That the Idea may not be immediately graspable in its evidence is, in any case, the sign of its profound historicity. The expanded title of "Philosophy as Mankind's Self-Reflection" is: "Philosophy as Mankind's Self-Reflection; the Self-Realization of Reason through Stages of Development Requires as its Own Function the Stages of Development of this Self-Reflection" (see "La Philosophie comme prise de conscience de l'humanité," tr. Paul Ricoeur, in *Deucalion*, 3: *Vérité et Liberté* [Cahiers de Philosophie], ed. Jean Wahl [Neuchatel: Edition de la Baconnière, October 1950], p. 116).

[170] Husserl rigorously distinguishes *Idea* from *eidos* (cf. *Ideas I,* Introd., p. 42). The Idea, then, is not essence. From which the difficulty, already indicated, of an *intuitive grasp* or *evidence* of what is neither an existent nor an essence. But it is also necessary to say of the Idea that it has *no* essence, for it is only the openness of the horizon for the emergence and determination of every essence. As the invisible condition of *evidence*, by preserving the *seen,* it loses any reference to *seeing* indicated in *eidos,* a notion from which it nevertheless results in its mysterious Platonic focus. The Idea can only be *understood* [or *heard: entendre*].

[171] Jean Cavaillès, *Sur la Logique,* p. 77.

the pure possibility of a genetic relation: the *of* can mark the subject's, *as well as* the object's, genealogically secondary and dependent status; then, through the very openness of its indetermination, it can mark their primordial interdependence. If that is clearly the case, why should we choose, as Cavaillès thought, between an "absolute logic" and a "transcendental logic" (*Sur la Logique,* p. 77), or between "a consciousness of progress" and a "progress of consciousness" (*ibid.,* p. 78)? All the more so, since the *dialectical* genesis that Cavaillès opposes to the "activity" of Husserlian consciousness is described precisely and copiously by Husserl on various levels, although the word is never mentioned. We have seen how much this "activity" of consciousness was both anterior and posterior to passivity; that the movement of primordial temporalization (the ultimate ground of all constitution) was dialectical through and through; and that (like every dialectic wants) this movement was only the dialectic between the dialectical (the indefinite mutual and irreducible implication of protentions and retentions) and the nondialectical (the absolute and concrete identity of the Living Present, the universal form of all consciousness). If the Absolute of transcendental history is indeed, as Husserl says in the *Origin,* the "vital movement of the coexistence and the interweaving *(des Miteinander und Ineinander)* of primordial formations and sedimentations of sense *(Sinnbildung und Sinnsedimentierung)*" (cited, p. 109 above), then the creative activity of sense implies in itself a passivity regarding constituted and sedimented sense—a sense which appears and acts as such only within the project of a new creativity, and so forth. What Cavaillès judges impossible or "difficult to admit for phenomenology—where the motive for research and the ground of objectivities are rightly the connection to a creative subjectivity" (*Sur la Logique,* p. 65)[172]—is precisely what Husserl describes in the *Origin,* each time the theme of sedimentation is the focus of his reflection. To again take up Cavaillès' terms, Husserl shows exactly that a subjectivity "normed" in its Present by a constituted objective sense (which is therefore its "absolute logic") "fastens" its "norms" to a "higher subjectivity," i.e., to *itself,* in the creative movement by which it goes beyond itself and produces a new sense, and so on. This new sense will also be the moment of a *higher* sense-investigation in which the past sense, sedimented and retained first in a sort of objectivist attitude, will be reawakened in its dependent relation to living sub-

---

[172] Cavaillès, who then referred above all to *Ideas I* and to *FTL,* moreover added: "Perhaps the last phenomenological investigations at least permit such a bluntly posed dilemma to be contested" (p. 65).

jectivity. Husserl never seems to have thought that this was "to abuse the singularity of the absolute—to reserve for it the coincidence between the constituting and the constituted moments" *(ibid.)*. For him this coincidence is simply nothing but the absolute unity of sense's *movement,* i.e., the unity of the noncoincidence and of the indefinite coimplication of the constituted and constituting moments *in the absolute identity* of a Living Present that dialectically projects and maintains *itself.*

Of course, all this remains paradoxical and contradictory as long as we continue to consider—implicitly or not—the Idea as *some thing* and Reason as an *ability*. We must constantly return, then:

1. To Husserl's concrete descriptions concerning the noema's being non-really included in consciousness, concerning the ideality of noematic sense (an includedness which is neither a subject nor an object, and therefore *is nothing but* the object's Objectivity, the appearing of its "as such" *for* a consciousness), and concerning the nonimaginary [*non fantastique*] irreality of the *eidos* (an irreality which is *nothing other than* the sense and possibility *of* factual reality to which it is always related, immediately or not, as the rigorous prescription of the *eidos'* essential mode of appearing). If we admit for just one instant, even were it an irreducible presumption, that there is in Husserl what perhaps there was not even in Plato (except in the literalness of his myths and pedagogy)—namely, a "Platonism" of the *eidos* or the Idea—then the whole phenomenological enterprise, especially when it concerns history, becomes a *novel*. The Idea is still less an existent than the *eidos,* if that is possible; for the *eidos* is an object that is determinable and accessible to a finite intuition. The Idea is not. It is always "beyond being" *(epekeina tēs ousias)*. As the Telos of the infinite determinability of being, it is but being's openness to the light of its own phenomenality, it is the light of light, the sun of the visible sun, a hidden sun which shows without being shown. And it is no doubt what a Plato muted by Platonism tells us about.

2. To Husserl's notion of Reason. Even if certain expressions at times might suggest this, "hidden Reason" is not an ability concealed in the shadows of a historical subjectivity or in the subworld [*arrière-monde*] of becoming.[173] Reason is not some eternity at work in history:

---

[173] Likewise, the transcendental *Ego* in the phenomenological sense *has no other* content *but* the empirical ego and, further, no real content of its own, although it is not the abstract *form* of a content either, as indeed might some falsely posed problems about this suggest. In its most radical moment, every transcendental reduction gives access to a

first because there is no history without Reason, i.e., no pure transmission of sense as the tradition of truth; then because (reciprocally) there is no Reason without history, i.e., without the concrete and instituting acts of transcendental subjectivity, without its objectifications and sedimentations. Now when we speak of Reason hidden in humankind, it is difficult to get rid of the psychological phantom of faculty or ability; when we speak of Reason hidden in history, the imaginative schema of noumenal substance is hard to efface. If we confine ourselves to these speculative prejudices, either history would only have an empirical and extrinsic signification, or else Reason would only be a myth. Once more we would have to choose between Reason and History. Yet very early, in his criticism of psychologism and in the "return to the things themselves" as the advent of "true positivism," Husserl urged getting rid of the spectrum of the soul's faculties and all the vestiges of classic substantialisms.

If Reason is but the essential structure of the transcendental *ego* and the transcendental *we*, it *is*, like them, historical through and through.[174] Conversely, historicity, as such, *is* rational through and through. But *being*, which articulates Reason and History in relation to each other, is a *"sense,"* a teleological ought-to-be which constitutes being as movement. The last pages of the *Origin* are engaged in this problem. "Do we not stand here before the great and profound problem-horizon of Reason, the same Reason that functions in every man, the *animal rationale*, no matter how primitive he is?" (180 [modified]).

Each type of factual humanity has this essence of *animal rationale*. Each type, Husserl continues, has "a root in the essential structure of what is universally human, through which a teleological Reason running throughout all historicity announces itself. With this is revealed a set of problems in its own right related to the totality of history and to the total sense which ultimately gives it its unity" (180 [modified]).

---

thoroughly *historical* subjectivity. In a letter of November 16, 1930, Husserl writes: "For, with the transcendental reduction, I attained, I am convinced, concrete and real subjectivity in the ultimate sense in all the fullness of its being and life, and in this subjectivity, universal constituting life (and not simply theoretical constituting life): absolute subjectivity in its historicity" (letter published by A. Diemer, French tr. Alexandre Lowit and Henri Colombié, in "La Phénoménologie de Husserl comme métaphysique," *Les Etudes Philosophiques*, NS 9 [1954], p. 36—hereafter cited as Diemer).

[174] *"Reason is not an accidental de facto ability,* not a title for possible accidental matters of fact, but rather a title for an *all-embracing essentially necessary structural form belonging to all transcendental subjectivity"* (*CM,* §23, p. 57).

Like the first geometrical act which supposes it, the first *philosophical* act is only the sense-investigation of this historical rationality *"in the constant movement of self-elucidation."*[175] Teleological Reason already occupied civilizations [*l'humanité dans ses types empiriques*] before the philosophical sense-investigation (a sense-investigation which awakened Reason to itself) and announced the pure sense of historicity, i.e., the very sense *of* Reason, to history. The sense-investigation of what was already there marks a rupture and, consequently, a radical and creative origin.[176] Every *self*-awakening [*naissance à soi*] of a latent intention is a rebirth. Having arrived at itself, philosophical Reason can thus exercise only the "archontic" function of beginning and prescription ("Philosophy and the Crisis of European Humanity," in *C,* p. 289). Insofar as the radical philosopher complies with the *demand* of the Logos, he must *prescribe* [*commander*]; insofar as he responds to and is responsible for it, he assumes the responsibility for a *mandate*. Only in this sense does Husserl define him as a *"functionary of mankind"* [*C,* §7, p. 17].

But what is the *self (selbst)* of this self-elucidation *(Selbsterhellung)?* Is human transcendental consciousness only the place of reflexive articulation, i.e., the *mediation* of a Logos retaking possession of *itself* through this consciousness? Certain manuscripts of the last period might suggest this, ones according to which the "absolute Logos" would be "beyond transcendental subjectivity."[177] But if this "be-

---

[175] "Thus philosophy is nothing other than rationalism, through and through, but it is rationalism differentiated within itself according to the different stages of the movement of intention and fulfillment; it is *ratio in the constant movement of self-elucidation (Selbsterhellung),* begun with the first breakthrough of philosophy into mankind, whose innate reason was previously in a state of concealment, of nocturnal obscurity" ("Philosophy as Mankind's Self-Reflection," in *C,* p. 338).

[176] "Just as man and even the Papuan represent a new stage of animal nature, i.e., as opposed to the beast, so philosophical reason represents a new stage of human nature and its reason" ("Philosophy and the Crisis of European Humanity," in *C,* p. 290; also cf. pp. 298–99).

[177] Cf. E III, 4, p. 60: "The absolute *polar ideal* Idea, that of an absolute in a new sense, of an absolute which is situated beyond the world, beyond man, beyond transcendental subjectivity: it is the absolute Logos, the absolute truth . . . as *unum, verum, bonum* . . ." (Diemer, p. 39).

If the Idea is thought here to have a transcendental sense and, as we will see in a moment, is "beyond" only compared with the *constituted* moment of transcendental subjectivity, we can observe that Husserl profoundly recuperates the original scholastic sense of the transcendental *(unum, verum, bonum,* etc., as the transcategorical of Aristotelian logic) over and above its Kantian meaning, but also in a development of the Kantian enterprise.

yond" designates only a teleological transcendence, it very clearly cannot deprive *historical* transcendental subjectivity of the absolute of the *Self;* because, since the Logos always has the form of a Telos, its transcendence would not be real transcendence but the ideal Pole for bringing about transcendental subjectivity *itself*. Other passages suggest this, passages which, without any doubt, more literally conform to all of Husserl's most lasting intentions.[178]

The fragments which mention God are marked with the same apparent ambiguity. God is no longer invoked, as for example in *Ideas I* (§44, p. 125, and §79, p. 210), only as the exemplary model and limit of all consciousness of impossibility in the proof of an eidetic truth, the latter being first what God himself could not call into question. God is no longer designated as the transcendent principle—and consequently also "reduced" in *Ideas I* (§58, pp. 157–58)—of every universal *factual* teleology, either of Nature or the spirit, i.e., of history. Divine consciousness, which reveals the intangibility of constituted essences, is a fictional content and the directing Telos for the real universe. As such, it is a factuality. The reduction of God as factual being and factual consciousness sets free the signification of transcendental divinity, such as it appears in the last writings. The ambiguity we announced a moment ago concerns precisely the relation of the transcendental Absolute as divinity and the transcendental Absolute as historical subjectivity. In its transcendental sense, God is sometimes designated as the one toward which "I am on the way" and "who speaks in us," at other times as what "is nothing other than the Pole."[179] At times the Logos expresses *itself through* a transcendental history, at other times it is only the absolute polar authenticity *of* transcendental historicity *itself*. In the first case, transcendental phenomenology would be only the most rigorous *language* of a speculative metaphysics or an absolute idealism. In the second case, the concepts borrowed from metaphysics would have only a *metaphorical* and indicative sense, which would not essentially affect the original purity of phenomenology as transcendental idealism. In the first case, the essential and present plenitude of an infinity would

---

[178] In the same fragment (Diemer, p. 40), the transcendence of the Logos is defined as a transcendental norm, "the infinitely distant Pole, the Idea of an absolutely perfect transcendental omni-community."

[179] K III, p. 106 (Diemer, p. 47). [Derrida translates his first cited phrase from the German found in Diemer on p. 48 rather than quoting the French given on p. 47.] In this sense, the Pole as "beyond" is always *beyond for the Self* of transcendental consciousness. It is *its own* beyond. It will never be a real transcendence: "the path which starts from the Ego . . . is *its own* path [our emphasis], but all these paths lead to the same pole, situated beyond the world and man: God" *(ibid.).*

be *unfolded* only in a historical discursiveness from which it would let itself be *derived*. In the second case, infinity would be only the indefinite *openness* to truth and to phenomenality for a subjectivity that is always finite in its factual being.

We could be no more unfaithful to Husserl than by seeing a dilemma here. To do so would surely be to strand ourselves in a speculative attitude (in the pejorative sense that Husserl always assigned to this). The phenomenological attitude is first an availability of attention for the future of a truth which is always already announced. Instead of frantically investigating the options, we must strive toward the necessarily *single* root of every dilemma. Does the sense of transcendental historicity make *itself* understood [or heard] *through* that historicity, like the Logos which is at the beginning? Is God, on the contrary, only the final fulfillment situated at the infinite, the name for the horizon of horizons, and the *Entelechy* of transcendental historicity itself?[180] The two at once, on the basis of a still deeper unity, such perhaps is the only possible response to the question of historicity. God speaks and passes *through constituted* history, he is *beyond* in relation to constituted history and all the constituted moments of transcendental life. But he is *only* the Pole *for itself* of *constituting* historicity and *constituting* historical transcendental subjectivity. The dia-historicity or the meta-historicity of the divine Logos only traverses and goes beyond "Fact" as the "ready-made" of history, yet the Logos is *but* the pure movement of its own historicity.

This situation of the Logos is profoundly analogous—and not by chance—to that of every ideality (such as our analysis of *language* has enabled us to specify this concept). Ideality is *at once* supratemporal and omnitemporal, and Husserl qualifies it sometimes in one fashion, sometimes in the other, according to whether or not he relates it to factual temporality. Only then can we say that pure sense, the ideality of ideality, which is *nothing other than* the appearing of being, is *at once* supratemporal (Husserl also often says timeless [*in-temporel*]) and omnitemporal, or again that "*supratemporality implies omnitemporality,*" the latter itself being only "*a mode of temporality*" (*EJ*, §64 *c*, p. 261 [modified]). Are not supratemporality and omnitemporality also the characteristics of *Time itself*? Are they not the characteristics of the Living Present, which is the absolute concrete Form of phenomenological temporality and the primordial Absolute of all transcendental life?[181]

---

[180] F I, 24, p. 68 (Diemer, p. 47: "God is the Entelechy . . .").

[181] "Die urzeitliche, überzeitliche 'Zeitlichkeit,' " Husserl says, speaking of "my Living Present" (C 2 III, 1932, pp. 8–9).

The hidden temporal unity of "dia"-, "supra"-, or "in"-temporality on the one hand and of *omni*temporality on the other is the unitary ground of all the significations [*instances*] dissociated by the various reductions: factuality and essentiality, worldliness and nonworldliness, reality and ideality, *empeiria* and transcendentality. This unity, as temporality's temporal unity for every *Geschehen,* for every history as the assemblage of what happens in general, is historicity itself.

*If there is any history,* then historicity can be only the passage of Speech [*Parole*], the pure tradition of a primordial Logos toward a polar Telos. But since there can be nothing outside the pure historicity of that passage, since there is no Being which has sense outside of this historicity or escapes its infinite horizon, since the Logos and the Telos *are* nothing outside the *interplay (Wechselspiel)* of their reciprocal inspiration, this signifies then that the *Absolute is Passage.* Traditionality is what circulates from one to the other, illuminating one by the other in a movement wherein consciousness discovers its path in an indefinite reduction, always already begun, and wherein every adventure is a change of direction [*conversion*] and every return to the origin an audacious move toward the horizon. This movement is also *Danger(ous) as the Absolute* [*l'Absolu d'un Danger*]. For if the light of sense is only through Passage, that is because the light can also be lost on the way. Like speech, light can be lost only in the inauthenticity of a *language* and by the abdication of a speaking being. In that respect, phenomenology as Method of Discourse is first of all *Selbstbesinnung* and *Verantwortung,* the free resolution to "take up one's own sense" (or regain consciousness [*reprendre son sens*]), in order to make oneself accountable, through speech, for an imperiled pathway.[182] This speech is historical, because it is always already a *response.* Responsibility here means shouldering a word one hears spoken [*une parole entendue*], as well as taking on oneself the transfer of sense, in order to look after its advance. In its most radical implications, then, Method is not the neutral preface or *preambulatory* exercise of thought. Rather, it is thought itself in the consciousness of its complete historicity.

[182] Since *The Idea of Phenomenology* [tr. William P. Alston and George Nakhnikain (The Hague: Nijhoff, 1973)] (cf. [Lecture I], pp. 18–19), Husserl's entire itinerary confirms the essence of phenomenology in its fundamental discovery, that of the transcendental reduction as the essence of Method, in the richest and perhaps most enigmatic sense of this word. Husserl says the transcendental reduction is "the Proto-Method of all philosophical methods" (C 2 II; S, 7; Diemer, p. 36). On the sense of phenomenology as Method, see particularly Beilage XIII: "Foreword to the Continuation of the Crisis," in *K,* pp. 435–45. [A French translation is presented by H. Dussort in *Revue Philosophique de France et de l'Etranger,* 149 (1959), pp. 447–62. Some passages are translated in *C,* p. 102, and pp. xxviii ff.]

All this rigorously develops the discovery of intentionality. The latter is also nothing but the Absolute of a living Movement without which neither its end nor its origin would have any chance of appearing. Intentionality is traditionality. At its greatest depth—i.e., in the pure movement of phenomenological temporalization as the going out from self to self of the Absolute of the Living Present—intentionality is the root of historicity. If that is so, we do not have to ask ourselves *what* is the sense of historicity. In all the significations of this term, historicity is *sense*.

Provided we respect its *phenomenological* value, such an assertion does not transgress sense itself, i.e., history's *appearing* and the *possibility* of its appearing. Such an assertion does not mix transcendental idealism and speculative metaphysics. Instead, it marks the moment phenomenology can be articulated, without confusion, with a "philosophy" posing the question of Being or History. This "ontological" question ("ontological" in the non-Husserlian sense of the term, which alone can be, and today often is, opposed to Husserl's phenomenological ontology) cannot stem from a phenomenology as such. But we do not believe either that this question can ever, *in philosophical discourse, simply* precede transcendental phenomenology as its presupposition or latent ground. On the contrary, this question would mark within philosophy in general the moment wherein phenomenology terminates as the philosophical propaedeutic for every philosophical *decision*—a moment conceived moreover by Husserl. Since this propaedeutic is always announced as infinite, that *moment* is not a factuality but an ideal sense, a right which will always remain under phenomenological jurisdiction, a right that phenomenology alone can exercise by explicitly anticipating the end of its itinerary.

We need to conclude this propaedeutic de jure or anticipate its factual end, so that we may pass from the question *"how"* to the question *"why"*—to know of what we speak. It is in this respect that all philosophical discourse must derive its authority from phenomenology. We must exhaust de jure the question of historicity's sense and of historicity as sense, i.e., of the *possibility of* historical factuality appearing, so that we can make full sense of the following questions: *Is there, and why is there, any historical factuality?* These two questions are irreducibly interrelated. The "why" can emerge only from the *possible* (in the metaphysical or ontological sense, and not in the phenomenological sense) nonbeing of historical factuality; and nonbeing *as* nonhistory only discloses its *eventuality* on the basis of a consciousness of pure sense and pure historicity, i.e., on the basis of a consciousness of *possibility* in the phenomenological sense. As we have sufficiently seen, this consciousness (which phenomenology alone can bring to light) can only be a teleological consciousness. This is because the sense to which we have access is not an event's being; because this sense can always not be incarnated, it can die out or not be born; because the "why" owes its seriousness to a phenomenological certainty and through this seriousness recovers the virulence of an *"in view of what?"* The ontological question, then, seems able to arise only out of a teleological affirmation, i.e., out of freedom. Teleology is the threatened unity of sense and being, of phenomenology and ontology. However, this teleology, which never ceased to ground and animate Husserl's thought, cannot be *determined* in a philosophical language without provisionally breaking this unity for the benefit of phenomenology.

Thus, knowing what the sense of an event is on the basis of a factual [*événementielle*] example, and what the sense of sense in general is on the basis of exemplariness in general, we can then ask ourselves a question which no longer proceeds from phenomenology as such. Not: *"What is a Fact?"*, a question to which a phenomenological ontology responds as a rule. But: *"Why are a factual starting point in factuality and a reduction possible in general?"* Or: *"What is the factuality of fact which supposes the exemplariness of fact?"* Or yet: *"What is the primordial unity of sense and fact, a unity for which, by themselves alone, neither can account?"* In other words, knowing what sense is as historicity, I can clearly ask myself why there would be any history rather than nothing.[183] On the condition that the taking seriously of pure factuality follows after the possibility of phenomenology and assumes its juridical priority, to take factuality seriously as such is no longer to return to empiricism or nonphilosophy. On the contrary, it completes philosophy. But because of that, it must stand in the precarious openness of a question: the question of the origin of Being as History. Every response to such a question can resurface only in a phenomenological process. Ontology only has a right to the question. In the always open breach [*brèche*] of this question, Being itself is *silently* shown under the negativity of the *apeiron*.[184] Undoubtedly, Being itself must always already be

---

[183] Such a question can be repeated about every single factuality and about all the particular forms of infinite historicity as the horizon of every phenomenon, about all the determined forms of the world in general as the horizon of every possible experience, singularly of this historical world right here.

[184] We have already cited the passage in which Husserl, gathering together the entire significance of his enterprise, affirms that, for phenomenology, pure existential [*existentielle*] factuality as wild singularity (always outside the reach of every eidetic subsumption) is "eternally the *apeiron*" ("PRS," p. 116). We pass from phenomenology to ontology (in the non-Husserlian sense) when we silently question the upsurge of stark fact and

given to thinking, in the pre-sumption—which is also a resumption—of Method.[185] And undoubtedly access to Being *and* Being's arrival must always already be *contracted* or *drawn together,* when phenomenology begins by claiming the right to speak [*droit à parole*]. And if Being did not *have* to be History through and through, the *delay* or *lateness* of Discourse *after* the showing of Being would be but a simple misfortune [*fautive misère*] of thought as phenomenology. That this cannot be so, because historicity is prescribed for Being; that delay is the destiny of Thought itself as Discourse—only a phenomenology can *say* this and make philosophy equal to it. For phenomenology alone can make infinite historicity appear: i.e., infinite discourse and infinite dialecticalness as the pure possibility and the very essence of Being in manifestation. It alone can open the absolute subjectivity of Sense to Being-History by making absolute transcendental subjectivity appear (at the end of the most radical reduction) as pure passive-active temporality, as pure auto-temporalization of the Living Present—i.e., as we *already* saw, as intersubjectivity. The discursive and dialectical intersubjectivity of Time with itself in the infinite multiplicity and infinite implication of its absolute origins entitles every other intersubjectivity in general to exist and makes the polemical unity of appearing and disappearing irreducible. Here delay is the philosophical absolute, because the beginning of methodic reflection can only consist in the consciousness of the implication of *another* previous, possible, and absolute origin in general. Since

---

cease to consider the Fact in its phenomenological "function." Then the latter can no longer be exhausted and reduced to its sense by a phenomenological operation, even were it pursued *ad infinitum.* The Fact is *always more* or *always less,* always other, in any case, than what Husserl defines it as when he writes, for example, in a formula which marks the highest ambition of his project: " *'fact',* with its *'irrationality',* is itself *a structural concept within the system of the concrete Apiori"* (*CM,* §39, p. 81; Husserl's emphasis). But phenomenology alone, by going to the end of eidetic determination, by exhausting itself, can strip pure materiality from the Fact. It alone can avoid the confusion of pure factuality with such and such of its determinations. Naturally, having reached this point, in order not to fall back into the philosophical nonsense of irrationalism or empiricism, the Fact *then* must not function: its sense must not be determined outside or independently of all phenomenology. Also, once we have become conscious of phenomenology's juridical priority in all philosophical discourse, perhaps it is permissible to regret again that Husserl had not *also* asked this ontological question about which there is nothing to *say* concerning the question itself. But how can we lament that phenomenology is not an ontology?

[185] [Derrida says of the neologism *présumption:* "I wanted to escape the current meaning of the word *présomption* (conjecture or hypothesis), in order to be nearer the metaphorical schema of anticipation and in order to set it more visibly over against the very rare French word *résumption* (I'm not even sure it exists)—which can only be written with a *u.*" Therefore, this word is translated as "pre-sumption" to emphasize its difference from "presumption."]

this alterity of the absolute origin structurally appears in *my Living Present* and since it can appear and be recognized only in the primordiality of something like *my Living Present,* this very fact signifies the authenticity of phenomenological delay and limitation. In the lackluster guise of a technique, the Reduction is only pure thought as that delay, pure thought investigating the sense of itself as delay within philosophy. Could there be an authentic thought of Being *as* History, as well as an authentic historicity of thought, if the consciousness of delay could be reduced? But could there be any philosophy, if this consciousness of delay was not primordial and pure? Now a primordial consciousness of delay can only have the pure form of anticipation. At the same time, pure consciousness of delay can only be a pure and legitimate, and therefore apriori, presumption, without which (once again) discourse and history would not be possible.

The impossibility of resting in the simple maintenance [nowness] of a Living Present, the sole and absolutely absolute origin of the De Facto *and* the De Jure, of Being *and* Sense, but always other in its self-identity; the inability to live enclosed in the innocent undividedness [*indivision*] of the primordial Absolute, because the Absolute is *present* only in being *deferred-delayed* [*différant*] without respite, this impotence and this impossibility are given in a primordial and pure consciousness of Difference. Such a *consciousness,* with its strange style of unity, must be able to be restored to its own light. Without such a consciousness, without its own proper dehiscence, nothing would appear.

The primordial Difference of the absolute Origin, which can and indefinitely must both retain and announce its pure concrete form with apriori security: i.e., the beyond or the this-side which gives sense to all empirical genius and all factual profusion, that is perhaps what has always been said under the concept of *"transcendental"* through the enigmatic history of its displacements. Difference would be transcendental. The pure and interminable disquietude of thought striving to "reduce" Difference by going beyond factual infinity toward the infinity of its sense and value, i.e., while maintaining Difference—that disquietude would be transcendental. And Thought's pure certainty would be transcendental, since it can look forward to the already announced Telos only by advancing on (or being in advance of [*en avancant sur*]) the Origin that indefinitely reserves itself. Such a certainty never had to learn that Thought would always be to come.

This strange procession of a *"Rückfrage"* is the movement sketched in *The Origin of Geometry,* whereby this piece of writing also holds, as Husserl says, "an exemplary significance" [157].

*July 1961*

# Appendix

# The Origin of Geometry[1]

THE INTEREST THAT propels us in this work makes it necessary to engage first of all in reflections which surely never occurred to Galileo. We must focus our gaze not merely upon the ready-made, handed-down geometry and upon the manner of being which its meaning had in his thinking; it was no different in his thinking from what it was in that of all the late inheritors of the older geometric wisdom, whenever they were at work, either as pure geometers or as making practical applications of geometry. Rather, indeed above all, we must also inquire back into the original meaning of the handed-down geometry, which continued to be valid with this very same meaning—continued and at the same time was developed further, remaining simply "geometry" in all its new forms. Our considerations will necessarily lead to the deepest problems of meaning, problems of science and of the history of science in general, and indeed in the end to problems of a universal history in general; so that our problems and expositions concerning Galilean geometry take on an exemplary significance.

Let it be noted in advance that, in the midst of our historical meditations on modern philosophy, there appears here for the first time with Galileo, through the disclosure of the depth-problems of the meaning-origin of geometry and, founded on this, of the meaning-origin of his new physics, a clarifying light for our whole undertaking: namely, [the idea of] seeking to carry out, in the form of historical meditations, self-reflections about our own present philosophical situation in the hope that in this way we can finally take possession of the meaning, method, and beginning of philosophy, the *one* philosophy to which our life seeks to be and ought to be devoted. For, as will become evident here, at first in connection with one example, our investigations are historical in an unusual sense, namely, in virtue of a thematic direction which opens up depth-problems quite unknown to ordinary history, problems which, [however,] in their own way, are undoubtedly histori-

[1] This manuscript was written in 1936 and was edited and published (beginning with the third paragraph) by Eugen Fink in the *Revue internationale de philosophie*, Vol. I, No. 2 (1939) under the title "Der Ursprung der Geometrie als intentional-historisches Problem." It appears in Biemel's edition of the *Crisis* as "Beilage III," pp. 365–86. The first paragraphs suggest it was meant for inclusion in the *Crisis*.

cal problems. Where a consistent pursuit of these depth-problems leads can naturally not yet be seen at the beginning.

The question of the origin of geometry (under which title here, for the sake of brevity, we include all disciplines that deal with shapes existing mathematically in pure space-time) shall not be considered here as the philological-historical question, i.e., as the search for the first geometers who actually uttered pure geometrical propositions, proofs, theories, or for the particular propositions they discovered, or the like. Rather than this, our interest shall be the inquiry back into the most original sense in which geometry once arose, was present as the tradition of millennia, is still present for us, and is still being worked on in a lively forward development;* we inquire into that sense in which it appeared in history for the first time—in which it had to appear, even though we know nothing of the first creators and are not even asking after them. Starting from what we know, from our geometry, or rather from the older handed-down forms (such as Euclidean geometry), there is an inquiry back into the submerged original beginnings of geometry as they necessarily must have been in their "primally establishing" function. This regressive inquiry unavoidably remains within the sphere of generalities, but, as we shall soon see, these are generalities which can be richly explicated, with prescribed possibilities of arriving at particular questions and self-evident claims as answers. The geometry which is ready-made, so to speak, from which the regressive inquiry begins, is a tradition. Our human existence moves within innumerable traditions. The whole cultural world, in all its forms, exists through tradition. These forms have arisen as such not merely causally; we also know already that tradition is precisely tradition, having arisen within our human space through human activity, i.e., spiritually, even though we generally know nothing, or as good as nothing, of the particular provenance and of the spiritual source that brought it about. And yet there lies in this lack of knowledge, everywhere and essentially, an implicit knowledge, which can thus also be made explicit, a knowledge of unassailable self-evidence. It begins with superficial commonplaces, such as: that everything traditional has arisen out of human activity, that accordingly past men and human civilizations existed, and among them their first inventors, who shaped the new out of materials at hand, whether raw or already spiritually shaped. From the superficial, however, one is led into the depths. Tradition is open in this general way to continued inquiry; and, if one consistently maintains

---

* So also for Galileo and all the periods following the Renaissance, continually being worked on in a lively forward development, and yet at the same time a tradition.

the direction of inquiry, an infinity of questions opens up, questions which lead to definite answers in accord with their sense. Their form of generality—indeed, as one can see, of unconditioned general validity—naturally allows for application to individually determined particular cases, though it determines only that in the individual that can be grasped through subsumption.

Let us begin, then, in connection with geometry, with the most obvious commonplaces that we have already expressed above in order to indicate the sense of our regressive inquiry. We understand our geometry, available to us through tradition (we have learned it, and so have our teachers), to be a total acquisition of spiritual accomplishments which grows through the continued work of new spiritual acts into new acquisitions. We know of its handed-down, earlier forms, as those from which it has arisen; but with every form the reference to an earlier one is repeated. Clearly, then, geometry must have arisen out of a *first* acquisition, out of first creative activities. We understand its persisting manner of being: it is not only a mobile forward process from one set of acquisitions to another but a continuous synthesis in which all acquisitions maintain their validity, all make up a totality such that, at every present stage, the total acquisition is, so to speak, the total premise for the acquisitions of the new level. Geometry necessarily has this mobility and has a horizon of geometrical future in precisely this style; this is its meaning for every geometer who has the consciousness (the constant implicit knowledge) of existing within a forward development understood as the progress of knowledge being built into the horizon. The same thing is true of every science. Also, every science is related to an open chain of the generations of those who work for and with one another, researchers either known or unknown to one another who are the accomplishing subjectivity of the whole living science. Science, and in particular geometry, with this ontic meaning, must have had a historical beginning; this meaning itself must have an origin in an accomplishment: first as a project and then in successful execution.

Obviously it is the same here as with every other invention. Every spiritual accomplishment proceeding from its first project to its execution is present for the first time in the self-evidence of actual success. But when we note that mathematics has the manner of being of a lively forward movement from acquisitions as premises to new acquisitions, in whose ontic meaning that of the premises is included (the process continuing in this manner), then it is clear that the *total* meaning of geometry (as a developed science, as in the case of every science) could not have been present as a project and then as mobile fulfillment at the beginning. A more primitive formation of meaning necessarily went before it as a preliminary stage, undoubtedly in such a way that it appeared for the first time in the self-evidence of successful realization. But this way of expressing it is actually overblown. Self-evidence means nothing more than grasping an entity with the consciousness of its original being-itself-there [*Selbst-da*]. Successful realization of a project is, for the acting subject, self-evidence; in this self-evidence, what has been realized is there, *originaliter,* as itself.

But now questions arise. This process of projecting and successfully realizing occurs, after all, purely within the *subject* of the inventor, and thus the meaning, as present *originaliter* with its whole content, lies exclusively, so to speak, within his mental space. But geometrical existence is not psychic existence; it does not exist as something personal within the personal sphere of consciousness: it is the existence of what is objectively there for "everyone" (for actual and possible geometers, or those who understand geometry). Indeed, it has, from its primal establishment, an existence which is peculiarly supertemporal and which—of this we are certain—is accessible to all men, first of all to the actual and possible mathematicians of all peoples, all ages; and this is true of all its particular forms. And all forms newly produced by someone on the basis of pregiven forms immediately take on the same objectivity. This is, we note, an "ideal" objectivity. It is proper to a whole class of spiritual products of the cultural world, to which not only all scientific constructions and the sciences themselves belong but also, for example, the constructions of fine literature.* Works of this class do not, like tools (hammers, pliers) or like architectural and other such products, have a repeatability in many like exemplars. The Pythagorean theorem, [indeed] all of geometry, exists only once, no matter how often or even in what language it may be expressed. It is identically the same in the "original language" of Euclid and in all "translations"; and within each language it is again the same, no matter how many times it has been sensibly uttered, from the original expression and writing-down to the innumerable oral utterances or written and other documentations. The sensible utterances have spatiotemporal individuation in the world like all corporeal occurrences, like everything embodied in bodies as such; but this is not true of the spiritual form itself,

---

* But the broadest concept of literature encompasses them all; that is, it belongs to their objective being that they be linguistically expressed and can be expressed again and again; or, more precisely, they have their objectivity, their existence-for-everyone, only as signification, as the meaning of speech. This is true in a peculiar fashion in the case of the objective sciences: for them the difference between the original language of the work and its translation into other languages does not remove its identical accessibility or change it into an inauthentic, indirect accessibility.

which is called an "ideal object" [*ideale Gegenständlichkeit*]. In a certain way ideal objects do exist objectively in the world, but it is only in virtue of these two-leveled repetitions and ultimately in virtue of sensibly embodying repetitions. For language itself, in all its particularizations (words, sentences, speeches), is, as can easily be seen from the grammatical point of view, thoroughly made up of ideal objects; for example, the word *Löwe* occurs only once in the German language; it is identical throughout its innumerable utterances by any given persons. But the idealities of geometrical words, sentences, theories—considered purely as linguistic structures—are not the idealities that make up what is expressed and brought to validity as truth in geometry; the latter are ideal geometrical objects, states of affairs, etc. Wherever something is asserted, one can distinguish what is thematic, that about which it is said (its meaning), from the assertion, which itself, during the asserting, is never and can never be thematic. And what is thematic here is precisely ideal objects, and quite different ones from those coming under the concept of language. Our problem now concerns precisely the ideal objects which are thematic in geometry: how does geometrical ideality (just like that of all sciences) proceed from its primary intrapersonal origin, where it is a structure within the conscious space of the first inventor's soul, to its ideal objectivity? In advance we see that it occurs by means of language, through which it receives, so to speak, its linguistic living body [*Sprachleib*]. But how does linguistic embodiment make out of the merely intrasubjective structure the *objective* structure which, e.g., as geometrical concept or state of affairs, is in fact present as understandable by all and is valid, already in its linguistic expression as geometrical speech, as geometrical proposition, for all the future in its geometrical sense?

Naturally, we shall not go into the general problem which also arises here of the origin of language in its ideal existence and its existence in the real world grounded in utterance and documentation; but we must say a few words here about the relation between language, as a function of man within human civilization, and the world as the horizon of human existence.

Living wakefully in the world we are constantly conscious of the world, whether we pay attention to it or not, conscious of it as the horizon of our life, as a horizon of "things" (real objects), of our actual and possible interests and activities. Always standing out against the world-horizon is the horizon of our fellow men, whether there are any of them present or not. Before even taking notice of it at all, we are conscious of the open horizon of our fellow men with its limited nucleus of our neighbors, those known to us. We are thereby coconscious of the men on our external horizon in each case as "others"; in each case "I" am conscious of them as "my" others, as those with whom I can enter into actual and potential, immediate and mediate relations of empathy; [this involves] a reciprocal "getting along" with others; and on the basis of these relations I can deal with them, enter into particular modes of community with them, and then know, in a habitual way, of my being so related. Like me, every human being—and this is how he is understood by me and everyone else—has his fellow men and, always counting himself, civilization in general, in which he knows himself to be living.

It is precisely to this horizon of civilization that common language belongs. One is conscious of civilization from the start as an immediate and mediate linguistic community. Clearly it is only through language and its far-reaching documentations, as possible communications, that the horizon of civilization can be an open and endless one, as it always is for men. What is privileged in consciousness as the horizon of civilization and as the linguistic community is mature normal civilization (taking away the abnormal and the world of children). In this sense civilization is, for every man whose we-horizon it is, a community of those who can reciprocally express themselves, normally, in a fully understandable fashion; and within this community everyone can talk about what is within the surrounding world of his civilization as objectively existing. Everything has its name, or is namable in the broadest sense, i.e., linguistically expressible. The objective world is from the start the world for all, the world which "everyone" has as world-horizon. Its objective being presupposes men, understood as men with a common language. Language, for its part, as function and exercised capacity, is related correlatively to the world, the universe of objects which is linguistically expressible in its being and its being-such. Thus men as men, fellow men, world—the world of which men, of which we, always talk and can talk—and, on the other hand, language, are inseparably intertwined; and one is always certain of their inseparable relational unity, though usually only implicitly, in the manner of a horizon.

This being presupposed, the primally establishing geometer can obviously also express his internal structure. But the question arises again: How does the latter, in its "ideality," thereby become objective? To be sure, something psychic which can be understood by others [*nachverstehbar*] and is communicable, as something psychic belonging to this man, is *eo ipso* objective, just as he himself, as concrete man, is experienceable and namable by everyone as a real thing in the world of things in general. People can agree about such things, can make common verifiable assertions on the basis of common experience, etc. But how does the intrapsychically constituted structure arrive at an intersubjective being of its own as an ideal object which, as "geometrical," is anything but a real psychic object, even though it has arisen psychically? Let us reflect. The original being-itself-there, in the immediacy [*Aktualität*] of its first production, i.e., in original "self-evidence," results in no persisting acquisition at all that could have objective existence. Vivid self-evidence passes—though in such a way that the activity immediately turns into the passivity of the flowingly fading consciousness of what-has-just-now-been. Finally this "retention" disappears, but the "disappeared" passing and being past has not become nothing for the subject in question: it can be reawakened. To the passivity of what is at first obscurely awakened and what perhaps emerges with greater and greater clarity there belongs the possible activity of a recollection in which the past experiencing [*Erleben*] is lived through in a quasi-new and quasi-active way. Now if the originally self-evident production, as the pure fulfillment of its intention, is what is renewed (recollected), there necessarily occurs, accompanying the active recollection of what is past, an activity of concurrent actual production, and there arises thereby, in original "coincidence," the self-evidence of identity: what has now been realized in original fashion is the same as what was previously self-evident. Also coestablished is the capacity for repetition at will with the self-evidence of the identity (coincidence of identity) of the structure throughout the chain of repetitions. Yet even with this, we have still not gone beyond the subject and his subjective, evident capacities; that is, we still have no "objectivity" given. It does arise, however—in a preliminary stage—in understandable fashion as soon as we take into consideration the function of empathy and fellow mankind as a community of empathy and of language. In the contact of reciprocal linguistic understanding, the original production and the product of one subject can be *actively* understood by the others. In this full understanding of what is produced by the other, as in the case of recollection, a present coaccomplishment on one's own part of the presentified activity necessarily takes place; but at the same time there is also the self-evident consciousness of the identity of the mental structure in the productions of both the receiver of the communication and the communicator; and this occurs reciprocally. The productions can reproduce their likenesses from person to person, and in the chain of the understanding of these repetitions what is self-evident turns up as the same in the consciousness of the other. In the unity of the community of communication among several persons the repeatedly produced structure becomes an object of consciousness, not as a likeness, but as the one structure common to all.

Now we must note that the objectivity of the ideal structure has not yet been fully constituted through such actual transferring of what has been originally produced in one to others who originally reproduce it. What is lacking is the *persisting existence* of the "ideal objects" even during periods in which the inventor and his fellows are no longer wakefully so related or even are no longer alive. What is lacking is their continuing-to-be even when no one has [consciously] realized them in self-evidence.

The important function of written, documenting linguistic expression is that it makes communications possible without immediate or mediate personal address; it is, so to speak, communication become virtual. Through this, the communalization of man is lifted to a new level. Written signs are, when considered from a purely corporeal point of view, straightforwardly, sensibly experienceable; and it is always possible that they be intersubjectively experienceable in common. But as linguistic signs they awaken, as do linguistic sounds, their familiar significations. The awakening is something passive; the awakened signification is thus given passively, similarly to the way in which any other activity which has sunk into obscurity, once associatively awakened, emerges at first *passively* as a more or less clear memory. In the passivity in question here, as in the case of memory, what is passively awakened can be transformed back,* so to speak, into the corresponding activity: this is the capacity for reactivation that belongs originally to every human being as a speaking being. Accordingly, then, the writing-down effects a transformation of the original mode of being of the meaning-structure, [e.g.,] within the geometrical sphere of self-evidence, of the geometrical structure which is put into words. It becomes sedimented, so to speak. But the reader can make it self-evident again, can reactivate the self-evidence.†

There is a distinction, then, between passively understanding the expression and making it self-evident by reactivating its meaning. But there also exist possibilities of a kind of activity, a thinking in terms of

* This is a transformation of which one is conscious as being in itself patterned after [what is passively awakened].

† But this is by no means necessary or even factually normal. Even without this he can understand; he can concur "as a matter of course" in the validity of what is understood without any activity of his own. In this case he comports himself purely passively and receptively.

things that have been taken up merely receptively, passively, which deals with significations only passively understood and taken over, without any of the self-evidence of original activity. Passivity in general is the realm of things that are bound together and melt into one another associatively, where all meaning that arises is put together passively. What often happens here is that a meaning arises which is apparently possible as a unity—i.e., can apparently be made self-evidence through a possible reactivation—whereas the attempt at actual reactivation can reactivate only the individual members of the combination, while the intention to unify them into a whole, instead of being fulfilled, comes to nothing; that is, the ontic validity is destroyed through the original consciousness of nullity.

It is easy to see that even in [ordinary] human life, and first of all in every individual life from childhood up to maturity, the originally intuitive life which creates its originally self-evident structures through activities on the basis of sense-experience very quickly and in increasing measure falls victim to the *seduction of language*. Greater and greater segments of this life lapse into a kind of talking and reading that is dominated purely by association; and often enough, in respect to the validities arrived at in this way, it is disappointed by subsequent experience.

Now one will say that in the sphere that interests us here—that of science, of thinking directed toward the attainment of truths and the avoidance of falsehood—one is obviously greatly concerned from the start to put a stop to the free play of associative constructions. In view of the unavoidable sedimentation of mental products in the form of persisting linguistic acquisitions, which can be taken up again at first merely passively and be taken over by anyone else, such constructions remain a constant danger. This danger is avoided if one not merely convinces oneself ex post facto that the particular construction can be reactivated but assures oneself from the start, after the self-evident primal establishment, of its capacity to be reactivated and enduringly maintained. This occurs when one has a view to the univocity of linguistic expression and to securing, by means of the most painstaking formation of the relevant words, propositions, and complexes of propositions, the results which are to be univocally expressed. This must be done by the individual scientist, and not only by the inventor but by every scientist as a member of the scientific community after he has taken over from the others what is to be taken over. This belongs, then, to the particulars of the scientific tradition within the corresponding community of scientists as a community of knowledge living in the unity of a common responsibility. In accord with the essence of science, then, its functionaries maintain the constant claim, the personal certainty, that everything they put into scientific assertions has been said "once and for all," that it "stands fast," forever identically repeatable with self-evidence and usable for further theoretical or practical ends—as indubitably reactivatable with the identity of its actual meaning.*

However, two more things are important here. First: we have not yet taken into account the fact that scientific thinking attains new results on the basis of those already attained, that the new ones serve as the foundation for still others, etc.—in the unity of a propagative process of transferred meaning.

In the finally immense proliferation of a science like geometry, what has become of the claim and the capacity for reactivation? When every researcher works on his part of the building, what of the vocational interruptions and time out for rest, which cannot be overlooked here? When he returns to the actual continuation of work, must he first run through the whole immense chain of groundings back to the original premises and actually reactivate the whole thing? If so, a science like our modern geometry would obviously not be possible at all. And yet it is of the essence of the results of each stage not only that their ideal ontic meaning in fact comes later [than that of earlier results] but that, since meaning is grounded upon meaning, the earlier meaning gives something of its validity to the later one, indeed becomes part of it to a certain extent. Thus no building block within the mental structure is self-sufficient; and none, then, can be immediately reactivated [by itself].

This is especially true of sciences which, like geometry, have their thematic sphere in ideal products, in idealities from which more and more idealities at higher levels are produced. It is quite different in the so-called descriptive sciences, where the theoretical interest, classifying and describing, remains within the sphere of sense-intuition, which for it represents self-evidence. Here, at least in general, every new proposition can by itself be "cashed in" for self-evidence.

How, by contrast, is a science like geometry possible? How, as a systematic, endlessly growing stratified structure of idealities, can it maintain its original meaningfulness through living reactivatability if its

---

* At first, of course, it is a matter of a firm direction of the will, which the scientist establishes in himself, aimed at the certain capacity for reactivation. If the goal of reactivatability can be only relatively fulfilled, then the claim which stems from the consciousness of being able to acquire something also has its relativity; and this relativity also makes itself noticeable and is driven out. Ultimately, objective, absolutely firm knowledge of truth is an infinite idea.

cognitive thinking is supposed to produce something new without being able to reactivate the previous levels of knowledge back to the first? Even if this could have succeeded at a more primitive stage of geometry, its energy would ultimately have been too much spent in the effort of procuring self-evidence and would not have been available for a higher productivity.

Here we must take into consideration the peculiar "logical" activity which is tied specifically to language, as well as to the ideal cognitive structures that arise specifically within it. To any sentence structures that emerge within a merely passive understanding there belongs essentially a peculiar sort of activity best described by the word "explication."[2] A passively emerging sentence (e.g., in memory), or one heard and passively understood, is at first merely received with a passive ego-participation, taken up as valid; and in this form it is already our meaning. From this we distinguish the peculiar and important activity of explicating our meaning. Whereas in its first form it was a straightforwardly valid meaning, taken up as unitary and undifferentiated—concretely speaking, a straightforwardly valid declarative sentence—now what in itself is vague and undifferentiated is actively explicated. Consider, for example, the way in which we understand, when superficially reading the newspaper, and simply receive the "news"; here there is a passive taking-over of ontic validity such that what is read straightway becomes our opinion.

But it is something special, as we have said, to have the intention to explicate, to engage in the activity which articulates what has been read (or an interesting sentence from it), extracting one by one, in separation from what has been vaguely, passively received as a unity, the elements of meaning, thus bringing the total validity to active performance in a new way on the basis of the individual validities. What was a passive meaning-pattern has now become one constructed through active production. This activity, then, is a peculiar sort of self-evidence; the structure arising out of it is in the mode of having been originally produced. And in connection with this self-evidence, too, there is communalization. The explicated judgment becomes an ideal object capable of being passed on. It is this object exclusively that is meant by logic when it speaks of sentences or judgments. And thus the *domain of logic* is universally designated; this is universally the sphere of being to which logic pertains insofar as it is the theory of the sentences [or propositions] in general.

Through this activity, now, further activities become possible—self-

---

[2] *Verdeutlichung,* i.e., making explicit.

evident constructions of new judgments on the basis of those already valid for us. This is the peculiar feature of logical thinking and of its purely logical self-evidences. All this remains intact even when judgments are transformed into assumptions, where, instead of ourselves asserting or judging, we think ourselves into the position of asserting or judging.

Here we shall concentrate on the sentences of language as they come to us passively and are merely received. In this connection it must also be noted that sentences give themselves in consciousness as reproductive transformations of an original meaning produced out of an actual, original activity; that is, in themselves they refer to such a genesis. In the sphere of logical self-evidence, deduction, or inference in forms of consequence, plays a constant and essential role. On the other hand, one must also take note of the constructive activities that operate with geometrical idealities which have been explicated but not brought to original self-evidence. (Original self-evidence must not be confused with the self-evidence of "axioms"; for axioms are in principle already the results of original meaning-construction and always have this behind them.)

Now what about the possibility of complete and genuine reactivation in full originality, through going back to the primal self-evidences, in the case of geometry and the so-called "deductive" sciences (so called, although they by no means merely deduce)? Here the fundamental law, with unconditionally general self-evidence, is: if the premises can actually be reactivated back to the most original self-evidence, then their self-evident consequences can be also. Accordingly it appears that, beginning with the primal self-evidences, the original genuineness must propagate itself through the chain of logical inference, no matter how long it is. However, if we consider the obvious finitude of the individual and even the social capacity to transform the logical chains of centuries, truly in the unity of one accomplishment, into originally genuine chains of self-evidence, we notice that the [above] law contains within itself an idealization: namely, the removal of limits from our capacity, in a certain sense its infinitization. The peculiar sort of self-evidence belonging to such idealizations will concern us later.

These are, then, the general essential insights which elucidate the whole methodical development of the "deductive" sciences and with it the manner of being which is essential to them.

These sciences are not handed down ready-made in the form of documented sentences; they involve a lively, productively advancing formation of meaning, which always has the documented, as a sediment of earlier production, at its disposal in that it deals with it logically. But out of sentences with sedimented signification, logical "dealing" can produce only other sentences of the same character. That all new acquisitions express an actual geometrical truth is certain a priori under the presupposition that the foundations of the deductive structure have truly been produced and objectified in original self-evidence, i.e., have become universally accessible acquisitions. A continuity from one person to another, from one time to another, must have been capable of being carried out. It is clear that the method of producing original idealities out of what is prescientifically given in the cultural world must have been written down and fixed in firm sentences prior to the existence of geometry; furthermore, the capacity for translating these sentences from vague linguistic understanding into the clarity of the reactivation of their self-evident meaning must have been, in its own way, handed down and ever capable of being handed down.

Only as long as this condition was satisfied, or only when the possibility of its fulfillment was perfectly secured for all time, could geometry preserve its genuine, original meaning as a deductive science throughout the progression of logical constructions. In other words, only in this case could every geometer be capable of bringing to mediate self-evidence the meaning borne by every sentence, not merely as its sedimented (logical) sentence-meaning but as its actual meaning, its truth-meaning. And so for all of geometry.

The progress of deduction follows formal-logical self-evidence; but without the actually developed capacity for reactivating the original activities contained within its fundamental concepts, i.e., without the "what" and the "how" of its prescientific materials, geometry would be a tradition empty of meaning; and if we ourselves did not have this capacity, we could never even know whether geometry had or ever did have a genuine meaning, one that could really be "cashed in."

Unfortunately, however, this is our situation, and that of the whole modern age.

The "presupposition" mentioned above has in fact never been fulfilled. How the living tradition of the meaning-formation of elementary concepts is actually carried on can be seen in elementary geometrical instruction and its textbooks; what we actually learn there is how to deal with *ready-made* concepts and sentences in a rigorously methodical way. Rendering the concepts sensibly intuitable by means of drawn figures is substituted for the actual production of the primal idealities. And the rest is done by success—not the success of actual insight extending beyond the logical method's own self-evidence, but the practical successes of applied geometry, its immense, though not understood, practical usefulness. To this we must add something that will become visible further on in the treatment of historical mathematics, namely, the dangers of a scientific life that is completely given over to logical activities. These dangers lie in certain progressive transformations of meaning* to which this sort of scientific treatment drives one.

By exhibiting the essential presuppositions upon which rests the historical possibility of a genuine tradition, true to its origins, of sciences like geometry, we can understand how such sciences can vitally develop throughout the centuries and still not be genuine. The inheritance of propositions and of the method of logically constructing new propositions and idealities can continue without interruption from one period to the next, while the capacity for reactivating the primal beginnings, i.e., the sources of meaning for everything that comes later, has not been handed down with it. What is lacking is thus precisely what had given and had to give meaning to all propositions and theories, a meaning arising from the primal sources which can be made self-evident again and again.

Of course, grammatically coherent propositions and concatenations of propositions, no matter how they have arisen and have achieved validity—even if it is through mere association—have in all circumstances their own logical meaning, i.e., their meaning that can be made self-evident through explication; this can then be identified again and again as the same proposition, which is either logically coherent or incoherent, where in the latter case it cannot be executed in the unity of an actual judgment. In propositions which belong together in one domain and in the deductive systems that can be made out of them we have a realm of ideal identities; and for these there exist easily understandable possibilities of lasting traditionalization. But propositions, like other cultural structures, appear on the scene in the form of tradition; they claim, so to speak, to be sedimentations of a truth-meaning that can be made originally self-evident; whereas it is by no means necessary that they [actually] have such a meaning, as in the case of associatively derived falsifications. Thus the whole pregiven deductive science, the total system of propositions in the unity of their validities, is first only a claim which can be justified as an expression of the alleged truth-meaning only through the actual capacity for reactivation.

Through this state of affairs we can understand the deeper reason for the demand, which has spread throughout the modern period and has finally been generally accepted, for a so-called "epistemological

---

* These work to the benefit of logical method, but they remove one further and further from the origins and make one insensitive to the problem of origin and thus to the actual ontic and truth-meaning of all these sciences.

grounding" of the sciences, though clarity has never been achieved about what the much-admired sciences are actually lacking.*

As for further details on the uprooting of an originally genuine tradition, i.e., one which involved original self-evidence at its actual first beginning, one can point to possible and easily understandable reasons. In the first oral cooperation of the beginning geometers, the need was understandably lacking for an exact fixing of descriptions of the prescientific primal material and of the ways in which, in relation to this material, geometrical idealities arose together with the first "axiomatic" propositions. Further, the logical superstructures did not yet rise so high that one could not return again and again to the original meaning. On the other hand, the possibility of the practical application of the derived laws, which was actually obvious in connection with the original developments, understandably led quickly, in the realm of praxis, to a habitually practiced method of using mathematics, if need be, to bring about useful things. This method could naturally be handed down even without the ability for original self-evidence. Thus mathematics, emptied of meaning, could generally propagate itself, constantly being added to logically, as could the methodics of technical application on the other side. The extraordinarily far-reaching practical usefulness became of itself a major motive for the advancement and appreciation of these sciences. Thus also it is understandable that the lost original truth-meaning made itself felt so little, indeed, that the need for the corresponding regressive inquiry had to be reawakened. More than this: the true sense of such an inquiry had to be discovered.

Our results based on principle are of a generality that extends over all the so-called deductive sciences and even indicates similar problems and investigations for all sciences. For all of them have the mobility of sedimented traditions that are worked upon, again and again, by an activity of producing new structures of meaning and handing them down. Existing in this way, they extend enduringly through time, since all new acquisitions are in turn sedimented and become working materials. Everywhere the problems, the clarifying investigations, the insights of principle are *historical*. We stand within the horizon of human civilization, the one in which we ourselves now live. We are constantly, vitally conscious of this horizon, and specifically as a temporal horizon implied in our given present horizon. To the one human civilization there corresponds essentially the one cultural world as the surrounding life-world with its [peculiar] manner of being; this world, for every

---

* What does Hume do but endeavor to inquire back into the primal impressions of developed ideas and, in general, scientific ideas?

historical period and civilization, has its particular features and is precisely the tradition. We stand, then, within the historical horizon in which everything is historical, even though we may know very little about it in a definite way. But it has its essential structure that can be revealed through methodical inquiry. This inquiry prescribes all the possible specialized questions, thus including, for the sciences, the inquiries back into origin which are peculiar to them in virtue of their historical manner of being. Here we are led back to the primal materials of the first formation of meaning, the primal premises, so to speak, which lie in the prescientific cultural world. Of course, this cultural world has in turn its own questions of origin, which at first remain unasked.

Naturally, problems of this particular sort immediately awaken the total problem of the universal historicity of the correlative manners of being of humanity and the cultural world and the a priori structure contained in this historicity. Still, questions like that of the clarification of the origin of geometry have a closed character, such that one need not inquire beyond those prescientific materials.

Further clarifications will be made in connection with two objections which are familiar to our own philosophical-historical situation.

In the first place, what sort of strange obstinacy is this, seeking to take the question of the origin of geometry back to some undiscoverable Thales of geometry, someone not even known to legend? Geometry is available to us in its propositions, its theories. Of course we must and we can answer for this logical edifice to the last detail in terms of self-evidence. Here, to be sure, we arrive at first axioms, and from them we proceed to the original self-evidence which the fundamental concepts make possible. What is this, if not the "theory of knowledge," in this case specifically the theory of geometrical knowledge? No one would think of tracing the epistemological problem back to such a supposed Thales. This is quite superfluous. The presently available concepts and propositions themselves contain their own meaning, first as nonself-evident opinion, but nevertheless as true propositions with a meant but still hidden truth which we can obviously bring to light by rendering the propositions themselves self-evident.

Our answer is as follows. Certainly the historical backward reference has not occurred to anyone; certainly theory of knowledge has never been seen as a peculiarly historical task. But this is precisely what we object to in the past. The ruling dogma of the separation in principle between epistemological elucidation and historical, even humanistic-psychological explanation, between epistemological and genetic origin, is fundamentally mistaken, unless one inadmissibly limits, in the usual way, the concepts of "history," "historical explanation," and "genesis." Or rather, what is fundamentally mistaken is the limitation through which precisely the deepest and most genuine problems of history are concealed. If one thinks over our expositions (which are of course still rough and will later of necessity lead us into new depth-dimensions), what they make obvious is precisely that what we know—namely, that the presently vital cultural configuration "geometry" is a tradition and is still being handed down—is not knowledge concerning an external causality which effects the succession of historical configurations, as if it were knowledge based on induction, the presupposition of which would amount to an absurdity here; rather, to understand geometry or any given cultural fact is to be conscious of its historicity, albeit "implicitly." This, however, is not an empty claim; for quite generally it is true for every fact given under the heading of "culture," whether it is a matter of the lowliest culture of necessities or the highest culture (science, state, church, economic organization, etc.), that every straightforward understanding of it as an experiential fact involves the "coconsciousness" that it is something constructed through human activity. No matter how hidden, no matter how merely "implicitly" coimplied this meaning is, there belongs to it the self-evident possibility of explication, of "making it explicit" and clarifying it. Every explication and every transition from making explicit to making self-evident (even perhaps in cases where one stops much too soon) is nothing other than historical disclosure; in itself, essentially, it is something historical, and as such it bears, with essential necessity, the horizon of its history within itself. This is of course also to say that the whole of the cultural present, understood as a totality, "implies" the whole of the cultural past in an undetermined but structurally determined generality. To put it more precisely, it implies a continuity of pasts which imply one another, each in itself being a past cultural present. And this whole continuity is a *unity* of traditionalization up to the present, which is our present *as* [a process of] traditionalizing itself in flowing-static vitality. This is, as has been said, an undetermined generality, but it has in principle a structure which can be much more widely explicated by proceeding from these indications, a structure which also grounds, "implies," the possibilities for every search for and determination of concrete, factual states of affairs.

Making geometry self-evident, then, whether one is clear about this or not, is the disclosure of its historical tradition. But this knowledge, if it is not to remain empty talk or undifferentiated generality, requires the methodical production, proceeding from the present and carried out as research in the present, of differentiated self-evidences of the type discovered above (in several fragmentary investigations of what belongs to such knowledge superficially, as it were). Carried out systematically, such self-evidences result in nothing other and nothing less than the universal a priori of history with all its highly abundant component elements.

We can also say now that history is from the start nothing other than the vital movement of the coexistence and the interweaving of original formations and sedimentations of meaning.

Anything that is shown to be a historical fact, either in the present through experience or by a historian as a fact in the past, necessarily has its *inner structure of meaning;* but especially the motivational inter-connections established about it in terms of everyday understanding have deep, further and further-reaching implications which must be interrogated, disclosed. All [merely] factual history remains incomprehensible because, always merely drawing its conclusions naïvely and straightforwardly from facts, it never makes thematic the general ground of meaning upon which all such conclusions rest, has never investigated the immense structural a priori which is proper to it. Only the disclosure of the essentially general structure* lying in our present and then in every past or future historical present as such, and, in totality, only the disclosure of the concrete, historical time in which we live, in which our total humanity lives in respect to its total, essentially general structure—only this disclosure can make possible historical inquiry [*Historie*] which is truly understanding, insightful, and in the genuine sense scientific. This is the concrete, historical a priori which encompasses everything that exists as historical becoming and having-become or exists in its essential being as tradition and handing-down. What has been said was related to the total form "historical present in general," historical time generally. But the particular configurations of culture, which find their place within its coherent historical being as tradition and as vitally handing themselves down, have within this totality only relatively self-sufficient being in traditionality, only the being of nonself-sufficient components. Correlatively, now, account would have to be taken of the subjects of historicity, the persons who create cultural formations, functioning in totality: creative personal civilization.†

* The superficial structure of the externally "ready-made" men within the social-historical only through the inner historicity of the individuals, who are individuals in their the inner historicities of the persons taking part. ["Structures" is Biemel's interpolation.]

† The historical world is, to be sure, first pregiven as a social-historical world. But it is historical only through the inner historicity of the individuals, who are individuals in their inner historicity, together with that of other communalized persons. Recall what was said in a few meager beginning expositions about memories and the constant historicity to be found in them [pp. 162f., above].

In respect to geometry one recognizes, now that we have pointed out the hiddenness of its fundamental concepts, which have become inaccessible, and have made them understandable as such in first basic outlines, that only the consciously set task of [discovering] the historical origin of geometry (within the total problem of the a priori of historicity in general) can provide the method for a geometry which is true to its origins and at the same time is to be understood in a universal-historical way; and the same is true for all sciences, for philosophy. In principle, then, a history of philosophy, a history of the particular sciences in the style of the usual factual history, can actually render nothing of their subject matter comprehensible. For a genuine history of philosophy, a genuine history of the particular sciences, is nothing other than the tracing of the historical meaning-structures given in the present, or their self-evidences, along the documented chain of historical back-references into the hidden dimension of the primal self-evidences which underlie them.* Even the very problem here can be made understandable only through recourse to the historical a priori as the universal source of all conceivable problems of understanding. The problem of genuine historical explanation comes together, in the case of the sciences, with "epistemological" grounding or clarification.

We must expect yet a second and very weighty objection. From the historicism which prevails extensively in different forms [today] I expect little receptivity for a depth-inquiry which goes beyond the usual factual history, as does the one outlined in this work, especially since, as the expression "a priori" indicates, it lays claim to a strictly unconditioned and truly apodictic self-evidence extending beyond all historical facticities. One will object: what naïveté, to seek to display, and to claim to have displayed, a historical a priori, an absolute, supertemporal validity, after we have obtained such abundant testimony for the relativity of everything historical, of all historically developed world-apperceptions, right back to those of the "primitive" tribes. Every people, large or small, has its world in which, for that people, everything fits well together, whether in mythical-magical or in European-rational terms, and in which everything can be explained perfectly. Every people has its "logic" and, accordingly, if this logic is explicated in propositions, "its" a priori.

However, let us consider the methodology of establishing historical

---

* But what counts as primal self-evidence for the sciences is determined by an educated person or a sphere of such persons who pose new questions, new historical questions, questions concerning the inner depth-dimension as well as those concerning an external historicity in the social-historical world.

facts in general, thus including that of the facts supporting the objection; and let us do this in regard to what such methodology presupposes. Does not the undertaking of a humanistic science of "how it really was" contain a presupposition taken for granted, a validity-ground never observed, never made thematic, of a strictly unassailable [type of] self-evidence, without which historical inquiry would be a meaningless enterprise? All questioning and demonstrating which is in the usual sense historical presupposes history [*Geschichte*] as the universal horizon of questioning, not explicitly, but still as a horizon of implicit certainty, which, in spite of all vague background-indeterminacy, is the presupposition of all determinability, or of all intention to seek and to establish determined facts.

What is historically primary in itself is our present. We always already know of our present world and that we live in it, always surrounded by an openly endless horizon of unknown actualities. This knowing, as horizon-certainty, is not something learned, not knowledge which was once actual and has merely sunk back to become part of the background; the horizon-certainty had to be already there in order to be capable of being laid out thematically; it is already presupposed in order that we can seek to know what we do not know. All not-knowing concerns the unknown world, which yet exists in advance for us *as* world, as the horizon of all questions of the present and thus also all questions which are specifically historical. These are the questions which concern men, as those who act and create in their communalized coexistence in the world and transform the constant cultural face of the world. Do we not know further—we have already had occasion to speak of this—that this historical present has its historical pasts behind it, that it has developed out of them, that historical past is a continuity of pasts which proceed from one another, each, as a past present, being a tradition producing tradition out of itself? Do we not know that the present and the whole of historical time implied in it is that of a historically coherent and unified civilization, coherent through its generative bond and constant communalization in cultivating what has already been cultivated before, whether in cooperative work or in reciprocal interaction, etc.? Does all this not announce a universal "knowing" of the horizon, an implicit knowing that can be made explicit systematically in its essential structure? Is not the resulting great problem here the horizon toward which all questions tend, and thus the horizon which is presupposed in all of them? Accordingly, we need not first enter into some kind of critical discussion of the facts set out by historicism; it is enough that even the claim of their factualness presupposes the historical a priori if this claim is to have a meaning.

But a doubt arises all the same. The horizon-exposition to which we recurred must not bog down in vague, superficial talk; it must itself arrive at its own sort of scientific discipline. The sentences in which it is expressed must be fixed and capable of being made self-evident again and again. Through what method do we obtain a universal and also fixed a priori of the historical world which is always originally genuine? Whenever we consider it, we find ourselves with the self-evident capacity to reflect—to turn to the horizon and to penetrate it in an expository way. But we also have, and know that we have, the capacity of complete freedom to transform, in thought and phantasy, our human historical existence and what is there exposed as its life-world. And precisely in this activity of free variation, and in running through the conceivable possibilities for the life-world, there arises, with apodictic self-evidence, an essentially general set of elements going through all the variants; and of this we can convince ourselves with truly apodictic certainty. Thereby we have removed every bond to the factually valid historical world and have regarded this world itself [merely] as one of the conceptual possibilities. This freedom, and the direction of our gaze upon the apodictically invariant, results in the latter again and again—with the self-evidence of being able to repeat the invariant structure at will—as what is identical, what can be made self-evident *originaliter* at any time, can be fixed in univocal language as the essence constantly implied in the flowing, vital horizon.

Through this method, going beyond the formal generalities we exhibited earlier, we can also make thematic that apodictic [aspect] of the prescientific world that the original founder of geometry had at his disposal, that which must have served as the material for his idealizations.

Geometry and the sciences most closely related to it have to do with space-time and the shapes, figures, also shapes of motion, alterations of deformation, etc., that are possible within space-time, particularly as measurable magnitudes. It is now clear that even if we know almost nothing about the historical surrounding world of the first geometers, this much is certain as an invariant, essential structure: that is was a world of "things" (including the human beings themselves as subjects of this world); that all things necessarily had to have a bodily character—although not all things could be mere bodies, since the necessarily coexisting human beings are not thinkable as mere bodies and, like even the cultural objects which belong with them structurally, are not exhausted in corporeal being. What is also clear, and can be secured at least in its essential nucleus through careful a priori explication, is that these pure bodies had spatiotemporal shapes and "mate-

rial'' [*stoffliche*] qualities (color, warmth, weight, hardness, etc.) related
to them. Further, it is clear that in the life of practical needs certain
particularizations of shape stood out and that a technical praxis always
[aimed at][3] the production of particular preferred shapes and the im-
provement of them according to certain directions of gradualness.

First to be singled out from the thing-shapes are surfaces—more or
less "smooth," more or less perfect surfaces; edges, more or less rough
or fairly "even"; in other words, more or less pure lines, angles, more
or less perfect points; then, again, among the lines, for example,
straight lines are especially preferred, and among the surfaces the even
surfaces; for example, for practical purposes boards limited by even
surfaces, straight lines, and points are preferred, whereas totally or
partially curved surfaces are undesirable for many kinds of practical
interests. Thus the production of even surfaces and their perfection
(polishing) always plays its role in praxis. So also in cases where just
distribution is intended. Here the rough estimate of magnitudes is
transformed into the measurement of magnitudes by counting the equal
parts. (Here, too, proceeding from the factual, an essential form becomes recognizable through a method of variation.) Measuring belongs
to every culture, varying only according to stages from primitive to
higher perfections. We can always presuppose some measuring technique, whether of a lower or higher type, in the essential forward
development of culture, [as well as] the growth of such a technique,
thus also including the art of design for buildings, of surveying fields,
pathways, etc.;[4] such a technique is always already there, already
abundantly developed and pregiven to the philosopher who did not yet
know geometry but who should be conceivable as its inventor. As a
philosopher proceeding from the practical, finite surrounding world (of
the room, the city, the landscape, etc., and temporally the world of
periodical occurrences: day, month, etc.) to the theoretical world-view
and world-knowledge, he has the finitely known and unknown spaces
and times as finite elements within the horizon of an open infinity. But
with this he does not yet have geometrical space, mathematical time,
and whatever else is to become a novel spiritual product out of these
finite elements which serve as material; and with his manifold finite
shapes in their space-time he does not yet have geometrical shapes, the
phoronomic shapes; [his shapes, as] formations developed out of praxis
and thought of in terms of [gradual] perfection, clearly serve only as

---

[3] Biemel's interpolation.

[4] "I have reverted to the original version of this sentence as given in the critical apparatus; I can make no sense of the emended version given in the text."—D. Carr.

bases for a new sort of praxis out of which similarly named new constructions grow.

It is evident in advance that this new sort of construction will be a product arising out of an idealizing, spiritual act, one of "pure" thinking, which has its materials in the designated general pregivens of this factual humanity and human surrounding world and creates "ideal objects" out of them.

Now the problem would be to discover, through recourse to what is essential to history [*Historie*], the historical original meaning which necessarily was able to give and did give to the whole becoming of geometry its persisting truth-meaning.

It is of particular importance now to bring into focus and establish the following insight: Only if the apodictically general content, invariant throughout all conceivable variation, of the spatiotemporal sphere of shapes is taken into account in the idealization can an ideal construction arise which can be understood for all future time and by all coming generations of men and thus be capable of being handed down and reproduced with the identical intersubjective meaning. This condition is valid far beyond geometry for all spiritual structures which are to be unconditionally and generally capable of being handed down. Were the thinking activity of a scientist to introduce something "time-bound" in his thinking, i.e., something bound to what is merely factual about his present or something valid for him as a merely factual tradition, his construction would likewise have a merely time-bound ontic meaning; this meaning would be understandable only by those men who shared the same merely factual presuppositions of understanding.

It is a general conviction that geometry, with all its truths, is valid with unconditioned generality for all men, all times, all peoples, and not merely for all historically factual ones but for all conceivable ones. The presuppositions of principle for this conviction have never been explored because they have never been seriously made a problem. But it has also become clear to us that every establishment of a historical fact which lays claim to unconditioned objectivity likewise presupposes this invariant or absolute a priori.

Only [through the disclosure of this a priori][5] can there be an a priori science extending beyond all historical facticities, all historical surrounding worlds, peoples, times, civilizations; only in this way can a science as *aeterna veritas* appear. Only on this fundament is based the secured capacity of inquiring back from the temporarily depleted self-evidence of a science to the primal self-evidences.

---

[5] Biemel's interpolation.

Do we not stand here before the great and profound problem-horizon of reason, the same reason that functions in every man, the *animal rationale,* no matter how primitive he is?

This is not the place to penetrate into those depths themselves.

In any case, we can now recognize from all this that historicism, which wishes to clarify the historical or epistemological essence of mathematics from the standpoint of the magical circumstances or other manners of apperception of a time-bound civilization, is mistaken in principle. For romantic spirits the mythical-magical elements of the historical and prehistorical aspects of mathematics may be particularly attractive; but to cling to this merely historically factual aspect of mathematics is precisely to lose oneself to a sort of romanticism and to overlook the genuine problem, the internal-historical problem, the epistemological problem. Also, one's gaze obviously cannot then become free to recognize that facticities of every type, including those involved in the [historicist] objection, have a root in the essential structure of what is generally human, through which a teleological reason running throughout all historicity announces itself. With this is revealed a set of problems in its own right related to the totality of history and to the full meaning which ultimately gives it its unity.

If the usual factual study of history in general, and in particular the history which in most recent times has achieved true universal extension over all humanity, is to have any meaning at all, such a meaning can only be grounded upon what we can here call internal history, and as such upon the foundations of the universal historical a priori. Such a meaning necessarily leads further to the indicated highest question of a universal teleology of reason.

If, after these expositions, which have illuminated very general and many-sided problem-horizons, we lay down the following as something completely secured, namely, that the human surrounding world is the same today and always, and thus also in respect to what is relevant to primal establishment and lasting tradition, then we can show in several steps, only in an exploratory way, in connection with our own surrounding world, what should be considered in more detail for the problem of the idealizing primal establishment of the meaning-structure "geometry."

# French and English Bibliography of Jacques Derrida

## Compiled by John Leavey and David B. Allison

## A. FRENCH AND ENGLISH WORKS BY JACQUES DERRIDA

### I. Books by Derrida

1962: Translation and Introduction to Edmund Husserl, *L'Origine de la géométrie*. Paris: Presses Universitaires de France. 2nd ed., 1974. ET: *Edmund Husserl's* Origin of Geometry: *An Introduction*. Tr. John P. Leavey. New York: Nicolas Hays, 1977.

1967: *De la Grammatologie*. Paris: Minuit. ET: *Of Grammatology*. Tr. Gayatri Chakravorty Spivak. Baltimore: The Johns Hopkins University Press, 1976. Ch. 2 of the ET, "Linguistics and Grammatology," was published in *Sub-Stance,* No. 10 (1974), 127–81.

*La Voix et le phénomène: Introduction au problème du signe dans la phénoménologie de Husserl*. Paris: Presses Universitaires de France. 2nd ed., 1972. ET: *Speech and Phenomena: And Other Essays on Husserl's Theory of Signs*. Tr. David B. Allison. Evanston: Northwestern University Press, 1973.

*L'Ecriture et la différence*. Paris: Seuil. ET by Alan Bass is forthcoming.

1972: *La Dissémination*. Paris: Seuil.

*Marges de la philosophie*. Paris: Minuit.

*Positions*. Paris: Minuit.

1974: *Glas*. Paris: Editions Galilée.

1976: *L'Archéologie du frivole: Lire Condillac*. Paris: Denoël/Gonthier. Rpt. of 1973 Introduction to Condillac's *Essai sur l'origine des connaissances humanies* (Paris: Editions Galilée).

*Eperons: Les Styles de Nietzsche.* Venice: Corbo e Fiore. Rpt. and tr. into English, Italian, and German of the 1972 "La Question du style."

## II. Articles by Derrida

1959:  " 'Genèse et structure' et la phénoménologie." *Entretiens sur les notions de genèse et de structure.* Ed. Maurice de Gandillac et al. Paris: Mouton, 1965, pp. 243–60. Discussion, pp. 261–68. Rpt. in *L'Ecriture.*

1963:  "Force et signification." *Critique,* 19, No. 193 (June 1963), 483–99, and No. 194 (July 1963), 619–36. Rpt. in *L'Ecriture.*

"Cogito et histoire de la folie." *Revue de Métaphysique et de Morale,* 68 (1963), 460–94. Rpt. in *L'Ecriture.*

1964:  "A propos de *Cogito et histoire de la folie." Revue de Métaphysique et de Morale,* 69 (1964), 116–19.

"Edmond Jabès et la question du livre." *Critique,* 20, No. 201 (February 1964), 99–115. Rpt. in *L'Ecriture.*

"Violence et métaphysique, essai sur la pensée d'Emmanuel Levinas." *Revue de Métaphysique et de Morale,* 69 (1964), 322–45 and 425–73. Rpt. in *L'Ecriture.*

1965:  "La Parole soufflée." *Tel Quel,* No. 20 (Winter 1965), 41–67. Rpt. in *L'Ecriture.*

"De la Grammatologie." *Critique,* 21, No. 233 (December 1965), 1016–42, and 22, No. 224 (January 1966), 23–53. Rpt. and adapted in *De la Grammatologie.*

1966:  "Le Théâtre de la cruaute et la clôture de la représentation." *Critique,* 22, No. 230 (July 1966), 595–618. Rpt. in *L'Ecriture.*

"La Structure, le signe et le jeu dans le discours des sciences humaines." In *L'Ecriture.* ET: "Structure, Sign, and Play in the Discourse of the Human Sciences." In *The Structuralist Controversy: The Languages of Criticism and the Sciences of Man.* Ed. Richard Macksey and Eugenio Donato. Baltimore: The Johns Hopkins University Press, 1972 (1970), pp. 247–65. Discussion, pp. 265–70.

"Freud et la scène de l'écriture." *Tel Quel,* No. 26 (Summer 1966), 10–41. Rpt. in *L'Ecriture.* ET: "Freud and the Scene of Writing." Tr. Jeffrey Mehlman. *Yale French Studies,* No. 48: *French Freud: Structural Studies in Psychoanalysis* (1972), 74–117.

"Nature, culture, écriture (de Lévi-Strauss à Rousseau)." *Les Cahiers pour l'analyse,* No. 4 (1966), 1–45.

1967:  "De l'Economie restreinte à l'économie générale: un hegelianisme sans réserve." *L'Arc: Georges Bataille,* No. 32 (May 1967), 24–44. Rpt. in *L'Ecriture.* ET: "From Restricted to General Economy: A Hegelianism

Without Reserves." Tr. Alan Bass. In *Semiotext(e)*, 2, No. 2 (1976), 25–55.

"La Forme et le vouloire-dire: note sur la phénoménologie du langage." *Revue Internationale de Philosophie*, 21, Fasc. 3, No. 81 (1967), 277–99. Rpt. in *Marges*. ET: *Speech and Phenomena*, pp. 107–28.

"La Linguistique de Rousseau." *Revue Internationale de Philosophie*, 21, Fasc. 4, No. 82 (1967), 443–62. Slightly changed in *Marges* as "Le Cercle linguistique de Genève."

"Implications: entretien avec Henri Ronse." *Les Lettres Françaises*, No. 1211, 6–12 December 1967, 12–13. Rpt. in *Positions*.

1968: "Le Puits et la pyramide: introduction à la sémiologie de Hegel." *Hegel et la pensée moderne* (Seminaire sur Hegel dirigé par Jean Hyppolite au Collège de France, 1967–68). Ed. Jacques d' Hondt. Paris: Presses Universitaires de France, 1970, pp. 27–84. Rpt. in *Marges*.

"La Pharmacie de Platon." *Tel Quel*, No. 32 (Winter 1968), 3–48, and No. 33 (Spring 1968), 18–59. Rpt. in *Dissémination*.

"OUSIA et GRAMME: note sur une note de *Sein und Zeit*." *L'Endurance de la pensée*. Ed. Marcel Jouhandeau. Paris: Plon, 1968, pp. 219–66. Rpt. in *Marges*. ET: "*'Ousia* and *Grammē*': A Note to a Footnote in *Being and Time*." Tr. Edward S. Casey. In *Phenomenology in Perspective*. Ed. F. Joseph Smith. The Hague: Nijhoff, 1970, pp. 54–93.

"Sémiologie et grammatologie: entretien avec Julia Kristeva." *Information sur les sciences sociales*, 7, No. 3 (June 1968), 135–48. Rpt. in *Positions*. Also rpt. in Julia Kristeva, Josette Rey-Debove, and Donna Jean Unicker, eds. *Essays in Semiotics: Essais de sémiotique*. (Approaches to Semiotics 4) The Hague and Paris: Mouton, 1971, pp. 11–27.

"La 'Différance.'" *Bulletin de la Société Francaise de Philosophie*, 62, No. 3 (July-September 1968), 73–101. Discussion, pp. 101–120. Rpt. in *Marges*. Also rpt. in *Théorie d'ensemble*. Paris: Seuil, 1968, pp. 41–66. ET: *Speech and Phenomena*, pp. 129–60.

"The Ends of Man." *Philosophy and Phenomenological Research*, 30, No. 1 (1969), 31–57. Tr. Edouard Morot-Sir, Wesley C. Puisol, Hubert L. Dreyfus, and Barbara Reid. Rpt. in *Marges*.

1969: "La Dissémination." *Critique*, 25, No. 261 (February 1969), 99-139, and No. 262 (March 1969), 215–49. Rpt. in *Dissémination*.

1970: "D'un Texte à l'écart." *Les Temps Modernes*, 25, No. 284 (March 1970), 1546–52.

"La Double Séance." *Tel Quel*, No. 41 (Spring 1970), 3–43, and No. 42 (Summer 1970), 3–45. Rpt. in *Dissémination*.

1971: "La Mythologie blanche (la métaphore dans le texte philosophique)."

*Poétique*, No. 5 (1971), 1–52. Rpt. in *Marges*. ET: "White Mythology: Metaphor in the Text of Philosophy." Tr. F. C. T. Moore. *New Literary History*, 6, No. 1 (Autumn 1974), 5–74.

"Signature, événement, contexte." *La Communication II*, Actes du XVᵉ Congrès de l'Association des Sociétés de Philosophie de Langue Française. Université de Montreal, Montreal: Editions Montmorency, 1973, pp. 49–76. Discussion, pp. 393–431. Rpt. in *Marges*. ET: "Signature Event Context." Tr. Samuel Weber and Jeffrey Mehlman. In *Glyph: Johns Hopkins Textual Studies*, Vol. I (Baltimore, 1977), pp. 172–97.

"Positions: entretien avec Jean Louis Houdebine et Guy Scarpetta." *Promesse*, Nos. 30–31 (Autumn and Winter 1971), 5–62. Rpt. in *Positions*. ET: "Positions." *Diacritics*, 2, No. 4 (Winter 1972), 35–43, and 3, No. 1 (Spring 1973), 33–59.

"Les Sources de Valéry: Qual, Quelle." *MLN*, 87, No. 4 (May 1972), 563–99. Rpt. in *Marges* as "Qual, Quelle: les sources de Valéry."

"Le Supplément de copule: la philosophie devant la linguistique." *Langages*, 24 (December 1971), 14–39. ET: "The Copula Supplement." Tr. David B. Allison. In *Dialogues in Phenomenology*. Ed. Don Ihde and Richard M. Zaner. The Hague: Nijhoff, 1975, pp. 7–48. Also: "The Supplement of Copula: Philosophy *Before* Linguistics." Tr. James Creech and Josué Harari. *The Georgia Review*, 30 (1976), 527–64. This translation is to be rpt. in the forthcoming *Textual Strategies: Criticism in the Wake of Structuralism*, ed. Josué Harari.

1972:  "Tympan." May 1972. In *Marges*.

"La Question du style." *Nietzsche aujourd'hui?* I: *Intensités*. Paris: Union Générale d'Editions, 1973, pp. 235–87. Discussion, pp. 288–99. Rpt. of a Modified Version in French and ET by Barbara Harlow in *Eperons*. Excerpts of another ET by Reuben Berezdivin published in *The New Nietzsche: Contemporary Styles of Interpretation*, ed. David B. Allison (New York: Dell Publishing, 1977), pp. 176–89.

"Avoir l'oreille de la philosophie." *La Quinzaine Littéraire*, No. 152, 30 November 1972, 213–16. This interview with Lucette Finas is rpt. in Lucette Finas et al., *Ecarts: Quatre essais à propos de Jacques Derrida*. (Paris: Fayard, 1973), pp. 303–12.

"Hors livre." In *Dissémination*

1973:  "Glas." *L'Arc: Jacques Derrida*. No. 54 (1973), 4–15. Excerpts of this appeared in *La Quinzaine Littéraire*, No. 172 (1973), 23–36.

"L'Archéologie du frivole." In Condillac, *Essai sur l'origine des connaissances humaines*. Ed. Charles Porset. Paris: Editions Galilée, 1973, pp. 9–95. Rpt. under separate cover as *L'Archéologie du frivole: Lire Condillac*.

1974:  "Mallarmé." In *Tableau de la littérature française: De Madame Staël à Rimbaud*. Paris: Gallimard, 1974, pp. 368–79.

"Le parergon." *Digraphe*, No. 2 (1974), 21–57.

"Le Sans de la coupure pure (Le parergon II)." *Digraphe,* No. 3 (1974), 5–31.

1975: "Economimesis." In Sylviane Agacinski, Jacques Derrida, et al. *Mimesis des articulations.* Paris: Aubier-Flammarion, 1975, pp. 55–93.

"Le Facteur de la vérité." *Poétique,* No. 21 (1975), 96–147. ET: "The Purveyor of Truth." Tr. Willis Domingo, James Hulbert, Moshe Ron, and Marie-Rose Logan. In *Yale French Studies,* No. 52: *Graphesis: Perspectives in Literature and Philosophy* (1975), 31–113.

"+ R (par dessus le marché)." In *Derriére le Miroir,* No. 214, May 1975 (Paris: Maeght Editeur), 1–23.

"Signéponge." In *Francis Ponge.* Colloque de Cerisy. Paris: Union Générale d'Editions, 1977, pp. 115–44. Discussion, pp. 145–51.

"Entre Crochets." *Digraphe,* No. 8 (April 1976), 97–114.

"Ja, ou le faux-bond." *Digraphe,* No. 11 (March 1977), 83–121. This is the second part of an interview with Derrida. The first part is "Entre Crochets."

"Pour la philosophie." *La Nouvelle Critique,* No. 84 (1975), 25–29. Rpt. as "Responses à *La Nouvelle Critique.*" In *Qui a peur de la philosophie.* Groupe de Recherches sur l'Enseignement Philosophique (GREPH). Paris: Flammarion, 1977, pp. 451–58.

Response to Questions on the Avant-Garde. *Digraphe,* No. 6 (October 1975), 152–53.

"La Philosophie et ses classes." In *Qui a peur de la philosophie.* GREPH. Paris: Flammarion, 1977, pp. 445–50. An extract of this, "La Philosophie refoulée," was published in *Le Monde de l'Education,* No. 4 (1975), 14–15.

1976: "Pas I." *Gramma: Lire Blanchot I,* Nos. 3–4 (1976), 111–215.

"Signéponge." *Digraphe,* No. 8 (April 1976), 17–39. This is a different fragment from the identically titled one listed under 1975. Both are extracts from a work in progress.

"Où commence et comment finit un corps enseignant." In *Politiques de la philosophie.* Ed. Dominique Grisoni. Paris: Bernard Grasset, 1976, pp. 55–97.

"Où sont les chasseurs de sorcières?" *Le Monde,* 1 July 1976.

"Fors: Les mots anglés de Nicolas Abraham and Maria Torok." Preface to Nicolas Abraham and Maria Torok. *Verbier de l'Homme aux Loups: Cryptonymie.* Paris: Aubier-Flammarion, 1976, 7–73. ET: "FORS: The Anglish Words of Nicolas Abraham and Maria Torok." Tr. Barbara Johnson. *The Georgia Review,* 31, No. 1 (Spring 1977), 64–116.

1977: "L'Age de Hegel." In *Qui a peur de la philosophie.* GREPH. Paris: Flammarion, 1977, pp. 73–107.

"Scribble." Preface to Warburton. *Essai sur les hiéroglyphes.* Paris: Aubier-Flammarion. To appear, Fall 1977.

## B. TEXTS CONCERNING DERRIDA

The special volume of *L'Arc: Jacques Derrida*, No. 54 (1973) will be referred to as *L'Arc*.

The special section of *Les Lettres Françaises, Grand Hebdomadaire Littéraire, Artistique et Politique*, No. 1429, 29 March 1972, devoted to Derrida will be referred to as *Les Lettres*.

Abel, Lionel. "Jacques Derrida: His *'Difference'* With Metaphysics." *Salmagundi*, No. 25 (Winter 1974), 3–21.

Allison, David Blair. Translator's Preface to Jacques Derrida's *Speech and Phenomena: And Other Essays on Husserl's Theory of Signs*. Evanston: Northwestern University Press, 1973, xxxi–xliii.

―――. "Derrida's Critique of Husserl: The Philosophy of Presence." Diss. The Pennsylvania State University 1974.

Altieri, Charles F. "Northrop Frye and the Problem of Spiritual Authority." *PMLA*, 87 (1972), 964–75.

Ames, Van Meter. "Art for Art's Sake Again?" *The Journal of Aesthetics and Art Criticism*, 33, No. 3 (1975), 303–07.

Anquetil, Gilles. "*Glas,* le nouveau livre de J. Derrida." *Les Nouvelles Littéraires*, No. 2457, 28 Oct.–3 Nov. 1974, p. 9.

Backes-Clement, Catherine. "La Dissémination: la méthode déplacée." *Les Lettres*, 4–5.

Bandera, Cesáreo. "The Crisis of Knowledge in *La Vida Es Sueño*." *SubStance*, No. 7 (Fall 1973), 27–47.

Barthes, Roland. Letter to Jean Ristat. *Les Lettres*, 3.

Beigbeder, Marc. "La Grammatologie de Jacques Derrida." In *Contradiction et nouvel entendement*. Paris: Bordas, 1972.

Benoist, Jean-Marie. "Le Colosse de Rhodes, quelques remarques à propos de *Glas* de Jacques Derrida." *L'Art Vivant*, No. 54 (December 1974–January 1975).

―――. "L'Inscription de Derrida." *La Quinzaine Littéraire*, No. 182 (1974), 18–19.

―――. " 'Présence' de Husserl." *Les Etudes Philosophiques*, 4 (1969), 525–31.

Bertherat, Y. Book Review of Derrida's *L'Ecriture et la différence*. *Esprit*, 35, No. 10 (Oct. 1967), 698–700.

Beyssade, Jean-Marie. " 'Mais quoi ce sont des fous': Sur un passage controversé de la 'Première Méditation.' " *Revue de Métaphysique et de Morale*, 78 (1973), 273–94.

Bonnefoy, Claude. "La Clôture et sa transgression." *Opus International*, 3 (1967).

Bothezat, T. "Lecturer to Visit Baltimore." *The Sun* (Baltimore), 2 Feb. 1968.

Bouazis, Charles. "Théorie de l'écriture et sémiotique narrative." *Semiotica*, 10 (1974), 305–31.

Boyer, Philippe. "Déconstruction: le désir à la lettre." *Change: La destruction*, 1, No. 2 (1969), 127–48. Rpt. in *L'Ecartée*. Paris: Seghers-Laffont, 1973.

———. "Le Point de la question." *Change: L'Imprononçable, l'écriture nomade,* No. 22 (1975), 41–72.

Brague, Rémi. "En Marge de 'La pharmacie de Platon' de J. Derrida." *Revue Philosophique de Louvain,* 71 (May 1973), 271–77.

Broekman, Jan M. *Structuralism: Moscow—Prague—Paris.* Tr. J. F. Beekman and B. Helm. Boston: D. Reidel, 1974, pp. 91–94 and 101–04.

Brykman, Geneviéve. Book Review of Derrida's *La Dissémination. Revue Philosophique de la France et de l'Etranger,* 164 (1974), 256.

Buci-Glucksmann, Christine. "Déconstruction et critique marxiste de la philosophie." *L'Arc,* 20–32.

Catesson, Jean. "A propos d'un pensée de l'intervalle." *Revue de Métaphysique et de Morale,* 74 (1969), 74–90.

Caws, Peter. "The Recent Literature of Structuralism, 1965–70." *Philosophische Rundschau,* 18, Heft 1–2 (1972), 63–77.

Chatelet, F. "Mort du livre?" *La Quinzaine Littéraire,* No. 37 (1967), 14.

———. "Qui est Jacques Derrida? La Métaphysique dans sa clôture." *Le Nouvel Observateur* (Spécial Littéraire), 20 Nov.–20 Dec. 1968.

Chumbley, Robert. " 'DELFICA' and 'LA DIFFERANCE': Toward a Nervalian System." *Sub-Stance,* No. 10 (1974), 33–37.

Cixous, Hélène. "L'Essort de Plusje." *L'Arc,* 46–52.

Clemens, Eric. "Sur Derrida: Alternance et dédoublement." *TXT,* Cahier No. 5 (1972).

Clément, Catherine. "A l'écoute de Derrida." *L'Arc,* 16–19.

———. "Le Sauvage." *L'Arc,* 1–2.

Corvez, Maurice. "Les Nouveaux Structuralistes." *Revue Philosophique de Louvain,* 67 (1969), 582–605.

"La Crise du signe et de l'imperalisme: Trotsky/Derrida." *Scription Rouge,* No. 5 (Sept.–Nov. 1973).

Culler, Jonathan. "Commentary." *New Literary History,* 6, No. 1 (Autumn 1974), 219–29.

———. *Structuralist Poetics: Structuralism, Linguistics, and the Study of Literature.* Ithaca, New York: Cornell University Press, 1975.

Daix, Pierre and François Wahl. "Qu'est-ce que le structuralisme?" *Les Lettres Françaises,* No. 1268, 29 Jan.–4 Feb 1969, pp. 4–6.

Dadoun, R. "Qu'est-ce que le structuralisme?" *La Quinzaine Littéraire,* No. 67 (1969), p. 15.

Damisch, Hubert. "Ceci (donc)." *Les Lettres,* 6.

Dauenhauer, Bernard P. "On Speech and Temporality: Jacques Derrida and Edmund Husserl." *Philosophy Today,* 18 (Fall 1974), 171–80.

Declève, H. Book Review of Derrida's *De la Grammatologie. Dialogue,* 9 (1970), 499–502.

Deese, James. "Mind and Metaphor: A Commentary." *New Literary History,* 6, No. 1 (Autumn 1974), 211–17.

De Greef, Jan. "De la Métaphore (à propos de *La Mythologie blanche,* de Derrida." *Cahiers de Littérature et de Linguisitque appliquée* (Kinshasa, Congo), Nos. 3–4 (1971), 45–50.

Deguy, Michel. "Husserl en seconde lecture." *Critique,* 19, No. 192 (May 1963), 434–448.

Delacampagne, Christian. "Condillac et le 'frivole.' " *Le Monde,* 20 December 1973, p. 24.

————. "Derrida et Deleuze." *Le Monde*, 30 April 1976.

————. "Derrida Hors de Soi." *Critique*, 30, No. 325 (June 1974), 503–14.

————. "Hegel et Gabrielle, le premier 'livre' de Jacques Derrida." *Le Monde*, 3 January 1975, p. 12.

————. "Six auteurs, une voix anonyme." *Le Monde*, 30 April 1976.

————. "Un Coup porté à la métaphysique." *Le Monde*, 14 June 1973, p. 22.

Detweiler, Robert. "The Moment of Death in Modern Fiction." *Contemporary Literature*, 13, No. 3 (Summer 1972), 269–94.

Donato, Eugenio. "Structuralism: The Aftermath." *Sub-Stance*, No. 7 (Fall 1973), 9–26.

Dufrenne, Mikel. "Pour une philosophie non théologique." In his *Le Poétique*. 2nd ed. Paris: Presses Universitaires de France, 1973, pp. 7–57.

Duval Raymond. "Présence et Solitude: La question de l'être et le destin de l'homme." *Revue des Sciences Philosophiques et Théologiques*, 57 (1973), 377–96.

Eco, Umberto. "La Structure et l'absence." In *La Structure absente*. Paris: Mercure de France, 1972.

Ehrmann, Jacques. "Sur le jeu et l'origine, où il est surtout question de la dissémination de Jacques Derrida." *Sub-Stance*, No. 7 (Fall 1973), 113–23.

Escarpit, Robert. *L'Ecrit et la communication*. Paris: Presses Universitaries de France, 1973, esp. pp. 17, 22, 44, 64–66.

Felman, Shoshana. "Madness and Philosophy *or* Literature's Reason." *Yale French Studies*, No. 52: *Graphesis: Perspectives in Literature and Philosophy* (1975), 206–28.

Ferguson, Frances C. "Reading Heidegger: Paul De Man and Jacques Derrida." *Boundary 2*, 4, No. 2 (Winter 1976), 593–610.

Ferguson, Margaret W. "Saint Augustine's Region of Unlikeness: The Crossing of Exile and Language." *The Georgia Review*, 29, No. 4 (Winter 1975), 842–64.

Finas, Lucette, Sarah Kofman, Roger Laporte, and Jean-Michel Rey. *Ecarts: Quatre essais à propos de Jacques Derrida*. Paris: Fayard, 1973.

Foucault, Michel. "Une petite pédagogie." *Le Monde*, 14 June 1973, p. 23. Excerpt from "Mon corps, ce papier, ce feu," Appendix to *Histoire de la folie à l'âge classique*. New ed. Paris: Gallimard, 1972, pp. 583–603.

Galay, J. L. Book Review of Derrida's *La Voix et le phénomène*. *Studia Philosophica*, 28 (1968).

Garelli, Jacques. "De quelques erreurs statistiques." *Les Temps Modernes*, 26, No. 286 (May 1970), 1929–36.

————. "L'Ecart du maintenant et l'extension de l'esprit." *Les Temps Modernes*, 25, No. 281 (December 1969), 874–96.

————. "Le Flux et l'instant." *Les Temps Modernes*, 26, No. 283 (Feb. 1970), 1239–63.

Garver, Newton. Preface to Jacques Derrida's *Speech and Phenomena: And Other Essays on Husserl's Theory of Signs*. Tr. David B. Allison. Evanston: Northwestern University Press, 1973, pp. ix–xxix.

Gelley, Alexander. "Form as Force." *Diacritics*, 2, No. 1 (Spring 1972), 9–13.

Genet, Jean. Letter to Jean Ristat. *Les Lettres*, 14.

Gillibert, Jean. "A propos de 'Freud et le Scène de l'écriture.' " *Les Lettres*, 8.

Giovannangeli, David. "Code et différence impure." *Littérature*, No. 12 (December 1973), 93–106.

————. "La Question de la littérature." *L'Arc*, 81–86.

————. "Vers un Dépassement de la phénoménologie et du structuralisme. La Réflexion sur la littérature dans la pensée de Jacques Derrida." Diss. Université de Mons 1974.

Girard, René. "Lévi-Strauss, Frye, Derrida, and Shakespeare Criticism." *Diacritics*, 3, No. 3 (Fall 1973), 34–38.

Goux, Jean-Joseph. "Du graphème au chromosome." *Les Lettres*, 6–7.

————. " 'La Dissémination' de Jacques Derrida." *Les Lettres Françaises*, No. 1455, 11–17 October 1972, p. 15.

Granel, Gérard. "Jacques Derrida et la rature de l'origine." *Critique*, 23, No. 246 (November 1967), 887–905. Rpt. in his *Traditionis traditio*. Paris: Gallimard, 1972, pp. 154–75.

Greisch, Jean. "La Crise de l'herméneutique. Réflexions méta-critiques sur un débat actuel." In Jean Greisch et al., *La Crise Contemporaine: Du modernisme à la crise des herméneutiques*. Paris: Beauchesne, 1973, pp. 135–90.

Grene, Marjorie. "Life, Death, and Language: Some Thoughts on Wittgenstein and Derrida," *Partisan Review*, 43 (1976), 265–79. Rpt. in her *Philosophy In and Out of Europe* (Berkeley: Univ. of California Press, 1976), pp. 142–54.

Guibal, Francis. "Philosophie, langage, écriture." *Etudes*, 5 (May 1972), 769–81.

Hartman, Geoffrey H. "Monsieur Texte: On Jacques Derrida, His *Glas*." *The Georgia Review*, 29, No. 4 (Winter 1975), 759–97.

————. "Monsieur Texte II: Epiphony in Echoland." *The Georgia Review*, 30, No. 1 (Spring 1976), 169–204.

Hector, J. "Jacques Derrida: la clôture de la métaphysique." *Techniques Nouvelles*, No. 6 (June 1972).

Hefner, R. W. "The *Tel Quel* Ideology: Material Practice upon Material Practice." *Sub-Stance*, No. 8 (1974), 127–38.

Hollier, Denis. "La Copulation labyrinthique (Un détail d'interférences)." *Les Lettres*, 14–15.

Irigaray, Luce. "Le v(i)ol de la lettre." *Tel Quel*, No. 39 (Fall 1969), 64–77.

Jabès, Edmond. "Sur la question du livre." *L'Arc*, 59–64.

Jacob, André. Book Review of Derrida's *L'Ecriture et la différence*. Les Etudes Philosophiques, 22 (1967).

————. Book Review of Derrida's *La Voix et le phénomène*. Les Etudes Philosophiques, 23 (1968).

————. Book Review of Edmund Husserl's *L'Origine de la géométrie*. Traduction et introduction de Jacques Derrida. *Les Etudes Philosophiques*, 18 (1963).

————. Book Review of Jacques Derrida's *Positions* and *Marges*. Les Etudes Philosophiques, 28 (1973), 389.

————. "De la socio-analyse à la grammatologie." Ch. 12 in his *Introduction à la philosophie du langage*. Paris: Gallimard, 1976, pp. 306–32.

Jameson, Fredric. *The Prison-House of Language: A Critical Account of Structuralism and Russian Formalism*. Princeton: Princeton University Press, 1972, esp. pp. 173–86.

Jannoud, Claude. "L'Evangile selon Derrida: sur Hegel et Genet." *Le Figaro Littéraire*, 30 November 1974.

Klein, Richard. "The Blindness of Hyperboles: The Ellipses of Insight." *Diacritics*, 3, No. 2 (Summer 1973), 33–44.

———. "Prolegomenon to Derrida." *Diacritics*, 2, No. 4 (Winter 1972), 29–34.

Krieger, Murray, ed. *Contemporary Literature:* "Directions for Criticism: Structuralism and its Alternatives," 17, No. 3 (Summer 1976), passim.

Kristeva, Julia. *La Révolution du langage poétique.* L'Avant-garde à la fin du XIX$^e$ siècle: Lautréamont et Mallarmé. Paris: Seuil, 1974, pp. 129–34.

Lacroix, J. "Ecriture et métaphysique selon Jacques Derrida." In *Panorama de la philosophie française contemporaine.* Paris: Presses Universitaires de France, 1968, p. 13.

———. "La Parole et l'écriture." *Le Monde,* 18 November 1967.

Lamizet, Bernard and Frederic Nef. "Entrave double: le glas et la chute (sur *Glas* de J. Derrida)." *Gramma,* No. 2 (April 1975), 129–50.

Laporte, Roger. "Bief." *L'Arc,* 65–70.

———. " 'Les "blancs" assument l'importance' (Mallarmé)." *Les Lettres,* 5.

Lapouge, Gilles. "Six philosophes occupés à déplacer la philosophie à propos de la mîmesis." *La Quinzaine Littéraire,* No. 231 (1976), 23.

Laruelle, François. "La Scène du vomi ou comment ça se détraque dans la théorie." *Critique,* 32, No. 347 (April 1976), 265–79.

———. "Le Style Di-phallique de Jacques Derrida." *Critique,* 31, No. 334 (March 1975), 320–29.

———. "Le Texte quatrième." *L'Arc, 38*–45.

———. *Machines textuelles: Déconstruction et libido d'écriture.* Paris: Seuil, 1976.

Leavey, John. "Derrida and Dante: Differance and the Eagle in the Sphere of Jupiter." *MLN,* 91, No. 1 (January 1976), 60–68.

Levers, A. "A Theory of Writing." *The Times Literary Supplement,* 15 February 1968, p. 153.

Levesque, Claude. *L'Etrangeté du texte: Essais sur Nietzsche, Freud, Blanchot et Derrida.* Montreal: VLB, 1976.

Levinas, Emmanuel. "Tout autrement." *L'Arc,* 33–37. Rpt. in his *Noms propres.* Montpellier: Fata Morgana, 1976, pp. 81–89.

Levine, Suzanne Jill. "Discourse as Bricolage." *Review,* No. 13 (Winter 1974), 32–37.

———. "Writing as Translation: *Three Trapped Tigers* and A *Cobra.*" *MLN,* 90, No. 2 (March 1975), 265–77.

Lévy, Bernard Henri. "Derrida n'est pas un gourou." *Magazine Littéraire,* 88 (May 1974), 60–62.

Logan, Marie-Rose. "Graphesis . . ." *Yale French Studies,* No. 52: *Graphesis: Perspectives in Literature and Philosophy* (1975), 4–15.

Loriot, P. Book Review of Derrida's *Glas. Le Nouvel Observateur,* No. 256, 9–15 December 1974.

Lotringer, Sylvère. "Le dernier mot de Saussure." *L'Arc,* 71–80.

M., A. Book Review of Derrida's *De la Grammatologie. Nice-Matin,* 12 January 1968.

Macann, Christopher. "Jacques Derrida's Theory of Writing and the Concept of Trace." *Journal of the British Society for Phenomenology,* 3, No. 2 (May 1972), 197–200.

Malmberg, Bertil. "Derrida et la sémiologie: Quelques notes marginales." *Semiotica,* 11, No. 2 (1974), 189–99.

de Man, Paul. "The Rhetoric of Blindness." In his *Blindness and Insight: Essays in the Rhetoric of Contemporary Criticism*. New York: Oxford University Press, 1971, pp. 102–41. A French translation by Jean Michel Rabeaté and Bernard Esmein appeared in *Poétique*, No. 4 (1970), 455–75, entitled "Rhétorique de la cécité."

———. Book Review of Derrida's *De la Grammatologie*. *Annales de la Societé J. J. Rousseau*, (1969).

Margolin, Jean-Claude. Book Review of Derrida's *La Dissémination*. *Les Etudes Philosophiques*, 28 (1973), 389–90.

Mehlman, Jeffrey. "Orphée scripteur: Blanchot, Rilke, Derrida." *Poétique*, No. 20 (1974), 458–82.

———. *A Structural Study of Autobiography: Proust, Leiris, Sartre, Lévi-Strauss*. Ithaca, N.Y.: Cornell University Press, 1974.

Merlin, Frédéric. "Après Mallarmé, Pour qui sonne le glas." *Les Nouvelles Littéraires*, No. 2461, 25 November 1974, p. 10.

———. "Derrida ou la philosophie en éclats." *Les Nouvelles Littéraires*, No. 2415, 7 January 1974, p. 15.

Meschonnic, Henri. "L'Ecriture de Derrida." *Les Cahiers du Chemin*, No. 24 (1975), 137–80.

———. *Le Signe et le poème*. Paris: Gallimard, 1975. Esp. pp. 401–92: "L'Ecriture de Derrida."

Miller, J. Hillis. "Deconstructing the Deconstructers." *Diacritics*, 5, No. 2 (Summer 1975), 24–31.

———. "Geneva or Paris? The Recent Work of Georges Poulet." *University of Toronto Quarterly*, 29, No. 3 (April 1970), 212–28.

———. "Stevens' Rock and Criticism as Cure, II." *The Georgia Review*, 30, No. 2 (Summer 1976), 330–48.

———. "Tradition and Difference." *Diacritics*, 2, No. 4 (Winter 1972), 6–13.

———. "Williams' *Spring and All* and the Progress of Poetry." *Daedalus*, 99 (Spring 1970), 405–34.

Nemo, Philippe. "L'Aventure collective d'un chercheur solitaire: Derrida et le GREPH." *Les Nouvelles Littéraires*, No. 2519, 12 February 1976.

Noguez, Dominique. Book Review of Derrida's *L'Ecriture et la différence*. *Nouvelle Revue Française*, No. 178 (Oct. 1967), 720.

Ollier, Claude. "Ouverture." *Les Lettres*, 11–13.

———. "Pulsion." *L'Arc*, 53–58.

Pachet, Pierre. "Une Entreprise troublante." *La Quinzaine Littéraire*, No. 197, 1 November 1974, pp. 19–20.

Paquet, Marcel. "Essai sur l'absolu." In *Morale et Enseignement*. Annals of the Institute of Philosophy. Brussels: Free University of Brussels, 1972, pp. 77–115.

Parenti, Claire. Book Review of Derrida's *Glas*. *Magazine Littéraire*, No. 96 (January 1975).

Parret, Herman. "Grammatology and Linguistics: A Note on Derrida's Interpretation of Linguistic Theories." *Poetics*, 4, No. 1 (13) (March 1975), 107–27.

———. "Jacques Derrida. Een wijsbergeerte van de schriftuur." *Tijdschrift voor Filosofie*, 30 (1968), 3–81. Resume: "Une philosophie de l'écriture," pp. 79–81.

Pavel, Toma. "Linguistique et phénoménologie du signe (Réflexions à propos de la philosophie de J. Derrida)." *Studi Italiani di Linguistica Teoretica ed Applicata*, 1 (1972), 51–68.

Penel, A. "Comment échapper à la philosophie? Jacques Derrida met en question la pensée occidentale." *La Tribune de Genève*, 15 November 1967.

Petitjean, Gérard. "Les grands prêtres de l'université française." *Le Nouvel Observateur*, No. 543, 7–13 April 1975.

Pierssens, Michel. "Introduction." *Sub-Stance*, No. 7 (Fall 1973), 3–7.

Poirot-Delpech, B. "Maîtres à dé-penser." *Le Monde*, 30 April 1976.

Popkin, Richard. "Comments on Professor Derrida's Paper ['The Ends of Man']." *Philosophy and Phenomenological Research*, 30, No. 1 (1969), 58–65.

Probst, Alain. "Une Critique de la métaphysique occidentale: la philosophie de Jacques Derrida." *Revue Reformée* (Société Calviniste de France), 24, No. 93 (1973), 29–43.

"A Propos de *L'Arc*, No. 54." *La Quinzaine Littéraire*, No. 175 (1973).

Rassam, J. "La Déconstruction de la métaphysique selon M. Derrida ou le retour au nominalisme le plus moyenâgeux." *Revue de l'Enseignement Philosophique*, 25, No. 2 (1975), 1–8.

Review of Derrida's *L'Ecriture et la différence*. *Bulletin Critique du livre français*, Nos. 260–61 (August–September 1967).

Rey, Jean-Michel. "De Saussure à Freud." *Les Lettres*, 9–10.

———. "La Scène du texte." *Critique*, 25, No. 271 (1969), 1059–1073.

Ricoeur, Paul. *La Métaphore vive*. Paris: Seuil, 1975, pp. 362–74.

Riddel, Joseph. "A Miller's Tale." *Diacritics*, 5, No. 3 (Fall 1975), 56–65.

———. "From Heidegger to Derrida to Chance: Doubling and (Poetic) Language." *Boundary 2*, 4, No. 2 (Winter 1976), 571–92.

———. *The Inverted Bell: Modernism and the Counterpoetics of William Carlos Williams*. Baton Rouge: Louisiana State University Press, 1974.

Ristat, Jean. "Le fil(s) perdu." *Les Lettres*, 13–14.

Robert, Jean-Dominique. "Voix et phénomène: à propos d'un ouvrage récent." *Revue Philosophique de Louvain*, 66 (1968), 309–24.

Roger, Philippe. "Les Philosophes saisis par la politique, un nouvel art de l'abordage." *Les Nouvelles Littéraires*, No. 2532, 13 May 1976.

Roudinesco, Elisabeth. "A propos du 'concept' de l'écriture. Lecture de Jacques Derrida." *Littérature et idéologies*. Colloque de Cluny II. *La Nouvelle Critique*, 39b (1970), 219–30.

———. "De Derrida à Jung: une tradition." In *Un Discours au réel*. Paris: Mame, 1973.

Ryan, Michael. "Self-De(con)struction." *Diacritics*, 6, No. 1 (Spring 1976), 34–41.

Said, Edward W. "*Abecedarium culturae*: structuralism, absence, writing." *Triquarterly*, No. 20 (Winter 1971), 33–71. Said's comments on Derrida have been taken up in his *Beginnings: Intention and Method*. New York: Basic Books, 1975, pp. 339–43.

Scarpetta, Guy. "Brecht et la Chine." *Littérature et idéologies*. Colloque de Cluny II. *La Nouvelle Critique*, 39b (1970), 231–36.

Schérer, René. "Clôture et faille dans la phénoménologie de Husserl." *Revue de Métaphysique et de Morale*, 73 (1968), 344–60.

"Scription, materialisme dialectique: Derrida-Marx." *Scription Rouge*, No. 1 (May 1972).

Singevin, Charles. "La Pensée, le langage, l'écriture et l'être." *Revue Philosophique de la France et de l'Etranger,* 162, No. 2 (April–June 1972), 129–48, and No. 3 (July–September 1972), 273–88.

Smith, F. Joseph. "Jacques Derrida's Husserl Interpretation." *Philosophy Today,* 9 (1967), 106–23.

Sollers, Philippe. "Transformer le statut même de la littérature." *Le Monde,* 14 June 1973, p. 23.

———. "Un Pas sur la lune." *Tel Quel,* No. 39 (Fall 1969), pp. 3–12. ET: "A Step on the Moon," *The Times Literary Supplement,* 25 September 1969, pp. 1085–87.

Spivak, Gayatri Chakravorty. Translator's Preface to Jacques Derrida's *Of Grammatology.* Baltimore: The Johns Hopkins University Press, 1976, ix–1xxxvii.

Stéfan, Jude. Book Review of Derrida's *L'Archéologie du frivole. Les Cahiers du Chemin,* No. 28 (1976), 157–59.

Thevenin, Paule. "Le hors-lieu." *Les Lettres,* 10–11.

Toubeau, Hélène. "Le Pharmakon et les aromates." *Critique,* 28, Nos. 303–04 (August–September 1972), 681–706.

Toyasaki, Koitchi. *Suppléments mobiles.* Tokyo: Editions Epaves, 1975.

Visscher, Luce Fontaine-De. "Des Privilèges d'une grammatologie." *Revue Philosophique de Louvain,* 67 (August 1969), 461–75.

Vuarnet, Jean-Noël. "Jacques Derrida." *Littérature de notre temps.* Recueil 4. Paris: Castermann, 1970.

———. "Sans titre." *Les Lettres,* 3–4.

Vuilleumier, J. "L'Irruption du dehors dans le dedans." *La Tribune de Genève,* 1–2 October 1966.

Wahl, François. "L'Ecriture avant la parole?" *La Quinzaine Littéraire,* No. 4 (1966).

———. "Forcer les limites." *La Quinzaine Littéraire,* No. 32 (1967).

———. "La Philosophie entre l'avant et l'après du structuralisme." In *Qu'est-ce que le structuralisme?,* ed. Francois Wahl. Paris: Seuil, 1968, pp. 299–442. Seuil reprinted this under separate cover in 1973 with the title of the article itself.

Wilden, Anthony. *System and Structure: Essays in Communication and Exchange.* London: Tavistock, 1972, pp. 395–400, 458–59.

Wood, Michael. "Deconstructing Derrida." *The New York Review of Books,* 3 March 1977, pp. 27–30.

Zaner, Richard M. "Discussion of Jacques Derrida, 'The Ends of Man.'" *Philosophy and Phenomenological Research,* 32, No. 3 (March 1972), 384–89.

# Index of Passages
# Cited from Husserl

[Page numbers refer to the present book.]

# Index